The Shakespeare Claimants

THE SHAKESPEARE CLAIMANTS

★

A Critical Survey of the Four
Principal Theories concerning the Authorship
of the Shakespearean Plays

★

H. N. GIBSON,
M.A., Ph.D.

BARNES & NOBLE, Inc.
New York
METHUEN & CO. Ltd
London

First published, 1962

This edition reprinted, 1971
by Barnes & Noble, Inc.
and Methuen & Co. Ltd.

Barnes & Noble ISBN 389 04144 0

Methuen ISBN 416 60770 5

Printed in the United States of America

TO
WINIFRED
MY WIFE

Your wit is of the true Pierian Spring
That can make anything of anything.

CHAPMAN

When once a man is determined to believe
the very absurdity of the doctrine confirms him
in his faith.

JUNIUS

One must know all the Elizabethans in order
to know Shakespeare.

HOTSON

Contents

Illustrations

Introduction

The Great Shakespeare Controversy, like History and Science, is a subject that goes on expanding. New generations of theorists are constantly putting forward new claimants for the authorship of the immortal plays, and orthodox scholars are constantly discovering new details about the life and background of the Stratford actor, which they beat into weapons to repel the new invaders or use to make fresh raids into the domains of the older schools of thought. There will therefore always be room for a new book that surveys the controversy historically, especially if it can introduce a little novelty into its presentation of the facts.

It has been my business for many years to lecture on Shakespeare to senior forms in schools and to adults in W.E.A. classes, and naturally from time to time I have been asked questions about the rival claimants to the authorship, followed by the inevitable one – what book would I recommend the questioners to read in order to get a general idea of the subject. This has never been easy to answer. The way in which the orthodox case has been presented is exceedingly diffuse. Sometimes it has consisted of a chapter or two in a biography of Shakespeare, sometimes it has been a special study of one type of argument, such as the Friedmans' work on the cryptograms, and sometimes a counter-attack on one particular school of thought, while of course there are numerous papers dealing with individual arguments.

Special studies, however, while of the greatest value to the expert, are of little use to the occasional student and the general reader, who want a bird's-eye view of the problem as a whole, and also the details of the theorist's main arguments and of the orthodox reply to them. And works of this sort are very rare. I know only of two, and neither of them is very suitable for the purpose I have in view. The first merely gives a summary of the main arguments of the theorists without the orthodox reply to them; the second includes every single theory – big or little – that has ever been put forward, and, as the rival candidates now number fifty-seven, it is obvious that the work has to be of a very general nature and cannot get down to the detailed examination of individual arguments.

There thus seemed to me to be a real need for a different kind of book, and this is what I have attempted to supply in the following pages. I have limited myself to the four main theories – the Baconian, the Oxfordian, the Derbyite, and the Marlovian. The first-named is the oldest theory, the last-named is the most recent, so the group forms a natural cross-section. The four are also the most interesting of the theories, and have been more fully studied and presented than any of the others. By limiting myself to them I have retained the advantage of being able to compare one theory with another and at the same time have left myself adequate space to describe the main arguments of each at some length and to subject these to a detailed analysis.

I may add that I began my research as a Shakespearean agnostic, not as a convinced adherent of the orthodox view. I believed that there were possible objections to the authorship of the Stratford actor, and from what I had read of works advocating the claims of others, I was ready to admit that there might be a case for one of them. I imagined that my ultimate conclusion would be that, while the actor remained the most probable, there was still a great deal to be said on the other side, and that I should be obliged to leave some problems unsolved. It was only when I began a detailed examination of the various theories that I discovered how really weak and unconvincing these were, and when brought together and compared, what a devastating wreck they made of one another.

In these circumstances it would be dishonest to claim, as my original intention was, that I wrote as a disinterested neutral with no decided opinions on the matter. I trust that I still retain what may be called an 'open mind'. I am quite prepared to consider any new evidence that may be forthcoming in the future, and to change my opinion if I felt this to be justified, but I must frankly admit that for the time being my studies have made me a convinced Stratfordian.

There are two kinds of evidence with which I deal in the

course of my survey – the first is that which is limited to one of the theories only; the second is that which is common to two or more of them. To facilitate comparison, and also to avoid the necessity of repetition, I have treated each of these two types separately. In the earlier chapters, each designated by the title of one of the theories, I deal with the evidence that pertains to that theory alone; while in the later chapters, each designated by the title of a single piece of evidence, I deal with what is common ground, examining the diverse use each theory makes of the same factors. This, the main section of my work, is preceded by an historical summary of the rise and development of the four theories that are my concern and a review of the case *against* the Stratford actor. I have also included a chapter on the case *for* him, as, of course, the other theories of authorship cannot be judged adequately without some reference to this, though to prove his case is in no way my purpose.

In order to make the book a handy guide for the general reader I have quoted my authorities with sufficient fullness to render reference to the originals unnecessary for a complete understanding of the matters discussed; but, of course, a more detailed examination of these authorities would be an advantage to all and is essential for the serious student. I have therefore added a bibliography and fully documented my references.

In this connection one not unimportant point arises. The classic work on this subject from the Stratfordian viewpoint is *The Baconian Heresy* by that very great Elizabethan scholar, J. M. Robertson. In the course of my investigations I have noticed a remarkable fact. *Not a single one of the theorists whose works I have read – and I have read many – ever mentions this important book.* Even A. J. Evans, who in his *Shakespeare's Magic Circle* thoughtfully provides his public with two reading lists – one anti- and one pro-Stratfordian, carefully refrains from including it in the latter. I can conjecture only one explanation for this strange suppression. One of the main props of all the theories is a book entitled *The Shakespeare Problem Restated*, in which Sir George Greenwood, while himself supporting no particular alternative candidate and always vigorously denying that he was a Baconian, delivered a trenchant attack on the authorship of the Stratford actor. This work J. M. Robertson, with his wealth of Elizabethan scholarship, subjected to such a merciless criticism in *The Baconian Heresy* that it was left incapable of supporting anything, even the wreckage of itself. But all the theorists still cling pathetically to it, and draw most of their arguments for attacking the orthodox position from its pages. Hence the apparent conspiracy of silence. I may add that my readers will find a great deal of reference to *The Baconian Heresy* in the following pages, and I urge all who have the opportunity to study it for themselves.

It is hardly necessary to state that I cannot include in my survey every individual argument put forward by every individual theorist. Their very number makes any such idea absolutely impossible. Hundreds of books and pamphlets have been produced in the course of the controversy, and the literature of the Baconians alone would stock a fair-sized library. It is true that there is much repetition and overlapping in these works, but even so it would require several bulky volumes to review them all adequately. What I can claim to have done is to include all the most important arguments in the four main theories, and to select for analysis those which tell most in favour of the various theories in which they appear. To have attempted more would have destroyed the main purpose of this work; that is, to serve as a handbook of the Great Shakespearean Controversy.

In order to economize as much as possible in space I usually refer to all the works in the accepted Shakespearean canon, which naturally are of frequent occurrence, either by their initial letters or by some other recognized abbreviation. The following is the key to my usage:

1 Hen. VI. *First Part of King Henry the Sixth.*
2 Hen. VI. *Second Part of King Henry the Sixth.*
3 Hen. VI. *Third Part of King Henry the Sixth.*
Ric. III. *King Richard the Third.*
T.A. *Titus Andronicus.*
C. of E. *Comedy of Errors.*
T.G. of V. *Two Gentlemen of Verona.*
L.L.L. *Love's Labour's Lost.*
R. & J. *Romeo and Juliet.*

M.N.D.	*A Midsummer Night's Dream.*
K.J.	*King John.*
T. of Sh.	*Taming of the Shrew.*
Ric. II.	*King Richard the Second.*
M. of V.	*The Merchant of Venice.*
1 Hen. IV.	*First Part of King Henry the Fourth.*
2 Hen. IV.	*Second Part of King Henry the Fourth.*
Hen. V.	*King Henry the Fifth.*
M. Ado.	*Much Ado About Nothing.*
M.W.W.	*Merry Wives of Windsor.*
J.C.	*Julius Caesar.*
A.Y.L.I.	*As You Like It.*
T.N.	*Twelfth Night.*
Ham.	*Hamlet.*
T. & C.	*Troilus and Cressida.*
A. Well.	*All's Well That Ends Well.*
M. for M.	*Measure for Measure.*
Oth.	*Othello.*
Mac.	*Macbeth.*
K.L.	*King Lear.*
A. & C.	*Antony and Cleopatra.*
Cor.	*Coriolanus.*
T. of A.	*Timon of Athens.*
Per.	*Pericles, Prince of Tyre.*
Cym.	*Cymbeline.*
W.T.	*The Winter's Tale.*
Temp.	*The Tempest.*
Hen. VIII.	*King Henry the Eighth.*
V. & A.	*Venus and Adonis.*
R. of L.	*The Rape of Lucrece.*
Son.	*Sonnets.*

There is only one other point that requires notice here. Throughout the book, except in the case of quotations from other works, when I refer to the Stratford actor I use the spelling 'Shakspere', which is one of the forms he himself used, and when I refer to the author of the plays and poems I use the spelling 'Shakespeare', which was attached to the First Folio and most of the other printed editions of his works. In the light of what I have said earlier about my views I shall not be suspected of any anti-Stratfordian tendencies, but it may occasion some surprise that I should adopt what is a favourite device of the theorists. My reason for so doing is that in a work which is primarily concerned with the claims of others to the name of the author of the plays, even if only as a pseudonym, it is convenient to make a distinction between the two in order to avoid ambiguity.

Acknowledgements

My thanks are due to Mr R. F. Hill of King's College, London University, for reading my original manuscript, and for the very valuable criticisms and suggestions he then made. I should also like to thank Messrs Methuen & Co. Ltd, for all the help they have given me in preparing this my first venture for the press. My indebtedness to the many Shakespearean scholars whose works I have consulted is acknowledged in the text.

H. N. GIBSON
BRADFORD, 1961

CHAPTER I

Theories and Theorists

If William Shakespeare the dramatist had not been such a supreme genius, and if what was known of William Shakspere the actor had not been so little and that little had not sometimes seemed incompatible with what the conventional mind usually associates with greatness, there would in all probability never have been a Shakespeare problem. Other obscure men have risen to greatness, and even less is known about many of the great Elizabethans, as we shall see later, than is known about the Stratford actor,[1] while great men, whatever their origin, have often displayed in private characteristics completely at variance with their public reputation. But the three things coming together were bound sooner or later to raise doubts in minds cast in the conventional mould whether the man distinguished by the first could be identical with the man distinguished by the other two. It is perhaps more surprising that these doubts were so long delayed than that they eventually became vocal.

It was not until 1857, more than 200 years after the great works had been written, that the storm actually broke, though, unknown to the world at large, there had been a forerunner of it in 1781. In that year the Rev. J. Wilmot, rector of Burton-in-the-Heath, who had spent a great deal of time searching for records of Shakspere in and around Stratford-on-Avon, came to the conclusion that such a man as he appeared to have been could never have possessed the necessary education and experience to write the plays ascribed to him. Wilmot also noticed

---

[1] As a matter of fact a considerable amount is now known about Shakspere, and many former difficulties have been cleared up, but nearly all the discoveries have been made in recent years. They were not known when the search for Shakespearean substitutes began, and most of them have been published in works seldom perused by the general reader, so the statement in the text remains true for the purpose of this book.

a certain similarity of ideas between Shakspere and Bacon, with whose works he was equally familiar, and the disturbing thought took possession of him that Bacon might be the real author of the plays. This so horrified him that he burnt all his notes, and never published a hint of his idea. He did, however, confide it to one man, J. C. Cowell, who left a record of it.

Cowell's record was not discovered until 1932, so it played no part in the development of the modern Baconian theory. This arose out of doubts expressed by certain writers, notably the American, J. C. Hart (1848), that Shakspere possessed the ability to write the plays. These doubts were taken up by W. H. Smith, who, in a pamphlet entitled *Bacon and Shakespeare* (1857), tentatively suggested that Bacon was the true author. Thereafter things moved rapidly. Others, both in this country and in America, advanced the claim more robustly; the Stratfordians, suddenly realizing that their hero was in danger, rallied to his defence; and thus the great Shakespearean controversy was launched.

During the closing years of the nineteenth century and the early years of the twentieth it was largely a straight fight between the Stratfordians and the Baconians; but between the two World Wars and since the Second World War new candidates for the authorship have been proposed thick and fast.

As early as 1919 a Frenchman, Professor Lefranc, put in a claim for the Earl of Derby. This was, however, temporarily side-tracked in this country by a counter-claim for the Earl of Oxford advanced by J. T. Looney, a Gateshead schoolmaster, in 1920. Looney proposed Oxford as the sole author, but his followers have modified this theory. According to their idea Oxford did not write all the works himself; he was the leader of a group of brilliant courtiers who jointly produced the plays. This view was most forcefully propagated by Gilbert Slater in 1931 in a work entitled *Seven Shakespeares*.

Since the Second World War the Derby theory has been revived by Dr Titherley in an exhaustive, not to say exhausting, study published in 1952. He has received some support from A. J. Evans as recently as 1956; but Evans really stands midway between Titherley and the Oxfordians. He accepts the latter's group theory, but maintains that it was Derby, not Oxford, who was the leader of the group.

The most recent candidate is Christopher Marlowe, already recognized in his own right as a dramatist inferior only to Shakespeare among the Elizabethans. A claim on his behalf as the sole author of the Shakespearean plays and poems was advanced by Calvin Hoffman, an American, in 1955.

Before proceeding to summarize separately the special features of each school of thought, there are two other points that we must consider. These are (a) the highly individual part played by Sir George Greenwood in the controversy, and (b) the connection of the Stratford actor with the plays if he were not their author.

The first need not detain us long. Sir George Greenwood entered the controversy in 1908 with a work entitled *The Shakespeare Problem Restated*, in which he argued very forcefully that the Stratford actor was totally incapable of writing the works attributed to him. Between 1908 and 1921 Greenwood produced another book, *Is There a Shakespeare Problem?*, and a number of papers and letters on the same subject. Unlike all the other theorists, however, he had no particular candidate to put in the actor's place, and he always indignantly repudiated the suggestion that he was a Baconian. The real author for him was an unknown lawyer. There is no need to say anything about his arguments here – except that they showed great forensic skill and an equally great lack of Elizabethan scholarship – for his work has provided the exponents of each theory in turn with most of their ammunition for bombarding the Stratfordian defences. His arguments therefore can be most conveniently dealt with where they occur in the various theories.

The second point requires fuller consideration. There is no doubt that the Stratford actor was generally regarded as the author of the plays during his lifetime, and his title to this honour was, as we have seen, never seriously disputed until nearly two hundred years later. The reader unacquainted with the details of the controversy may well ask how, if he were not really the author, the name of 'William Shakespeare' came to be attached to the plays; and why the fraud, if it were a fraud, was allowed to continue for so long without being challenged.

To the first of these questions the members of all the schools of thought answer with complete unanimity that for certain reasons of the utmost gravity their own particular candidate was obliged to keep his authorship secret; he therefore engaged the Stratford actor to lend his name and act as a cover or mask, for which service he was handsomely rewarded.

The supporters of the noble lords, and also the Baconians, explain that the reasons which prevented their candidates from acknowledging their work were two in number. First, it was *infra dig* for a nobleman to allow any poetry or play to be made public under his own name during his lifetime, and to do so would lower his prestige at Court. Second, historical plays at least could hardly avoid expressing political opinions, and if these should prove displeasing to the Government, the author, especially if he were a person of consequence, might well find himself in danger of imprisonment and even of execution.

There is no doubt some truth in both these contentions. Courtiers did not as a rule publish dramatic or poetical works under their own names; but there were many exceptions to this rule, and, among others, both Oxford and Bacon broke it by publishing poems. Moreover, it was apparently known that Oxford and Derby wrote plays. In an intercepted letter of a Jesuit spy, preserved in the State Papers of Elizabeth's reign for the year 1599, this sentence occurs – 'Our Earle of Darby is busye in penning commodyes for the commoun players'; and Francis Meres, in his *Palladis Tamia* (1598), gives a list of seventeen writers, headed – no doubt because of his rank – by the Earl of Oxford, who are, he says 'The best for Comedy among us'.

It is also true that Queen Elizabeth was greatly enraged at a performance of *Richard II* arranged by the conspirators in the hope of influencing the London populace to favour the Essex rebellion, an episode we shall have to consider at greater length later (see Chapter X). But such incidents could rarely happen, for all plays had to be submitted to the Master of the Revels, who was an officer of the Lord Chamberlain's staff, for censorship, and it was his business to see that nothing of a dangerously political nature was performed. It should be noted that even in this case, though the players were summoned for questioning, neither they nor the author were punished.[1]

It is therefore obvious that the suggestion of the Stratford actor's being used as a cover, though essential for all the theories, is by no means a completely convincing one as far as the nobles are concerned. With the Marlowe theory the case is different. Marlowe was no courtier, and had already had several plays produced under his own name. There could therefore be no question of either of the reasons just discussed applying to him; but, since the explanation put forward by Hoffman is peculiar to his own theory, it will be more convenient to postpone an account of it until we deal with that theory in detail.

The question why the authorship of the Stratford actor should not have been challenged earlier can be answered much more briefly. All the theorists are agreed that the secret was most skilfully and cunningly concealed, though the evidence they offer in support of their own candidate's authorship is often, as we shall see, a direct contradiction of this. The Baconians hold that Francis Bacon, though he dare not acknowledge the works in his own day, was determined that posterity should know the truth, and accordingly left behind him a number of clues, which they have been the first clever enough to discover and interpret. The other theorists believe that their candidates never meant the secret to be revealed, and it is only through their ingenuity that it has been torn from the oblivion in which it was intended to remain.

We may now turn to the task of summarizing the main features that characterize each theory.

THE BACONIAN THEORY

The Baconians, as we have seen, were the first in the field. They had a clear fifty years' start of all rivals, and in consequence have collected a greater number of adherents and produced a much

---

[1] It is true, as Ben Jonson told Drummond of Hawthornden, that he, Chapman, and Marston were imprisoned and threatened with mutilation for a reference in a joint play, but the reference was libellous, not political. Moreover the sentence was never carried out, and they were soon pardoned and released.

larger literature than any of the other schools of thought. Their starting-point was that Shakspere of Stratford, even if he had been a genius – a quality they emphatically deny him – could never have written the Shakespearean plays. In these they found what they consider such a profound knowledge of the Law that only a practising lawyer could have written them, and as they also found in them a number of alleged parallelisms in expression and thought with the acknowledged works of Bacon, the latter was in their view the only possible candidate for the authorship.

There are slight variations in this theory as treated by different exponents, but the following is, I believe, a not unfair general outline of it. Bacon was not enamoured of a legal career, which he only adopted under parental pressure and the urge of his own ambition, while he found an outlet for his desire to be a man of letters by secretly writing plays and poems. Then came the trouble, to which reference has already been made (see p. 20), over *Richard II*, and Bacon felt that his authorship was suspected by the Queen; so to disarm her suspicions he hastily looked around for someone to use as a cover. He had adopted the name 'William Shakespeare' as a pseudonym for his secret works, and finding by an extraordinary coincidence an actor with a similar sounding name, he engaged him for the purpose.

As the years have passed the Baconians have supported this bare outline with an increasing number of details culled from the plays themselves and from the social history of the times, until they have built up an imposing façade which we shall have to examine very closely in a subsequent chapter.

As is natural in an association that has been in existence for so long and has attracted a comparatively large number of adherents, the Baconian school has included many types of mind with a corresponding diversity of attitude. There are some whose approach is restrained and scholarly, while others are naïve and credulous, and often indulge in the wildest fantasy. With many Bacon has become a sort of cult. They hold that he was really a Tudor Prince – the illegitimate son of Queen Elizabeth and the Earl of Leicester – and not content with assigning to him the whole of the Shakespearean canon, they also credit him with having written Lyly's *Euphues*, Spenser's *Faerie Queene*, Puttenham's *Arte of English Poesy*, Burton's *Anatomy of Melancholy*, all the works of Nashe, all the plays of Marlowe, Peele, Kyd, and Greene, and many other gems of Elizabethan literature. To this modest output some add the translation of the Authorized Version of the Bible, and Sir Edwin Durning-Lawrence has even claimed that he wrote Montaigne's *Essays* in French. These absurd claims should be kept in mind when evaluating that of the authorship of the Shakespearean works, for they depend on the same kind of evidence.

The wildest of the Baconians are the cryptologists. They believe that Bacon, to ensure that posterity gave him full credit for all he had achieved in secret, filled the Shakespearean and other works with cryptograms and similar clues which, to the seeing eye, reveal the full story of his life and work.

It must not be thought that these groups within the Baconian circle are sharply divided. Such grading as can be made is of individuals, some accepting more and some less of these manifold claims. Thus there are those who, like Dr R. M. Theobald and Lord Penzance, reject the cryptograms altogether, and others are content to claim for Bacon no more than the Shakespearean works; but B. G. Theobald, who is not unscholarly, maintains the claim to the works of Marlowe, Peele, and Greene, and thinks that the cryptograms, if used with discretion, can supply valuable corroborative evidence; while there is nothing too fantastic to find a welcome in the seething pages of Sir Edwin Durning-Lawrence.

A marked feature of the Baconian theory is the intense hatred its adherents display towards William Shakspere the actor. To read what they have to say about him one would imagine the wretched fellow had deliberately stolen the credit of writing the plays from Bacon instead of merely doing what, according to their own theory, Bacon had asked him to do – that is, to act as a cover or mask to protect the latter's life and dignity. This hatred not only takes the form of violent abuse and the accusation of every kind of disreputable conduct, but also of the rather childish trick of hunting up all the most outlandish Elizabethan variations of the spelling of his name, and filling their pages with 'Shagspurs', 'Shaxpers', and similar atrocities;

while Sir Edwin Durning-Lawrence concludes each chapter in his book with the legend 'Bacon is Shakespeare' in block capitals. Such are the Baconians and their theory.

THE OXFORD THEORY

It was, as already stated, a Gateshead schoolmaster named Looney who first put forward the claim for Edward de Vere, seventeenth Earl of Oxford, in a work entitled *Shakespeare Identified*, published in 1920. His own account of its origin is that the constant teaching of *The Merchant of Venice* to senior forms at school convinced him that the author of that play must have been a man who knew Italy and Italian life at first hand, and therefore could not have been the Stratford actor. He determined if possible to identify the true author, and with this purpose in view he began to examine Elizabethen literature in search of a poet whose style resembled that of the Shakespearean works. He paid particular attention to poems written in the same metre as *Venus and Adonis*. At length he came across in Palgrave's *Golden Treasury* the poem by Oxford beginning – 'If women could be fair and yet not fond', which seemed to him to be exactly the piece of evidence for which he was in search. He thereupon began to study the life and interests of Oxford, and came to the conclusion that these fitted perfectly with what was required by the author of the plays. Oxford was, of course, intimate with kings and queens and other high authorities; he had travelled extensively, had been lampooned as an Italianate Englishman, and though no specimen of a dramatic work acknowledged as his has survived, there was the statement of Francis Meres (see p. 20) as evidence that he had written plays. Moreover, there were incidents in the Shakespearean plays that Looney felt might well have been suggested by episodes in the career of Oxford and his relatives. He therefore decided that his case was complete, and accordingly published his theory.

This theory was taken up and developed by others both in this country and in America, and it was not long before it underwent the groupist modification already mentioned. In its final form, as laid down by Professor Gilbert Slater, though the poems and sonnets were left to Oxford, he was no longer regarded as the sole author of the plays. These were produced by a syndicate consisting of himself as leader, the Earl of Derby, Francis Bacon, Sir Walter Ralegh, the Earl of Rutland, the Countess of Pembroke, and Christopher Marlowe, the last-named, as a professional dramatist, acting in an advisory capacity.[1] William Shakspere came into it as the honest broker who negotiated with the theatres and printers for the production and publication of the plays. He also lent his name as a pseudonym for the authors, as of course it would have been politically dangerous as well as *infra dig* for the courtiers to use any of theirs, and he may well, with his practical knowledge as an actor, have lent his aid in rendering the literary productions suitable for performance on the stage.

From this summary it will be seen that the Oxfordians are as pleasant as the Baconians are unpleasant. Instead of the bitter hatred of the latter, they are full of the milk of human kindness. All the candidates put forward by the other schools of thought are welcome at their hospitable board. Even the Stratford actor is an honoured guest, and the whole atmosphere is refined and sweetened by the gracious feminine presence of the Countess of Pembroke.

The foregoing is not intended as ridicule. The Oxfordian theory is an attractive one, and, if it could be established, it would help to clear up one or two problems of Shakespearean criticism. For instance the author's uncanny insight into female psychology is most easily explained by postulating a woman collaborator, and none could fill such a rôle better than the brilliant and much-admired sister of Sir Philip Sidney. Mere attractiveness, however, is not evidence, and we shall have to examine the Oxford case very critically.

THE DERBY THEORY

The Derby theory owes its origin to a Frenchman, Professor Lefranc, whose approach somewhat resembled that of Looney. He became convinced that *Love's Labour's Lost* could only have been written by a man who was resident at the Court of

[1] Some of the Oxfordians have produced even longer lists, but this is sufficient for our purpose.

Navarre at Nerac in or about 1583, when certain events, which he considers gave rise to the play, took place. As this ruled out the Stratford actor, he embarked on a search for a possible substitute. He discovered that William Stanley, afterwards sixth Earl of Derby, who, according to the Jesuit spy (see p. 20), wrote plays for the public theatre, was at that time travelling through France on his way to Spain, and although there is no direct evidence that he did visit Nerac, Lefranc considered him a likely candidate. He further investigated Derby's life and interests, and having found a number of episodes and incidents to which he considered reference was made in the plays, he published his views in 1919.

Side-tracked in this country for a time by Looney's Oxford theory, the Derby claim was later taken up by Dr Titherley, who published in 1952 a very full and detailed study of the question in a work entitled *Shakespeare's Identity*. Titherley not only made full use of the kind of evidence collected by Lefranc, but also called to his aid the sciences of genetics and mathematics, and a number of other techniques in addition.

In his version the Stratford actor's connection with the plays follows the usual pattern, namely to protect the safety and dignity of the noble author. Derby, long before he unexpectedly inherited the earldom, had been publishing poems under his initials W. S. (William Stanley), and was contemplating writing plays for the public theatres. His elder brother, Lord Strange and later fifth Earl of Derby, kept a company of players, and among these Derby discovered a young recruit with the name of William Shakspere.[1] Struck by the identity of their initials, he decided to adopt the young player's name and employ him as his agent for placing the plays, of course paying him well for these services.

The Derby theory has enjoyed a considerable vogue in France, the country of its origin, and between 1951 and 1953 another Frenchman, Professor Lambin, published a series of papers containing alleged evidence similar to that of Lefranc; while in England, as already stated, A. J. Evans has proposed a

---

[1] It may be well to state here that there is no evidence that Shakspere was ever a member of Lord Strange's company, though of course it is by no means impossible that he was. Some Stratfordians have certainly held this view.

modification of the theory, which is merely the Oxford groupist idea, but with Oxford and Derby changing places, so that the latter becomes its leader and therefore the true Shakespeare.

THE MARLOWE THEORY

The theory that Christopher Marlowe was the sole author of the Shakespearean works is the most recent, having been put forward by Calvin Hoffman, an American, in 1955. It begins in a way reminiscent of the Baconians. Just as they found numerous parallelisms between Bacon's acknowledged works and those of Shakespeare, and deduced from this that Bacon was Shakespeare, so Hoffman found numerous parallelisms between Marlowe's acknowledged works and those of Shakespeare, and deduced from this that Marlowe was Shakespeare.

At this point, however, he was confronted by a difficulty encountered by none of the other theorists. In 1593, long before many of the great works were written, Christopher Marlowe, according to the verdict of the Queen's Coroner, was dead – killed in a drunken brawl. In the face of this most men would have hastily abandoned the theory, but not so Mr Hoffman. He is of sterner stuff, and one cannot but admire both his persistence and his ingenuity in circumventing such an intractable obstacle.

We shall have to deal with the whole story at some length when we come to analyse Hoffman's theory, so we may content ourselves with a brief outline here. Just before his alleged death Marlowe had been in trouble with the Privy Council for propagating Atheistical views. He also had a powerful patron in the person of Sir Thomas Walsingham, a rich Kentish landowner. So much is historical fact; what follows is Hoffman's speculation. Walsingham and Marlowe were bound together by the romantic tie of a homosexual relationship, and, believing Marlowe's life might be in danger as the result of his reckless expression of heretical opinions, Walsingham decided to save his young lover at all costs. Three ruffians in his employ were ordered to go to Deptford and murder some foreign sailor. They were not to avoid arrest, but were to say that the victim was Marlowe, and to plead self-defence. Walsingham would bribe the Coroner to accept both the plea and also the body as

27

that of Marlowe. This hastily-arranged and somewhat complicated plot was successfully carried out.

Meanwhile Marlowe was smuggled out of the country and settled somewhere on the continent, probably in North Italy. There he continued to write, sending his manuscripts to Walsingham for disposal. Naturally they could not be made public under Marlowe's name – if a suspicion of what had happened reached the ears of authority Walsingham's own life would be forfeit. So Walsingham looked around for a suitable cover, and of course he found a steady, unimaginative actor named William Shakspere, who, for a consideration, was willing to father the plays and dispose of them to the theatres as occasion required.

Hoffman naturally does not rely on speculation alone. He supports his theory with a number of other arguments of the same kind as, and some even identical with, those of the other theorists. We shall deal with these, as well as with his speculations, in subsequent chapters.

When all these theories are brought into juxtaposition, even in the summary form just given, it at once raises doubts about their validity. And it is right that it should do so, for it provides a striking illustration of the ease with which the same set of factors can be moulded into evidence for the most diverse and contradictory conclusions. This will become even more obvious when we proceed to the detailed examination of the various pieces of common evidence. We must, however, beware of over-emphasizing the point. The doubts it raises are reasonable, but it does not *necessarily* prove that all the theories are false. It might be that the evidence does really support one of them, while all the others have misappropriated it.

On the other hand we must be equally on our guard against accepting the arguments of the theorists too readily. Almost any one of their books, read in isolation and with little knowledge of the historical background, will be found startlingly convincing. The reason for this is that the author is not genuinely examining the problem in search of truth, but is making the best possible case for his own particular view. This is not to impute dishonesty to him. He may be sincerely convinced of the truth of that view; but this does not alter the fact that in presenting his case he is an advocate, not an investigator. Moreover, unless he possesses unusual powers of self-discipline, his very enthusiasm for his theory will often lead him into the suppression of awkward facts and the glossing over of contradictory evidence. We shall come across numerous instances of both in the course of our survey.

Again there is the vexed question of 'assumptions'. There are enormous gaps in our knowledge both of the lives of persons and the details of their background in Elizabethan times, and we often have no clue to the significance of certain isolated references and incidents we occasionally come across. The temptation to bridge such gaps with surmises and guesses is therefore almost irresistible. At times this practice may be not unreasonable, but it is always dangerous in a problem such as the one with which we are dealing because it is so easily abused. We encounter an assumption, introduced quite correctly with a 'probably' or even a 'possibly', only to find a few pages later that its author, consciously or unconsciously, has turned it into a certainty, and is using it in support of another assumption even less probable or possible. The works of the theorists abound with such cases, and I shall have occasion, as we pursue our survey, to draw attention to some of them.

Although it is not properly my business, I feel that in the interests of fairness I ought to point out that most of the sins of omission and commission I have just laid to the charge of the theorists can also be found among the orthodox Stratfordians when they write a panegyric on their hero. They even have a group – the Bardolators – who are almost as wild and woolly, as the Baconian Cryptologists; indeed it is this group, with its extravagant claims, that has provided the theorists with much of the ammunition they use to attack the orthodox position. This, however, will not concern us to any great extent since the purpose of our survey is not to prove Shakspere's authorship, but to criticize the rival claims.

In conclusion it may be of interest and not without importance to say a word or two about the theorists themselves as distinct from the theories they support. Very few of them are Elizabethan scholars in any real sense; many are not even professional men of letters, and, while it is good to find the amateur displaying an interest in such problems, we must keep in mind the fact that, unless his circumstances are unusual, he has neither the time nor the training for delving deeply into the necessary studies. As might be expected, many of the Baconians are eminent lawyers, men skilled in making the best of a case, but in practice not much concerned with arriving at the truth – it would often be unfortunate for their clients if they were. The Oxfordians were founded by a schoolmaster responsible for teaching English literature, but a number of its exponents have come from the Church, the Army, and the Navy. Like the Baconians, they have strong American support of a mixed character.

The Derbyites, in spite of their French allies, are fewer in number than either of the schools just mentioned. Their chief exponent in this country, Dr Titherley, is a scientist, a former lecturer in chemistry in the University of Liverpool, who, as we shall see, is inclined to treat unpredictable human genius and eccentricity as if they were predictable elements in a laboratory experiment. He has, however, probably because he is a scientist, introduced into the controversy one or two interesting novelties which we shall have to examine in due course. A. J. Evans, who must be considered a Derbyite in spite of his slight deviation in the direction of the Oxfordian groupists, has many admirers, of whom I am one, both for his thrilling 'escape' stories and for his former prowess on the cricket field, but neither of these activities is a guarantee of literary scholarship. Calvin Hoffman, at present the sole exponent of the Marlowe theory, is an American journalist.

As the two preceding paragraphs suggest, most of the great Shakespearean scholars are to be found in the Stratfordian camp; but too much must not be made of this fact, for many of them display comparatively little interest in the controversy with which we are dealing. Their chief concerns are textual criticism, interpretation, and the internal problems of the plays, and they accept the orthodox view mainly because it is orthodox. The Stratfordians can, however, legitimately claim that almost all the great Elizabethan scholars who *have* interested themselves in the controversy have been on their side.

CHAPTER II

Denigration of an Actor

It is obvious that anyone who sets out deliberately to deny that the Stratford actor, William Shakspere, wrote the works commonly ascribed to him and to substitute the name of some other person as the true author, must challenge Shakspere's ability to perform the task. Unless this were done the case for any other claimant, even if not entirely ruled out, would lose much of its force. It was therefore a *sine qua non* that, as a starting point for his exposition, every one of the theorists should make an attack on the actor's qualifications for writing the immortal works.

All of them, however, with the exception of those genial spirits among the Oxfordian groupists who, as we have seen (p. 25), accord him an honourable if minor rôle in the great task, have gone far beyond this. Not only have they denied his literary ability and other necessary qualifications, but they have made the most vituperative attacks on his personal character. Even A. J. Evans, who otherwise displays little bitterness, bemoans the fact that his publishers vetoed many of the things he would have liked to say about the wretched actor; while the Baconians, after the manner of their kind, have heaped mountains of abuse on his dishonoured name.

With this by way of introduction, we can turn to the actual accounts given by the different schools of thought. We will begin with that of the Baconians, for it includes almost everything that has been, or could be, said on the matter, and when we have dealt with it we shall not need to spend much time on those of the other schools. For a similar reason we shall select Sir Edwin Durning-Lawrence as the chief exponent of their case, for he expresses this much more freely and forcefully than anyone else. It is possible that the more scholarly Baconians might hesitate to identify themselves with some of the extreme opinions he expresses, but to the best of my knowledge they have never openly repudiated him in this matter, as some of them did in the matter of his cryptograms, and later writers on the Baconian theory still include his book in their bibliographies. We are therefore entitled to regard him as an official spokesman.

Durning-Lawrence states his case in *Bacon is Shakespeare*, a sumptuous volume he produced in 1910. According to this Shakespere was illiterate in the full sense of the term; that is, he could neither read nor write a single word. Moreover he was not even a good actor or a successful theatre manager, for he never played a part of any importance, and his share in the management was very small indeed. He was just an ignorant drunken rustic, disliked and despised by all who knew him, who made a small fortune out of usury and blackmailing his betters.

Some of his *dicta* Durning-Lawrence delivers *ex cathedra*, and clearly expects them to be accepted as matters of faith alone, but others he attempts to support by arguments and evidence, and it is to the examination of these arguments and this evidence that we must now give our attention.

There are in existence six signatures claimed to be those of William Shakspere. The first is on the purchase deed for a house in Blackfriars, bought by him in 1612, and the second on a mortgage on the same house taken out the following day; the third is on a document containing his 'deposition' in the Belott-Mountjoy suit, a legal case in which Shakspere was called as a witness; and the remaining three come from his will, which consists of three sheets of paper each bearing his name. The writing of these signatures is indisputably bad, and the spelling of the name varied[1] and in four cases abbreviated.

Not only the Stratfordians, but also the Oxfordians and Derbyites, accept these signatures as genuine, the Derbyites even attempting to make a little capital out of the badness of the handwriting; while Calvin Hoffman, since he makes no mention of them, apparently does not dispute their authenticity.

Sir Edwin Durning-Lawrence, however, will have none of this. To accept even these scrawls as genuine signatures would conflict with his dogma that Shakspere was totally illiterate. He

[1] The variations in spelling of course are in accordance with the free and easy custom of the time, and have no significance.

therefore proceeds to make a frontal attack on their authenticity.[1] He points out that the Blackfriars deeds are both sealed, and explains that when a legal document was sealed a signature was unnecessary, but that a lawyer or his clerk often wrote in the client's name near the seal in order to facilitate future reference. This, he declares, is what happened in the present instance; while he dismisses the three signatures on the will with the remark that they and the text are obviously in the same handwriting, and that they were therefore written by Collyns, the solicitor who drew up the document.

The Belott-Mountjoy 'deposition' confronts him with a problem of a slightly different nature. This was a legal document that the person making the statements recorded in it was obliged to sign or, if he could not write, to set his mark to it. Now just under Shakspere's name, which is here in an abbreviated form, there is a small blot. And it is this small blot that enables Sir Edwin once again to ride off triumphantly. To his all-seeing eye the blot is no ordinary blot; it is Shakspere's mark, made because the ignorant fellow could not write his own name, and the name is added by the lawyer *in an abbreviated form* to show that it is not a true signature.

Such then is Durning-Lawrence's case against the signatures. One might of course summarily dismiss it by merely pointing out that, even if all he claims were true, it would not prove that Shakspere was illiterate. In those days, when so many people could not write, lawyers, either from force of habit or because they preferred their own handwriting, would occasionally write in the names of even literate clients and get the latter to make their mark.[2] But there is no need to avoid the issue by any such means. A very brief analysis will show the utter untenability of Durning-Lawrence's whole case.

Before proceeding to this analysis, however, it is necessary to

---

[1] *Bacon is Shakespeare*, pp. 35–39 and 167–174.

[2] One example of this is provided by no less a person than Christopher Marlowe's father, the master-cobbler of Canterbury. There are extant a legal document on which he has made his mark and the lawyer has written in his name and a letter written and signed by himself. The same is true of Adrian Quiney, an Alderman of Stratford-on-Avon and a close friend of the Shakspere family.

draw attention to a particular fact, a mere triviality it may seem, yet one that has a considerable bearing on the matter in question. In the Elizabethan age the only kind of pen in general use was the quill. Now the quill pen in action very quickly loses its point, and becomes an awkward and intractable instrument. The lawyers and their clerks of course had 'pen-knives' handy, and kept their private pens well sharpened; but anyone who has used even the more durable steel pens provided today in post offices and other public places will have little difficulty in imagining the horror of the quill kept for the use of clients in an Elizabethan lawyer's office, where certainly most, probably all, the Shakspere signatures were made.

Now a glance at the documents, either the originals or good facsimiles – Durning-Lawrence has provided the latter in his book to his own undoing – is enough to enable anyone to recognize that all the signatures belong to the same class of scrawl one would expect to be made by such a pen as I have described, while the text of the documents consists in every case of the neat and well-formed script of a man whose profession compelled him to keep his pen in good order and who could never be guilty of such calligraphy as that of the signatures. Not only is the penmanship of the two different, but so are the pens with which they were written, and if Sir Edwin Durning-Lawrence saw them as 'obviously' the same, then it was only because he was determined that that was how he would see them. Many other persons, some of them experts on such questions, have examined the documents with the opposite result.

With regard to the 'deposition' there are some additional points to be observed. The usual mark made by an illiterate was a cross,[1] not a blot. This is significant, for another of the witnesses in the same case, who really was an illiterate, does in fact sign with a cross; and strangely enough the lawyer, who, according to Durning-Lawrence, wrote Shakspere's name *in an abbreviated form to show that it was not a true signature*, has written this witness's name *in full*. Moreover in this second case there

---

[1] Some persons, illiterate or otherwise, having occasion to sign frequently, adopted as a mark the symbolic form of a tool of their trade and similar devices, but a mere smudge of ink never occurs.

is no mistaking that the name was written by the same hand as the text and with the same well-sharpened pen. To complete Durning-Lawrence's discomfiture it may be mentioned that there is a second small blot – not shown in Durning-Lawrence's facsimile – just beyond the end of the signature, making it obvious that both came from a dripping pen.

That the signatures are genuine is proved for all practical purposes, as Feuillerat has pointed out,[1] by the fact that they all contain two very striking characteristics. First, all are written in the old English Secretary hand except for the second 's', which is in the new Italian hand; and, second, the signature is always in an abbreviated form except once on the will, and there it was obviously first written in an abbreviated form and the completing letters added as an afterthought. Now this repetition of the same characteristics on every occasion is natural enough if Shakspere wrote the signatures himself, but it is quite impossible to believe that several different lawyers' clerks could all display identical tricks in writing Shakspere's name for him.

So much for Durning-Lawrence on the signatures. His next charge against Shakspere is that he could not even act. He bases this on a passage in Rowe's *Life of Shakespeare*, first published in 1709. The passage runs as follows – 'His Name is printed, as the Custom was in those Times, amongst those of the other Players, before some old Plays,[2] but without any particular Account of what parts he us'd to play; and tho' I have inquir'd I could never meet with any further Account of him this way than that the top of his Performance was the Ghost in his own Hamlet.'

On this Durning-Lawrence, after suggesting with singular lack of dramatic appreciation that the part of the ghost was not worth playing, offers the following characteristic comment[3] –

---

[1] *Composition of Shakespeare's Plays*, p. 48.

[2] As Rowe himself points out, it was not the custom in Tudor times to print the names of the actors opposite the parts they played. When the names were included they were usually given in a list preceding the play. It is therefore impossible to identify the player and his part from the printed version, and nothing about Shakspere's ability can be deduced from this.

[3] *Bacon is Shakespeare*, p. 141 footnote.

35

'The appearance of Shakespeare's name in the list of Actors in Ben Jonson's plays and the plays known as Shakespeare's was, of course, part of the plot to place Shakespeare's name in a prominent position while the pseudonym had to be preserved.'

And that is the whole of his 'evidence'. Let us see what it amounts to.

Rowe's statement, written nearly a hundred years after the death of Shakspere, is not evidence at all, and was never intended as such. To anyone not the victim of wishful thinking it only means that the biographer, like so many others who have written on Shakspere, is bemoaning the lack of detailed information about his subject. As for Durning-Lawrence's own statement, it is clearly an *ex cathedra* utterance. Its pontifical tone, together with the fact that he offers nothing in support of it, is ample proof of this. In any case it is manifestly absurd, for apart from the difficulties of arranging for Shakspere's name to be printed in the casts of plays in which he had never acted, there would be hundreds of playgoers who would know that he had not done so, and the falsehood would only arouse suspicion and draw attention to the very 'plot' which, by Durning-Lawrence's own hypothesis, it was designed to conceal. It may be added that Dr Titherley, the leading Derbyite, not only accepts Shakspere's acting in Jonson's plays as a fact, but sees no reason to doubt the tradition that Shakspere was instrumental in persuading his own company to stage Jonson's *Sejanus*.

There is, however, no need to depend on tradition to rebut the dogmatic assertions of Durning-Lawrence. There is contemporary documentary evidence that William Shakspere ranked high as an actor, and incidentally was an important member of the management of the company to which he belonged. In the accounts of the Treasurer of the Chamber for the year 1594–95 the following entry occurs:

> To William Kempe William Shakespeare and Richard Burbage, servaunts to the Lord Chamberleyne, upon the Councille's warrant dated at Whitehall XVth. Marcij 1594, for two severall comedies or enterludes shewed by them before her maiestie in Christmas tyme laste parte viz St. Stephen's daye and Inocentes daye xiij[li] vj[s] vij[d], and by waye of her majesties Reward vj[li] xiij[s] iiij[d], in all xx[li].

In 1603 Shakspere's name occurs in the list of actors who received the new King's licence to continue playing, and in March 1604 it appears again in the list of actors who each received 4½ yards of scarlet cloth at the King's cost to provide a uniform for the Royal Procession through London.

From these official documents it is clear that as early as 1595 Shakspere was a leading member of the Lord Chamberlain's Company, and, since this was the principal company of players in the country and was later to become the King's Company, it is most unlikely that it would contain any but the best actors. Shakspere can therefore hardly have been less than good, an estimate that is confirmed by the King's renewal of his licence, for James was no mean judge where the drama was concerned. Moreover, as he is named with Kempe and Burbage, recognized managers, as a person to whom payment for the performances of the company was made, it is obvious that he must have had a considerable share in the management. So another of Durning-Lawrence's canards goes up in smoke.

Before turning to the next charge, we may pause just for a moment to note the light our conclusion about Shakspere as an actor throws on the question of his literacy. If he were an actor playing parts in the theatre and before Royalty, as we have seen that he was, then he must have been able to read. Parts have to be learnt, and even a Baconian can hardly believe that Burbage sat beside him, script in hand, and taught him his lines orally.

Now let us see what Durning-Lawrence has to say about him as a drunken rustic. His sole evidence for this charge is a story recorded by one, John Ward, who was vicar of Stratford from 1662 to 1681, that Shakspere attended a party, got drunk, and shortly afterwards developed a fever of which he died. As Ivor Brown has pointed out,[1] the dear vicar is not a very reliable witness for, apart from the fact that he is repeating mere hearsay more than fifty years after the event, he confesses that he had been so little interested in Shakspere that he had never read his works. Moreover, according to the story, Ben Jonson, a man whom Durning-Lawrence greatly admires, and who, the Baconians allege, had such a contempt for the 'Stratford clown', formed one of the merry party.

[1] *Amazing Monument*, p. 27.

Even Durning-Lawrence seems to have felt that this particular story required some reinforcement. Unfortunately, no more such stories or any other kind of evidence existed, but Durning-Lawrence was equal to the occasion. He claimed,[1] of course without any grounds whatever for so doing, that Christopher Sly, the drunken tinker who appears in the Prologue to *The Taming of the Shrew*, is a portrait of Shakspere, whom Bacon, the true author, thus castigates, which seems rather ungrateful conduct on the part of Bacon towards the man who was acting as his cover against Royal displeasure.

Of course all this is incredibly silly and childish, and I only include it because it illustrates the Baconians' methods and the lengths to which they will go to vilify Shakspere. It may well be that Shakspere did get drunk on occasion, as many eminent literary men and men eminent in other lines have done, or he may – though this is unlikely – have been a total abstainer. We do not know. But whether he drank heavily, moderately, or not at all, the matter is entirely irrelevant and throws no light whatever on the authorship of the Shakespearean works.

The next charge that Durning-Lawrence brings against Shakspere is that of usury.[2] The term 'usury', of course, is chosen because it has unpleasant associations even today, and thus serves to blacken the character of the person to whose activities it is applied. All it really means is that, among his multifarious affairs, like banks, building societies, and many business men at the present time, Shakspere lent capital to those who needed it, and charged interest on the sum lent.

The evidence that he did so consists of nothing more than documentary references to two prosecutions initiated by him for the recovery of debts – one at least for goods purchased from him, *not for money lent*, and the accusation that Greene made in his *Groatsworth of Wit* against actors in general that they indulged in usury. This is a very fragile foundation for the charge against Shakspere as an individual, but, as it is just a bare possibility, I am prepared to accept and answer it. To our modern minds, of course, there is nothing immoral about charging interest – it is a commonplace of business, but in Elizabethan times the practice, though freely used, was still regarded with

[1] *Bacon is Shakespeare*, p. 140. [2] Ibid., p. 51 ff.

much of the repugnance it had excited in the Middle Ages. This is the crux of the matter. Can we conceive, the Baconians demand, with a chorus of other theorists to assist them,[1] that the man who wrote *The Merchant of Venice* in condemnation of this very thing, would himself indulge in the practice?

Our answer to this question must be an unhesitating 'Yes, we can'. Modern psychologists tell us that a very common reaction to a feeling of guilt is loudly to condemn the fault occasioning it, and even to accuse others of the same fault. If Shakspere, assuming of course that he really was a usurer, were suffering from a guilt-complex, as he well might be in view of the prevailing attitude towards the practice, then to write such a play as *The Merchant of Venice* would be a very natural way to discharge it. That this was actually the case can be nothing but a surmise, but it does gain a little support from internal evidence. The play as a whole is a stern condemnation of usury, but when Shylock, the usurer, speaks for himself his defence is always superior to the attacks of his opponents, and he generally behaves with much greater dignity than they; indeed it is quite easy for a clever actor to play the part so as to win the sympathy of the audience. This is exactly what we should expect to find if the author were struggling with the task of simultaneously discharging a guilt complex and defending the sin. Of course the play really proves nothing; but, if it is to be dragged in as evidence, it certainly favours the Stratfordians rather than their opponents.

We come now to the climax of Durning-Lawrence's indictment of Shakspere – the blackmail charge.[2] He accuses Shakspere of bleeding poor Bacon with ever increasing demands, long after he had been fully rewarded for his services, under the threat of revealing the truth about the authorship of the Shakespearean plays. In support of this he quotes an extract from a pamphlet entitled *Ratsei's Ghost*, which was entered at the Stationers' Hall in 1605. I reproduce the 'relevant' passage, which is from a speech by the robber, Ratsei. The remarks enclosed in brackets also occur in Durning-Lawrence's text, and are his own scholarly comments on the subject matter.

[1] See, for example, Titherley, *Shakespeare's Identity*, pp. 105 and 114.
[2] *Bacon is Shakespeare*, p. 136 f.

39

Let thy hand be a stranger to thy pocket (*like the miser, Shakespeare*), thy hart slow to perform thy tongues promise (*like the lying rascal, Shakespeare*), and when thou feelest thy purse well lined, buy thee a place of lordship in the country (*as Shakespeare had bought New Place, Stratford*) that, growing weary of playing, thy mony may thus bring thee to dignitie and reputation (*as Shakespeare obtained a coat of arms*), then thou needst care for no man, no not for them that before made thee prowd with speaking their words upon the stage.

Durning-Lawrence then adds this final comment, 'This manifestly refers to two things, one that Shakespeare, when he bought New Place, quitted London and ceased to act; the other that he continually tried to exact more and more blackmail from those to whom he had sold his name'.

There are two comments to be made on this. First, most critics have taken the passage to refer to the famous tragedian, Edward Alleyn. He completed the purchase of Dulwich Manor in 1605, the same year as that in which *Ratsei's Ghost* was published, whereas Shakspere had bought New Place in 1597, no less than eight years earlier. The author of the pamphlet could hardly suppose that his readers would appreciate the point of his satire if it referred to such ancient history, even if they had ever heard of an event that took place so far from London as Stratford.

Second, no matter who the intended victim was, where is the reference to blackmail? I have read the quotation through carefully a number of times, and I cannot find the slightest suggestion of blackmail in it. If Durning-Lawrence can see one, then it is only because, like Humpty-Dumpty in *Alice Through the Looking-Glass*, words to him mean exactly what he chooses them to mean – neither more nor less.[1]

[1] There are two other details worthy of note in passing. The first occurs in the quotation, and is what Durning-Lawrence says in a reference to Shakspere's speaking other men's words on the stage, which implies that he could both read and act, talents that Durning-Lawrence has previously denied him. The second is an inaccuracy in the earlier part of Durning-Lawrence's own comment. Shakspere did *not* leave London and cease to act when he bought New Place. The purchase was completed in 1597, and in 1603, as we have seen (p. 37), James I granted him a licence to continue acting. He could hardly '*continue* acting' if he had already given it up.

The Baconians, however, are not the only theorists to accuse Shakspere of blackmail. Dr Titherley, the leading exponent of the Derbyites, does the same.[1] He says that the actor, in order to increase his ill-gotten gains, abused his position as Derby's agent by selling to publishers, without permission, copies of the Shakespearean (that is, Derby's) plays and also plays by inferior writers under the Shakespearean pseudonym. At length, however, he overreached himself. He sold a revised version of *Hamlet*,[2] and Derby, who had no doubt long suspected his false dealings, then had the proof of them in his hands, for the revised version had never been performed and was known only to himself and Shakspere. He thereupon dismissed his dishonest agent; but Shakspere, not wishing to lose such a lucrative position, threatened to reveal the secret of the plays' authorship, and Derby was obliged to buy his silence with a large sum of money.

The reply to this is that there is not a single scrap of evidence to support such a story, nor does Titherley attempt to produce any. It is nothing more than one of those assumptions referred to in the preceding chapter (see p. 29) which every theorist is driven to make on occasion in order to account for facts that are otherwise irreconcilable with his case. In this particular instance it is offered as an explanation of the means by which Shakspere acquired his very considerable fortune – an indisputable fact – if he were not the author of the plays. It has thus the additional weakness of begging the question, since it could not be true unless the rest of Titherley's theory were true and Derby wrote the plays, and this of course is the whole point at issue.

Another accusation Titherley makes[3] in order to blacken the character of Shakspere is that he tried to marry a certain Anne Whateley on the day before his actual marriage, but was prevented by the Hathaway faction. His only evidence for this suggestion is an entry, dated 27 November, 1582, in the

---

[1] *Shakespeare's Identity*, pp. 120 f.
[2] A bad Quarto of *Hamlet* was published in 1603 and a good Quarto a year later. While more or less plausible conjectures have been made, the actual circumstances responsible for these two publications are unknown.
[3] Ibid., p. 108.

Worcester Diocesan Register of the issue of a licence for the marriage of 'Willelmum Shaxpere et Annem Whateley'. The very next day Shakspere married Anne Hathaway, and two local farmers, Sandalls and Richardson, bound themselves in the sum of £40 to indemnify the Bishop of Worcester for issuing a licence for the pair to be married when their banns had been called once only. Now, since there is no entry in the Diocesan Register for a second licence, since nothing is known of any such person as 'Anne Whateley' apart from this one entry, and since the Christian name is 'Anne' in both cases, most critics have assumed that 'Whateley' is merely a scribal error for 'Hathaway'.[1] But even if Titherley's assumption were correct, shabby treatment of women could hardly be considered as evidence of inability to write poetry. On the contrary the biographies of many poets – Shelley and Byron, for example – might even suggest that it was by way of being a qualification. Moreover Derby himself was far from being impeccable in this respect. Like so many of the theorists' arguments, the incident cannot possibly have any bearing on the subject. It throws no light on Shakspere's literary ability or lack of it, and I, for one, am left completely puzzled why such a matter should have ever been introduced.

The specific charges against Shakspere therefore all fall to the ground. They are ridiculous in themselves, and, with one exception, are entirely unsupported by any evidence worth the paper on which it is written. The exception is the so-called 'usury' charge, and though this, if true, might be unpleasing to a bardolator, it is certainly no proof of Shakspere's inability to write plays; on the contrary, as we have seen, it is favourable rather than unfavourable to the thesis that he wrote *The Merchant of Venice*.

There is, however, another form of attack on the character of Shakspere, of which *Ratsei's Ghost* has given us a foretaste, that must be examined before we bring this chapter to a conclusion. It consists of a number of satiric references which most of the theorists claim are aimed at Shakspere, and which, they say, show that his contemporaries despised him as a brainless dolt,

[1] Such scribal errors were far from uncommon in Elizabethan times. We shall have to deal with a very important example in Chapter VI.

capable of any trick to gain the reputation of an author. For reasons of space I can quote only three of these – two by Ben Jonson and the other by an anonymous author – but as the rest are all of the same type and, as the theorists draw exactly the same conclusions from all of them, these three will be quite sufficient for our purpose.

The first comes from the play *Every Man Out Of His Humour* (III, iv). Puntarvolo and Sogliardo, two of the *dramatis personae*, are on the stage. The former is congratulating his companion, whose name, the Baconians hasten to tell us, means 'filth', on having received the patent for a coat-of-arms from the Heralds. The dialogue continues:

> SOG. I' faith I thank them; I can write myself gentleman now; here 's my patent, it cost me thirty pound by this breath.
> PUNT. A very fair coat, well charged and full of armoury.
> SOG. Nay, it has as much variety of colours in it, as you have seen a coat have; how like you the crest, sir?
> PUNT. I understand it not well, what is't?
> SOG. Marry, sir, it is your boar without a head, *rampante*.
> PUNT. A boar without a head; that's very rare.

And, after some more dialogue of the same kind, comes:

> PUNT. Let the word be 'Not without mustard'. Your crest is very rare, sir.

The second is No. 56 of Jonson's *Epigrams*, published in 1616, but written some years earlier. It runs as follows:

> Poor poet ape, that would be thought our chief,
> Whose works are e'en the frippery of wit
> From brokage is become so bold a thief,
> As we, the robbed, leave rage and pity it.
> At first he made low shifts, would pick and glean,
> Buy the reversion of old plays; now grown
> To a little wealth and credit in the scene
> He takes up all, makes each man's wit his own,
> And told of this he slights it, etc.

The third is another play, entitled *The Return from Parnassus*, which was performed at Cambridge University, probably by an

43

amateur cast of undergraduates. It contains a speech by one of the *dramatis personae*, Studioso, bemoaning the sad lot of the dramatic poet and the poor payment he receives from the players, who gain fame through his plays. The speech continues:

> *England* affords these glorious vagabonds,
> That carried earst their fardels on their backes,
> Coursers to ride on through the gazing streetes,
> Sooping it in their glaring Satten sutes,
> And pages to attend their maisterships;
> With mouthing words that better wits haue framed,
> They purchase lands, and now esquiers are namde.

To which another character, Philomusus, replies:

> What ere they seeme being even at the best
> They are but sporting fortunes *scornfull* iest.

It is clear that in these references we are picking up echoes of those literary quarrels in which writers in the Elizabethan age, as in some others, freely indulged. The first belongs to the famous 'War of the Theatres'. In this Jonson mercilessly attacked many of his fellow-dramatists, and was belaboured by them with equal ruthlessness, as for instance by Dekker and Marston in *Satiromastix*. There can be little doubt that Shakspere was one of his victims in *Every Man Out Of His Humour*. The play was produced soon after he had been granted his coat-of-arms, and Sir Puntarvolo's words 'Not without mustard' are an obvious parody on Shakspere's actual motto 'Non sanz Droict'. Moreover there are various suggestions in what we know of him that Shakspere did aspire to gentility. So much may be freely accorded to the theorists; but what does it all amount to? Jonson's references to some other dramatists of the opposing party, particularly to Marston, were much more biting than those he applied to Shakspere, and, as already stated, he received as good as he gave. If the attacks on Shakspere are to be taken at their face value, then logically so must all the others, which would leave nearly all the great Elizabethan men of letters without a shred of reputation among them. But of course the attacks cannot be taken at their face value; they are satire, and the essence of satire is exaggera-

44

tion. Moreover, these literary squabbles were only passing phases. Jonson's and Marston's antipathy for each other did not prevent them from collaborating on occasion. The theorists' attempt to write literary criticism based on *Every Man Out Of His Humour* is just about as nonsensical as trying to write modern history based on a *Punch* article.

When we turn to the *Epigram*, we cannot even be sure that the sketch was meant for Shakspere; there are several other candidates for the rôle of victim. The phrase 'Poet ape', invented by Sir Philip Sidney, was the current term for actor-dramatists, in a hostile sense of course, and Jonson used it freely. In this poem he is making an attack on an actor-dramatist, whom he accuses of plagiarism – first by writing over old plays and later by lifting the best bits out of his contemporaries' works. He may have had Shakspere in mind when he wrote, or he may have been referring to someone else. We have no means of telling. In any case it has the character of satire – exaggeration.

The Return From Parnassus is an attack on actors in general by some disgruntled dramatist, who is also a snob and resents their improved and improving social status. Shakspere must clearly be included with the rest, for it is known that he rode in the Royal Procession through London (see p. 37), to which there is an obvious reference; but there is nothing in the pasasge to suggest that the author had him specially in mind when he wrote it.

Precisely the same result emerges from a study of the other references of the same sort collected by the theorists. Some are certainly aimed at Shakspere; others may be, but may equally well have another target. They prove two things only, neither favourable to the anti-Stratfordians. The first is that Shakspere was an eminent man in his own day, for only someone who was well-known could be treated as a subject for satire in plays intended for public performance and poems intended for publication; and the second is that his contemporaries clearly believed that he was the author of the works that bore his name, though they did not think much of the works themselves. The charges of rewriting old plays and plagiarizing from new ones can mean nothing else.

Of course the Baconians are not content with these conclusions. They claim the references imply that Shakspere appropriated Bacon's plays, but this is obvious nonsense. Apart from the fact that the words simply cannot support such an interpretation, Bacon's authorship was, by their own theory, a closely guarded secret, and even if Jonson might be supposed to share it, as some of them say he did, he would not risk giving it away in this manner, nor would he be so stupid as to offer his audiences and readers something which they could not possibly understand, thus depriving his work of its point. Moreover Jonson is not the only author to be considered; there are those of the other references. By the same reasoning they also must have shared the secret, in which case it could hardly have been a secret at all, and all the elaborate arrangements made to preserve it would merely be so much wasted effort. We encounter this confusion of 'secret' and 'no secret' over and over again in the Baconian arguments, for they can never make up their minds whether the whole population of the country from the throne downwards recognized the hand of their hero in the immortal works, or whether the knowledge of his authorship, so dangerous to his dignity and perhaps to his life, remained locked in the breasts of a devoted few.

The Baconians, however, are not the only people who suffer from confusion of thought. Most of the theorists are afflicted with the same weakness to a greater or less degree, and their excessive denigration of Shakspere provides a good example of their aberration.

It is an essential of all their theories that the true author, whoever he was, for good and sufficient reasons desired to remain anonymous, and paid Shakspere handsomely to lend his name to the works and pose as their author. In such circumstances one would suppose that the true author, or his agent, would carefully select a substitute who, superficially at least, would appear the brilliant author he was supposed to be. In no other way could the deception possibly be sustained, and, since the true author's life might depend upon it, he would hardly be likely to overlook such an obvious point.

Instead of this, however, we are told that he chose a drunken rustic, an ignorant clown who could not write his own name, a person whom no one in his senses could possibly believe to be the author of anything. Of course all the theorists do not go to the same extremes as Durning-Lawrence, though many of his fellow-Baconians and some of the others follow him a long way. Others, however, are a little more cautious. To Calvin Hoffman Shakspere was nothing worse than 'a steady, not too imaginative fellow . . . who did not mind lending his name to anything as long as . . . gold flowed freely'. Dr Titherley even allows him some verbal agility and the ability to hold his own in the wit combats at the Mermaid Tavern, though he too at times tends to overdo the 'writing down'.

It is of course a trap easy for people who are 'making a case' to fall into. The deeper Shakspere can be driven into the mire of illiteracy and degradation the clearer will be the path to the authorship for their own candidate; but, while they are enthusiastically labouring for this desirable end, they forget the other leg of their argument, namely that Shakspere has to make a convincing 'stand-in' for the true author. Hence arose the mass of contradictions found in their theories.

The only theorists entirely to escape this dilemma are certain of the Oxford groupists. Their picture of Shakspere as the honest broker and technical adviser of the coterie of literary courtiers, and perhaps also a bit of a dramatist himself, is much more convincing. Such a man might well be able to pass himself off as the author of plays with the details of the construction of which he had assisted, although he had not written them. This is not, of course, meant to imply that I accept the Oxfordian theory; I merely mention the matter to show that the only way to avoid the perils of the denigration tactic is not to make use of it.

As for the denigration employed by the other schools, it fails both as a whole and in its details to establish the case for which it was intended to be a proof. The only thing it does prove is the varying degree of confusion of thought in the minds of its practitioners, a fact that should be remembered when their other arguments are under consideration.

CHAPTER III

The Case for Francis Bacon[1]

The Baconians were not only the originators of the great Shakespearean controversy; they also devised the pattern for it that all the other schools of thought have followed. This pattern consists of four sections – (1) arguments for the rejection of William Shakspere as author; (2) arguments for the recognition of some other candidate as author; (3) reasons for the long concealment of the identity of the new claimant; and (4) reasons for the former ascription of the authorship to William Shakspere. Apart from the fact that Calvin Hoffman, the advocate of Marlowe's authorship, differs from the others in the third item of this pattern, the arguments put forward by all schools for the first, third, and fourth items are very nearly identical. It is in the second item that the greatest differences occur, though even here there is considerable overlapping where the same factor, or series of factors, is merely given a slight twist to make it apply to a different candidate. In this chapter we shall confine our attention to the evidence peculiar to the case for Francis Bacon.

The main plank in the Baconian platform is that the plays show such a remarkable familiarity with the Law and all its processes that they could only have been written by a practising

---

[1] It is to be noted that the leading authorities on Francis Bacon, almost without exception, reject the theory of his authorship of the Shakespearean works. James Spedding, by universal consent the greatest expert on the subject, the man who edited the standard editions of Bacon's works and letters, who wrote the history of his life and times, who was his most devoted admirer, and who spared no pains to clear Bacon's character of the stigma thrown upon it by Macaulay, always combated the Baconian Theory in season and out; while Charles Williams, a recent biographer, in addition to a number of scathing references to the Baconian Theory, remarks (*Bacon*, p. 310) that if there were any concealed work to be ascribed to Bacon it would be something like *Paradise Lost*, not the Shakespearean works, which would be completely alien to him.

I FRANCIS BACON
Engraving by Simon de Passe in the British Museum

lawyer. This is known technically as 'the argument from legal phraseology', and it is true that the plays do exhibit a considerable amount of legal expertise. Not only are legal matters sometimes introduced into the action, but much use is made of the terminology of the Law in similes and imagery. The Baconians grow almost lyrical themselves as they contemplate these. B. G. Theobald[1] cries in delight that the author actually thinks in legal terms. He claims that only trained lawyers can fully understand the plays, and that they are astounded at the depths of legal knowledge these contain. He quotes the eminent luminaries, including a Lord Chief Justice, who have agreed with this finding, and inevitably he refers to the use made of it by the non-Baconian, Sir George Greenwood, in his slashing attack on Shakspere's authorship.

As I can lay claim to no legal expertise myself, I rely very largely for my criticism of this part of the Baconian case on J. M. Robertson, who was not only a great Elizabethan scholar, but spent five years of his life in a lawyer's office. He devotes nearly 200 pages of his vast work, *The Baconian Heresy*, to exposing the fallacies which underlie all the Baconian arguments on this matter, giving chapter and verse from Elizabethan literature for every claim he makes. His work should be read by all who desire a full understanding of this aspect of the controversy. All I can do here is to give a brief summary of his arguments.

Robertson begins his destructive analysis by tracing the genesis of the legal theory.[2] Like so many of the Baconian ideas it was originated by a Stratfordian, J. P. Collier, who about 1859 wrote to Lord Chief Justice Campbell to ask if he did not think the legal references in the plays suggested that Shakespeare had at one time been a lawyer's clerk. In reply Lord Campbell prepared a disquisition on the subject entitled *Shakespeare's Legal Acquirements Considered*, in which he stated that the legal knowledge was undoubtedly great, but not more so than might have been picked up by a man who 'for some years had occupied a desk in the office of a country attorney in good business'. The list of quotations Lord Campbell compiled to illustrate this contention was taken over unaltered by Sir

---

[1] *Enter Francis Bacon*, p. 107.   [2] *The Baconian Heresy*, pp. 36 f.

George Greenwood in 1908, but he rejected Lord Campbell's finding that they might emanate from a mere clerk, and maintained that the author must have been a trained lawyer, versed in all the fundamentals of the Law. The Baconians, since that time, have merely repeated Greenwood's arguments and referred their readers to his work.

Robertson next asks a very pertinent question.[1] If the author really filled his plays with legal references that only trained lawyers could understand, did not this imply that his *dramatis personae* talked 'out of character', and thus detracted from his artistry as a dramatist? Moreover there was the audience to be considered. Would the writer have become the most popular dramatist of his day if his plays had contained so much that could not be understood? This point need not detain us long; the questions answer themselves. It is obvious that the Shakespearean plays do not contain the defects mentioned or they could never have attained their universal popularity.

Robertson then proceeds to make his main point. The lawyers, who so largely constitute the ranks of the Baconians, are not Elizabethan scholars. They have certainly studied the Shakespearean plays to find in them what they wanted, and have done as much with the works of Bacon for the same purpose, but they are totally ignorant of the rest of Elizabethan literature. Had they not been so they would have known that almost every other dramatist of the time, and other writers too, made as much use of legal phraseology as did Shakespeare, many a great deal more, and not a few handled it more adroitly, for Shakespeare's knowledge is far from being as impeccable as the Baconians claim. If Shakespeare's familiarity with the Law proves that he was a trained lawyer, then by the same reasoning so was almost every other writer of the time, and we are driven to the absurd conclusion that the whole of Elizabethan literature was written by trained lawyers.

To prove his point Robertson takes a wide range of legal expressions from the Campbell–Greenwood list, and in well over a hundred pages[2] of closely printed matter shows that every one of them is used in precisely the same way by other authors of the day. Here considerations of space allow me to

[1] *The Baconian Heresy*, p. 33.   [2] Ibid., pp. 39–177.

quote only two examples by way of illustration of the thoroughness of Robertson's work. The two I have chosen are 'Extent' and 'Praemunire', the use of which by the author of the Shakespearean plays proves, so the Baconians claim, that he had a deep technical knowledge of the Law.

An example of his use of the first occurs in *As You Like It* (III, i), 'Make an extent upon his house and lands'; and the second, used only on this one occasion in all the Shakespearean works, occurs in *Henry VIII* (III, ii), 'Fall into the compass of a praemunire'.

Robertson gives a list of nine other contemporary works out of many in which these words are used in their strict legal sense. In the pre-Shakespearean play *Selimus* (sc. I, l. 21), usually ascribed to Greene, is the phrase 'Through all the world make extent'; and in the same author's undoubted work, *A Defence of Coney-Catching*, there is 'They have you in suit, and I doubt not will ere long have some extent against your lands'.

Thomas Nashe, in his *Pierce Pennilesse, His Supplication To The Devill*, causes his hero to suggest to the Infernal Potentate that he might 'make extent upon the souls of a number of uncharitable cormorants' who have 'incurred the danger of a praemunire with meddling with matters that properly concern your own person'. Again, in *Christ's Tears Over Jerusalem*, the same author has 'Oh pride, of all heaven-relapsing praemunires the most fearful'; in *The Unfortunate Traveller*, 'lamenting my Jewish Praemunire that body and goods I should light into the hands of such a cursed generation'; and, in the same tale, 'to extend upon' in the sense of 'to make extent upon'.

Massinger makes frequent use of the terms. The following are a few examples:

From *The City Madam* (V, ii),

> There lives a foolish creature
> Called an under-sheriff, who, being well paid, will serve
> An extent on lords' and lowns' lands.

From *A New Way To Pay Old Debts*,

> When
> This manor is extended to my use
> You 'll speak in a humbler key.

51

And from the same play, spoken by Sir Giles Overreach,

> If I were a justice, besides the trouble,
> I might, or out of wilfulness or error,
> Run myself into a praemunire,
> And so become a prey to the informer.

And from *The Old Lady*,

> That 's a shrewd praemunire.

Ben Jonson also uses the second term in *A Staple Of News* (V, ii):

> Lest what I have done to them, and against law,
> Be a praemunire.

So much for the Baconian argument from the use of legal phraseology. This, however, does not exhaust that school's appeal to the Law. Another claim is that the author of the Shakespearean plays was so familiar with lawyers' language that he could make his *dramatis personae* utter whole long speeches in a burlesque legal terminology, as he does in the case of Don Adriano in L.L.L. (I, 11). To which Robertson replies[1] that this is perfectly true, but it is equally true of many other Elizabethan dramatists, and that there is nothing of this type of humour in the Shakespearean plays to compare with the speech Ben Jonson puts into the mouth of Sir Puntarvolo in *Every Man Out Of His Humour*:

> That, after receipt of his money, he shall neither in his own person or any other, either by direct or indirect means, as magic, witchcraft, or other exotic arts, attempt, practise, or complot anything to the prejudice of me, my dog or my cat; neither shall I use the help of any such sorceries or enchantments, as unctions to make our skins impenetrable, or travel invisible by virtue of a powder, or a ring, or to hang any three-forked chains about my dog's neck, secretly conveyed into his collar; but all be performed sincerely, without fraud or imposture.

Moreover there are Shakespeare's legal lapses to be taken into account. A barrister named Devecmon – for not all lawyers are Baconians – in his *Re Shakespeare's Legal Acquire-*

---

[1] *The Baconian Heresy*, p. 53.

ments, another work conspicuous by its absence from Baconian bibliographies, calls attention to some of these. More particularly he attacks the trial scene in M. of V. as a romantic travesty of both justice and Law Courts, good theatre no doubt, but, as regards the sober processes of the Law, absolute nonsense. He contrasts with this Webster's realistic handling of trial scenes in three of his plays – *The White Devil*, *The Devil's Law Case*, and *Appius And Virginia*. With regard to the second, Devecmon says that it contains in the one scene 'more legal expressions, some of them highly technical, and all correctly used, than any single one of Shakespeare's works'. We can hardly imagine Francis Bacon, the premier lawyer of his age, being beaten in such a matter by Webster.

Baconian lawyers, not being Elizabethan scholars, do not understand that in the Tudor period there grew up a positive 'craze' for the Law, which affected all classes. Hubert Hall, an official of H.M. Records Office about the middle of last century, says in his *Society In The Elizabethan Age*[1] that 'Every man in those days was up to a certain point his own lawyer; that is, he was well versed in all the technical forms and procedure'. Bringing legal actions was a favourite pastime, as Nashe tells us. In *Pierce Pennilesse* he says, 'Lawyers cannot divise which way in the world to beg, they are so troubled with brabblements and suits every term, of yeomen and gentlemen that fall out for nothing. If John a Nokes his hen do but leap into Elizabeth de Yappe's close, she will never leave to haunt her husband till he bring it to a *Nisi prius*. One while the parson sueth the parishioner for bringing home his tithes; another while the parishioner sueth the parson for not taking away his tithes in time'. So great was this mania for litigation that Bishop Latimer felt impelled to preach a sermon against the bringing of frivolous lawsuits.

In those days too, when entertainment was not so easily come by as at the present time, the Law Courts drew crowds of people, who eagerly followed the cases tried there, which explains why dramatists could rely on their audiences' appreciating the legal references in their plays. Moreover, it was quite normal for the sons of the wealthy to go into residence at one

[1] Page 141.

of the Inns of Court, after completing their university course, for a period of study, not with the idea of practising the Law, but merely to set the seal on their education.

All this preoccupation with the Law naturally produced a legalistic fashion of writing poetry, just as preoccupation with euphuism had produced a euphuistic fashion of writing poetry. Robertson deals with this fully,[1] mentioning the names of many poets who indulged in the practice and quoting copiously from their works.

When this kind of poetry was general it is not surprising that we should find a large number of legal allusions in the Shakespearean plays. This would hold good whoever the author might be; that is, *unless he were Francis Bacon.*

There is a sting in the tail of the legalistic argument for the Baconians themselves. We have seen (p. 22) that according to their theory Bacon disliked the practice of the Law, and only followed it as a profession because of his ambition to make a career for himself. They have certainly good grounds for this view. Except in the very few of his acknowledged writings which dealt specifically with legal subjects, he never mentioned the Law in his works. When other writers were filling theirs with legal allusions, he steadfastly refused to discuss what would have been to him 'shop'. Now do the Baconians, who tell us that Bacon took to writing plays in his spare time as a relief from the frets of the Law, seriously ask us to believe that, contrary to his practice in the works that bear his name, he filled these labours of love with references to the hated topic? This suggestion is another example of the confusion of thought to which the Baconians so easily fall victims.

The argument from legal allusions then, so far from proving that Bacon wrote the Shakespearean plays, actually points in the opposite direction.

The next point we must consider is the Baconians' claim that Bacon had an absorbing interest in the drama. The point is vitally important for their theory, for without such an interest he could not, and would not, have wanted to write the Shakespearean plays either secretly or in any other way. Moreover, unlike Oxford and Derby – scions of a leisured aristocracy, and

[1] *The Baconian Heresy*, pp. 86–93.

known to have at least a dilettantish interest in dramatic art –
Bacon lived an exceedingly busy life, much of it public, and
none of it in any way associated with the theatre. His modern
supporters therefore labour strenuously to establish the only
factor that could be a sufficient incentive for such a mighty
additional task.

As far as his more youthful days are concerned they have no
great difficulty in making some sort of case for this. The members of the Inns of Court at the time he was in residence were
very interested in all theatrical activities. Not only did they
engage professional companies to come and act before them,
but they frequently indulged in amateur productions of their
own. And in these activities and others like them Bacon took a
full share. Gradually, however, a change came about, and soon
his name ceased to appear in such a connection. An ordinary
person might conclude that this was simply because Bacon,
having made up his mind that the Law must be his career,
felt that he could no longer spare the time from his studies for
such frivolities. Not so the Baconians; they see in it something
far deeper. B. G. Theobald[1] informs us that it was because
Bacon had even at that early date decided to write plays
secretly, and, in order to avoid the slightest suspicion of his
authorship when the time to do so came, he withdrew from all
open association with the drama. 'Even where harmless
amateur theatricals were concerned,' Theobald says, 'he
(Bacon) was somewhat cautious in allowing his name to appear
too prominently.'

It is at this point that the Baconians usually stop the story;
and indeed without a little *suppressio veri* they would soon be in
difficulties, for in his great work *De Augmentis* Bacon makes two
attacks upon the contemporary drama. In the first (ii, 13) he
states that 'the stage is capable of no small influence both of
discipline and corruption', and 'of corruptions of this kind we
have enough, but the discipline has in our times been plainly
neglected'. In other words, the drama may be an influence for
good or evil; in Elizabethan and Jacobean times it had been for
evil. Again, at the end of Book vi, after describing the Jesuits'
use of amateur theatricals in education, he says, 'stage-playing

---

[1] *Enter Francis Bacon*, p. 34.

is a thing indeed, if practised professionally, of low repute; but if it be made a part of discipline – of excellent use'; that is, the drama of the playhouse is an evil thing, but didactic plays, produced by amateurs under the supervision of school-masters, may be very helpful in education. As Robertson points out,[1] *De Augmentis* was published in the same year as the First Folio, the very volume in which Bacon, according to the Baconians, gave with such loving care his dramatic treasures to the world, after these had been enjoying performances on the *professional* stage for more than twenty years.

Moreover Bacon gave a practical demonstration of his lack of sympathy with the theatre in 1614. In that year the players were contemplating removing their theatres from the south to the north bank of the river, a far more convenient site for their audiences. The Thames watermen thereupon presented a petition to James I, protesting that if this were done they would lose half their livelihood. The King's Company, that which had the monopoly of the Shakespearean plays, at once presented a counter-petition, pointing out the necessity for the players to make the change. James referred the matter to the Commissioners for Suits, of whom Bacon was one, and these decided in favour of the watermen. John Taylor, the watermen's leader, thus describes what took place:

> Our extremities and cause being judiciously pondered by the Honourable and Worshipfull Commissioners, Sir Francis Bacon very worthily said that so farre forth as the Publike weal was to be regarded before pastimes, or a serviceable decaying multitude before a handful of particular men, or profit before pleasure, so far was our suit to be preferred before theirs.

It is not merely the decision but Bacon's language in announcing that decision which is so revealing of his attitude of mind. It is clear that he regarded the drama as mere frivolous entertainment, not to be compared in importance to the community with the services of those who plied for hire in boats on the Thames. This is hardly the attitude of an enthusiast, and if what he wrote about the Elizabethan and Jacobean drama in *De Augmentis* represents his sincere opinion, as coming in such

[1] *The Baconian Heresy*, p. 532.

an important work it undoubtedly does, then he would scarcely feel grateful to his modern admirers for their attempt to father a share of this drama on him. Once again the Baconians fail to establish their claim.

The next subject for examination is a small group of miscellaneous items of the kind that form the staple of the Baconian case. I have taken my examples from B. G. Theobald's book, *Enter Francis Bacon*, which, he claims, summarizes all the principle arguments in favour of Bacon's authorship. The first is concerned with a letter which Bacon wrote to Sir John Davies when the latter was on the point of setting out to meet James I, then on his way from Scotland to ascend the Throne of England. In the letter Bacon begged Sir John to use his influence with the new King to obtain for him (Bacon) some office. To it Bacon added a postscript which contained the words, 'So desiring you to be good to concealed poets'.[1]

The Baconian argument from this is beautiful in its simplicity. It runs as follows – Bacon here acknowledges himself to be a concealed poet, and if a concealed poet, then *ipso facto* the author of the Shakespearean plays. The term 'concealed poet' was in general use for all courtly writers who considered it *infra dig* to publish their work under their own names. Bacon may well have been a concealed poet in this sense, and was sometimes an unconcealed one, for he published a rather inferior metrical version of the Psalms under his own name. Sir John Davies was well-known as a patron of poets, and Bacon was obviously trying 'to get on the right side of him' by appealing to this soft spot in his nature. Dozens of young gentlemen at that time could have addressed exactly the same words to him. There is not the remotest suggestion of any connection with the Shakespearean plays in them, and as evidence of Bacon's authorship they are invalid.

The second item is another postscript, this time in a letter addressed to Bacon by his friend, Sir Tobie Mathew, in 1624. It runs as follows: 'The most prodigious wit that I ever knew, of my nation and this side the sea, is of your lordship's name, though he be known by another.'[2]

The Baconians interpret this as meaning that Bacon was

[1] *Enter Francis Bacon*, p. 22. [2] Ibid., p. 24.

writing works of wit under a pseudonym, Theobald remarking that the Stratfordians had never been able to counter 'this deadly evidence'. Clearly Theobald had not read the anti-Baconian evidence very carefully, otherwise he would have discovered that a Stratfordian, Mrs Stopes, had countered the point most effectively as far back as 1888. She pointed out in her *Bacon–Shakspere Question Answered* that Sir Tobie Mathew wrote his letter from abroad, as, of course, his own words 'this side the sea' make perfectly obvious. At this time Bacon's brother, Anthony, was also abroad on secret service, travelling under an assumed name. Such a circumstance is more than adequate to explain Mathew's remark. In any case he would scarcely be such a fool as to risk betraying Bacon's secret, if Bacon had one, by hinting at it in the frivolous fashion the Baconians suggest, in a letter that might well have been opened by the authorities on reaching England.

The third item that Theobald offers us is of a rather different nature. It consists of three lines from an anonymous poem, entitled *Wits Recreations*, published in 1640. The three lines are as follows:

> Shakespeare, we must be silent in thy praise
> 'Cause our encomions will but blast thy bayes,
> Which envy could not.

I give Theobald's interpretation of them in full.[1] He writes, 'What a remarkable statement! Why, forsooth, were the literary men of those days to be "silent" about Shakespeare? And why would their praise injure his reputation? Can any reasonable explanation be given which fits in with the orthodox theory? I think not. There would be no reason why the man of Stratford should not be praised had he really been the author. But with Bacon the case was different. He could not be publicly praised as a poet.'

To such incredible blindness can an *idée fixe* bring a man. The plain meaning of these lines is that Shakespeare stands so high that he is beyond all praise, and any tributes from lesser men will only detract from his glory, not add to it. To put it another

---

[1] *Enter Francis Bacon*, pp. 26 f.

way, Shakespeare *is* being praised under the poetic pretence that this is impossible. Hundreds of compliments in verse and prose have been paid in this form, as Theobald must have known when he penned this absurd passage if the Baconian fog had not obscured his mental vision. Has he himself never said, 'No words of mine can describe how wonderful he, she, or it, is'? That, in short, is all there is in the lines, and like the preceding item they are evidence of nothing.[1]

Theobald's next argument is, in my opinion, the one piece of evidence in the whole Baconian case that demands serious consideration. It is the claim that two Elizabethan satirists, Hall and Marston, recognized Bacon as the author of *Venus and Adonis* and *The Rape of Lucrece*. This claim was first put forward by Bagley at the beginning of the present century. I give Theobald's account of it in full. He writes:

'In Hall's Satires, 1597, Book II, p. 25, the following passage occurs:

> For shame write better *Labeo*, or write none
> Or better write, or Labeo write alone.

[1] In addition to this, Theobald's argument is fallible on several other counts. I briefly summarize these in order to illustrate the utter worthlessness of all such so-called evidence. They are as follows:

(1) *Wits Recreations* mentions that Shakespeare was a poet (i.e. he wore the 'Bayes'), and if this did not betray Bacon's secret, how could the mere addition that he was a *good* poet do so?

(2) Shakespeare had been highly praised in verse and prose, not only by the contributors to the First Folio, but also independently by Drayton, Cowley, Milton, Habington, Suckling, and at least seven other men of letters, all before 1640. If all this eulogy of Shakespeare's name had done Bacon no harm, how could any similar praise in *Wits Recreations* do so?

(3) Bacon died in 1626, fourteen years before *Wits Recreations* was published. How then could the betrayal of Bacon's secret by this work do him any more harm than the Baconians' own more recent betrayal of it?

(4) If Theobald's view of the quotation is correct, then the anonymous author of *Wits Recreations* must have known Bacon's secret, and, what is more, he must have believed that most of his readers would be privy to it also, or there would have been no point in his remark. And this brings us once again to the Baconians' mental confusion about 'secret' and 'no secret'.

59

Nay, call the Cynic but a wittie fool,
Thence to obscure his handsome drinking bole;
Because the thirstie swaine with hollow hand
Conveyed the streame to weet his drie weasand.
Write they that can, tho they that cannot do;
But who knows that, but they that do not know.

'From the orthodox standpoint these lines are by no means clear, and editors have been unable to identify *Labeo* and the *Cynic*. But if Francis Bacon was the author of *Venus and Adonis* published under the name of "Shakespeare" the whole passage becomes plain. Hall may easily have been slightly shocked, or pretended to be, at the theme of his poem, even though it is handled with delicacy and not in a lascivious manner; and so he took the opportunity of reproving the author for writing in such a strain. He also rebukes him for writing in conjunction with someone else, but leaves us to conjecture what is the nature of the partnership with some other person un-named.[1]

'Hall is telling Bacon bluntly that he is a fool to let "the thirstie swaine" (Shakspere) moisten his parched throat with draughts from the Muses' spring, i.e. to obtain credit for the poetical inspiration from the Muses which was not really his but Bacon's. The Cynic is also meant for Bacon. But what is the meaning of those quizzical lines which Hall has specially italicized? They may be paraphrased as follows: Do let us have literary work from those who *can* write properly, and not from those who cannot, but yet appear in print as authors (e.g. Shakspere). Who are the persons who are aware of this deception? Those who pretend not to know, but really do know,

[1] It is really very naïve of Theobald to put it like this in order to keep up the suggestion of Shakspere's illiteracy. The plain sense of Hall's words is 'collaboration'. He does not like a poem, which he believes is the joint work of two writers, and he tells the principal that he would probably have done better if he had written it alone, though it might be better still if he had left it unwritten. The word 'swaine', like that of 'shepherd', was a conventional pseudonym for poet, and accordingly confers this rank on the supposed junior partner. The names Shakspere and Bacon are, of course, read in by Theobald; there is nothing in the lines, as we shall see, to suggest the identity of either of the writers concerned.

i.e. Hall himself and others who, like him, had guessed the secret.[1]

'When we turn to the Fourth Book, Satire 1, the evidence becomes much stronger. Here is the passage alluding to Labeo.

> *Labeo* is whip't, and laughs me in the face.
> Why? for I smite and hide the galled place,
> Gird but the Cynicks Helmet on his head,
> Cares he for *Talus* or his flayle of lead?
> Long as the craftie Cuttle lieth sure
> In the black *Cloud* of his thick vomiture;
> Who list complaine of wronged faith or fame
> When he may shift it on to anothers name?

On the third line is another reference to the Cynick, i.e. the author, and from this it is tolerably plain that Hall is speaking of the "Honourable Order of the Knights of the Helmet", described in Bacon's *Gesta Grayorum*, produced at Gray's Inn in 1594, and thus pointing to him as the author of *Venus and Adonis*; while the concluding lines once more emphasize the fact that he was writing under a pen-name.

'Still another passage may be quoted where Hall satirizes *Labeo*, though here in a more good-natured manner. It is from Book VI, Satire I. The passage begins thus:

> Tho *Labeo* reaches right; (who can deny)
> The true straynes of Heroicke Poesie,
> For he can tell how fury reft his sense
> And Phoebus fild him with intelligence,

and shortly after comes the line:

> While big But Ohs each stanza can begin,

[1] While the second part of this paraphrase may represent roughly Hall's meaning, the first part cannot be accepted as correct. What Theobald attempts to make it mean is that Hall thought Bacon's work good, and blamed him for publishing it under a pseudonym and letting the credit go to Shakspere. But this is in direct conflict with the opening couplet of the lines quoted. In this Hall clearly suggests that the work is bad. He tells Labeo (Theobald's Bacon) that he ought not to write at all, but if he must do so, he should try to write better; and he should write what is all his own, not collaborate with anyone else. Theobald thus ignores part of his own evidence in order to produce the conclusion his theory requires.

a pointed allusion to *Lucrece*, where it is noticeable how many stanzas commence with "But" or "Oh". Another marked feature of both *Venus and Adonis* and *Lucrece* is the use of hyphened words as epithets; and this did not escape Hall's satirical comment, since he writes:

> In Epithets to join two words as one,
> Forsooth for Adjectives cannot stand alone.

'It is abundantly clear from these Satires that Hall identified Bacon as the author of *Venus and Adonis* and *Lucrece*, and alluded to him under the names of Labeo and the Cynick.

'Now turn to John Marston. In 1598 he published his *Pigmalion's Image*, in which occurs the following passage:

> So *Labeo* did complaine his loue was stone,
> Obdurate, flinty, so relentless none;
> Yet *Lynceus* knows, that in the end of this
> He wrought as strange a metamorphosis.
> Ends not my poem thus surprising ill?
> Come, come, Augustus, crowne my laureat quill.

'The first two lines are an obvious allusion to lines 200, 201 of *Venus and Adonis*, since he compares the metamorphosis of Pygmalion, as given in his own work, to that of Adonis described by "Shakespeare" in *Venus and Adonis*.

'In Satire 1 is another covert allusion to an author who "presumst as if thou wert unseene", and in Satire 4 Marston defends various authors whom Hall had attacked, and without actually naming *Labeo* refers to him in the following line:

> What, not *medioca firma* from thy spite!

i.e. has not even *medioca firma* escaped thy spite? Now as these two Latin words form Bacon's family motto, we have the strongest proof that Marston was referring to Bacon in this line; and since a study of all these passages shows that both Hall and Marston point to the same man as *Labeo*, we reach the conclusion that both of them definitely identified Francis Bacon as the author of *Venus and Adonis* and *Lucrece*.'

I have said that I regard this as the most telling piece of evidence produced by the Baconians in favour of their theory.

This, however, does not imply that the Baconians' interpretation of it is not open to criticism, or that they can be allowed to make it mean more than it actually does mean; and the concluding sentence of the passage I have just quoted certainly claims more than is justified.

We may agree that Hall is patting himself on the back because he thinks he has guessed the identity of an author writing under a pseudonym and collaborating with an inferior poet, and that he is aiming his satire at this author; but that he believed Bacon to be the author in question is not so certain. He denotes his victim by the name of Labeo, and as Labeo was a Roman lawyer the Baconians are within their rights in assuming that Hall's victim was a lawyer. There were, however, other lawyers and men who had studied Law besides Bacon who were 'concealed poets', so this proves nothing. Theobald attempts to fix the identification by claiming, no doubt correctly, that the Cynick also stands for the author. The Cynick wears a helmet, and this, says Theobald, is a reference to Bacon's *Gesta Grayorum*, in which there is a comic Order of Chivalry, the Knights of the Helmet. Quite apart from the fact that this is rather far-fetched in any case, what Theobald gratuitously calls 'Bacon's' *Gesta Grayorum* was a masque produced by the members of Gray's Inn *after* Bacon had withdrawn from open association with such revelries (see p. 55), and, while he may along with others have assisted with the production, *his name nowhere appears in connection with it*. Such being the case, Hall would be most unlikely to deprive his satire of its point by choosing as a symbol for his victim something with which that victim had no acknowledged connection, and if the reference is to *Gesta Grayorum* it would count against Bacon rather than for him, while if it is not, we are left without a clue to the identity of Labeo and the Cynick.

Theobald is more probably correct in his identification of the poems concerned. In *The Rape of Lucrece* a number of stanzas do begin with 'Oh' or 'But', and both this poem and *Venus and Adonis* contain hyphened epithets. Such details, however, are found in other poems too, so here again there is no absolute certainty.

With Marston's work there are no such difficulties. The

introduction of the family motto into the poem makes it clear that he had Bacon, and no one else, in mind, and his own echoes of the lines in *Venus and Adonis* prove the same for the poem concerned. But here a *caveat* must be entered. Though he does not actually say so, Theobald writes as if Hall and Marston had each arrived at the same conclusion independently. This was most certainly not the case. Marston was in no sense independent of Hall. It was specifically Hall's work that he had in mind, and what he wrote resulted from what he thought, rightly or wrongly, Hall meant by his cryptic remarks. It follows then that only two facts can be deduced with absolute certainty from the works of Hall and Marston. They are:

(1) That Hall believed he had guessed the real author, or rather part-author, of some poem published under a pseudonym, but does not clearly indicate either.

(2) That Marston believed that Hall meant Bacon as the author and *Venus and Adonis* as the poem.

Anything further takes us into the realm of surmise.

Still it must be admitted that the possibility that both writers did actually believe that Bacon was the author of the poem in question exists. When Bagley first put forward the case quoted by Theobald, some Stratfordians accepted it at its face value, but said that Hall and Marston were mistaken. At such a suggestion Theobald throws up his hands in pious horror. How could two such shrewd satirists, with their fingers on the pulse of the London literary world, possibly be mistaken? This question can only be answered by another – Why not? There have been other cases in the course of literary history when shrewd critics have believed they have penetrated a well-preserved pseudonym; sometimes they have been right, but sometimes quite wrong. Hall and Marston were not infallible. The former was certainly mistaken, as both Stratfordians and Baconians would agree, in believing that *Venus and Adonis* was a collaboration by two authors. In Elizabethan and Jacobean times there were many eminent literary men, quite as shrewd as Hall and Marston, who believed that William Shakspere was the author of the Shakespearean plays.[1] The Baconians say that these were

[1] Examples are given later in this book. They include Drayton, Heywood, and Webster (see pp. 260 f.) and Leonard Digges (see pp. 298 f.).

mistaken. If Hall and Marston had appeared to favour another candidate the Baconians would unhesitatingly have declared that they were mistaken. Evidence of this kind, depending as it does on personal opinion, must necessarily be of a doubtful nature. Stripped of the Baconian verbiage with which it is surrounded, all it amounts to is that two minor writers, encountering a new poetic work with a new name attached to it as author, hazarded a guess that this name concealed the identity of a well-known public man, and one at least, possibly both, thought that public man might be Francis Bacon. It may prove that Hall and Marston were the first exponents of the Baconian theory, but it does not, and cannot, prove that the Baconian theory is true.

We must now turn our attention to the cryptograms,[1] which make up a considerable part of the Baconian evidence, though it is only fair to remember that some of the more scholarly supporters of the theory have repudiated them. It appears, according to the authors of these phantasies, that Bacon, when as a young law-student he first conceived the idea of writing plays and poems secretly, determined that although the fact must be kept from his contemporaries, posterity should give him full credit for all his writings – which included not only the Shakespearean works and those bearing the names of most of the other Elizabethans, but also the translation of the Authorized Version of the Bible and the Essays of Montaigne in French. In order to achieve this modest purpose he made the most elaborate arrangements. Clues of all sorts were included in the designs of title pages, chapter headings, and tail-pieces; tricks

---

[1] The cryptograms fall into two classes. Those in the first class maintain nothing more than the alleged claims of Bacon to the authorship of the Shakespearean and other works; those in the second class purport to reveal a fantastic secret history of Bacon's life – that he was the son of Queen Elizabeth by the Earl of Leicester and the hero of a number of episodes that make the wildest of the Romances read like sober fact. It is only with the first that we are concerned. The second, though of course they make the authorship claim incidentally, are interested mainly in matters that have nothing to do with our inquiry. I have, however, included the titles of a few specimens of the second class – such as the bulky volumes of Mrs Gallup – in the Bibliography as they certainly throw a very interesting sidelight on the Baconian type of mind.

were played with the pagination of books; and ciphers, anagrams, and other forms of concealed message, introduced into
the text of the works themselves. That the literary detectives of
the future might the more readily solve these puzzles, Bacon
'caused to be issued' such English books as Meres' *Palladis
Tamia* and Camden's archaeological works, together with a
number of other volumes by foreign authors and published in
France and Germany, all of which contain keys for the reading
of his ciphers.[1] How Bacon made all these arrangements with
such a host of authors, publishers, and printers, and still managed to preserve his secret, the cryptologists do not inform us.

While this book was in preparation Colonel and Mrs Friedman's exhaustive work, *The Shakespearean Ciphers Examined*, was
published, and since the colonel and his wife are undoubtedly
the greatest living authorities on the subject of cryptography, I
have gladly availed myself of the benefit of the information and
criticism they supply. I may say that no one whose mind is not
steeped in prejudice could possibly put an atom of faith in any
of the ciphers after the Friedmans' exposures, and I recommend all who are interested in the question to read their book
for themselves, for I, of course, can give only the most meagre
indications of its contents here.

The Friedmans begin with a description of the various kinds
of cipher that exist and the rules they must obey before their
alleged meaning may be accepted as genuine. These are two in
number. First every cipher must rigidly conform to a system;
that is, it must correspond to a specific key and be capable of
one solution only, absolutely and without any ambiguities or
variations, for obviously if it were open to more than one the
correct solution could never be certain. Second, the deciphered
message must be coherent and logical, making complete sense,
and that without the necessity for any manipulation additional
to the application of the key, such as anagramming, since such
manipulation could only be guess-work.

The Friedmans point out that not one of the theorists'
ciphers, except that of Mrs Gallup, which breaks down on
other grounds, conforms to these simple rules. One or two
examples will make this clear.

[1] Durning-Lawrence, *Bacon is Shakespeare*, pp. 89 and 108–133.

In the closing years of last century an American lawyer, Ignatius Donnelly, a convinced Baconian, conceived the idea that Bacon had left concealed messages claiming the authorship of the Shakespearean plays in the plays themselves,[1] and set himself to discover them. He worked on a facsimile of the First Folio, as this was of course the only version of any of them which Bacon himself could have influenced. His idea seems to have been that the messages were expressed in words spaced through the double columns that formed each page of the Folio. He found some suggestive word in a column, counted its number from the beginning of the column, and took this as his basic number. The next word in the message should, of course, have been at the same numerical distance from the suggestive word as the latter was from the beginning of the column, or at least at some regularly related distance, and so on for every word in the message. Donnelly found no such simple system as this, but inevitably, considering the mass of material with which he was dealing, he found scattered at random about the various columns words that would serve his purpose. The question therefore for him was how to bring these into some regular system. He did this by introducing an increasing number of what he called 'modifiers'. These were arbitrarily selected figures that could be added to or subtracted from the basic numbers in order to bring him in his counts to the required word. He also sometimes counted hyphened words as two, sometimes as one; and sometimes included and sometimes omitted words in brackets with the same end in view. Finally he surmounted any more than usually intractable difficulty by further 'computations' with an additional group of figures that he designated 'subordinate root numbers'. By such means he read off the desired messages. The following, in which 'b' and 'h' stand respectively for brackets and hyphens, is an example of his method:

	Word.	Page and Column.	
$516 - 167 = 349 - 22$ b & h $= 327 - 30 = 297 -$			
$245 = 43 - 15$ b & h $= 28$.	28	75·2	Shak'st⎫
$516 - 167 = 349 - 22$ b & h $= 327 - 248 = 79$.			⎬
$193 - 79 = 114 + 1 = 115 + $ b & h $= (121)$.	(121)	75·1	spur ⎭

[1] Friedman, *The Shakespearean Ciphers Examined*, pp. 27–50.

		Page and Column.
Word.		
$516 - 167 = 349 - 22$ b & h $= 327 - 254 = 73 -$ 15 b & h $= 58$. $498 - 58 = 440 + 1 = 441$.	441	76·1	never
$516 - 167 = 349 - 22$ b & h $= 327 - 50 =$ $227 - 7$ b & h $= 516 - 167 = 349 - 22$ b & h $= 327$.	220 327	76·2 76·1	writ a
$516 - 167 = 349 - 22$ b & h $= 327 - 145 (76·2) =$ 182, $498 - 182 = 316 + 1 = 317$.	317	76·2	word
$516 - 167 = 349 - 22$ b & h $= 327 - 193 = 134$. $248 - 134 = 114 + 1 = 115$.	115	74·2	of
$516 - 167 = 349 - 22$ b & h $= 327 - 254 = 73 -$ 15 b & h $= 58 - 5$ b $= 53$.	53	74·1	them.

As the Friedmans say, Donnelly seems to have found his word first and then proceeded to bolster up his find by arithmetical manipulation. Clearly such a method fails completely to comply with the cryptogrammatic rules – there is no logical system about it. Any message whatever could be manufactured by this means. This was demonstrated by the Rev R. Nicholson, who answered Donnelly's claims in his *No Cipher in Shakespeare* by extracting messages that flatly contradicted Donnelly's. Taking Donnelly's own root numbers and modifiers, delving into Donnelly's own favourite columns in the First Folio, and following exactly Donnelly's own method, he produced the message: 'Master Will-I-am Shak'st-spurre writ the Play and was engaged at the Curtain.' And he produced it not once, but five times, using each of Donnelly's five root numbers in turn. No refutation could be more complete.

Our second example is that known as the String Cipher, claimed as his discovery by W. S. Booth in his *Some Acrostic Signatures of Francis Bacon*.[1] His method was as simple as Donnelly's was complicated. He found a passage in one of the Shakespearean plays in which the initial letter of the first word was F and of the last word N, or the converse, for the cipher might be read up or down. Provided that these two points were fixed, any initial letter of any word between them might be taken, reading along the lines alternately from right to left and from left to right. Any number of intervening lines might be neglected if they did not happen to contain a word with the required initial letter or if the required initial letter had already been found elsewhere. To illustrate this method we will take

[1] Friedman, *The Shakespearean Ciphers Examined*, pp. 120–121.

one of Booth's examples – one in which he used the Epilogue from *The Tempest*:

→	*N*ow my *C*harmes are all *o*re-throwne		CO	NO
	And what *s*trength I have 's my *o*wne.	←	S	O
→	Which is most faint; now 'tis true			
	I must be heere *c*onfinde by you	←	IC	C
→	Or sent to Naples, Let me not			
	Since I haue my Dukedom got.	←		
→	And pardon'd the deceiuer, dwell			
	In this bare Island, by your Spell,	←		
→	But release me from my bands			
	With the helpe of your good hands;	←		
→	Gentle breath of yours, my Sailes			
	Must fill, or else my project failes,	←		
→	Which was to please; *N*ow I want		N	
	Spirits to enforce; Art to inchant,	←		
→	*A*nd my ending is despaire,		A	
	Vnlesse I be *r*elieu'd by praier	←	R	
→	Which pierces so, that it assaults			
	Mercy it selfe, and frees *a*ll faults	←		A
→	As you from crimes would pardon'd *b*e			B
	Let your Indulgence set me *f*ree.	←	F	

The Friedmans point out that with such a system any name could be extracted, provided the cryptologist took enough lines between his first and last letters. To prove their point they took the same passage, and, starting from Booth's 'b' in the penultimate line and traversing the lines in the opposite direction to his, they produced the 'signature' Ben Ionson ('I' and 'J' were, of course, the same letter in Elizabethan times). They also point out that, using a variant of this cipher, one that Booth himself sometimes employed – that of taking the last letter of a word instead of the first – the 'signatures' of several other claimants may be read; namely those of Edmund Spenser, Sir William Dyer, Sir Francis Drake, William Stanley, and Christopher Marlowe. Moreover, by the same method Friedman's own name, or in fact almost any name beginning with F and ending with N that does not contain an unusual letter, such as 'x', can be detected.

As an example of this I append one of my own devising.

69

I have taken the name of Fynes Moryson, incidentally one of the few contemporary men of letters for whom no theorist has claimed the Shakespearean works. It appears as follows:

→	*N*ow my Charmes are all ore-throwne		N
	And what strength I have 's my owne.	←	
→	Which is most faint; now 'tis true		
	I must be heere confinde by you,	←	
→	*O*r sent to Naples, Let me not		O
	*S*ince I haue my Dukedom got.	←	S
→	And pardon'd the deceiuer, dwell		
	In this bare Island, by *y*our Spell,	←	Y
→	But *r*elease me from my bands		R
	With the help *o*f your good hands;	←	O
→	Gentle breath of yours, my *S*ailes	S	
	Must fill, or *e*lse my project failes,	← E	
→	Which was to please; *N*ow I want	N	
	Spirits to enforce; Art to inchant,	←	
→	And my ending is despaire,		
	Vnlesse I be reliue'd by praire	←	
→	Which pierces so, that it assaults		
	*M*ercy it selfe, and frees all faults.	←	M
→	As *y*ou from crimes would pardon'd be.	Y	
	Let your Indulgence set me *f*ree.	← F	

It will be noticed that I have followed Booth's method exactly – starting on the initial letter of the last word, ending on the initial letter of the first word, and traversing the lines in the same direction as he does. I have not troubled to add the rather silly pseudo-Latinizations, CO and O, but obviously it can be done if required, and 'Fynesco Morysono' looks and reads quite as well as 'Francisco Bacono'.

This is not mere frivolity. It is a serious demonstration of the absurdity of the cryptologists' claims. What is true of the two ciphers we have examined is equally true of all the alleged ciphers, anagrams, acrostics, and other gleanings from 'Puzzle Corner' that the theorists have ever produced. Those who read the Friedmans' expert treatise will find them all there, minutely described, scientifically examined, and ruthlessly exposed for the worthless rubbish they are.

I can spare no more space for their details here. There is,

however, a point which, in my opinion, constitutes even stronger argument against them. It is impossible to imagine a man of Bacon's intellectual calibre indulging in such puerilities. If he were really the author of works other than those which bear his name, and for some reason did not wish this authorship to be announced until some fixed date in the future, his simplest plan to attain this end would be to write down a full account of the facts, enclose the script in a sealed packet, and deliver it into the hands of some trustworthy person with instructions to make the facts public on some specific date. For security several copies of the letter could have been made and entrusted to different persons; and, if the date for publication lay in the distant future – though one is scarcely able to conceive of an adequate reason for this – these persons could have been asked to leave all the necessary instructions for dealing with the matter to their descendants.

Such a method would not only be simpler, but also much safer in every respect. The cryptogram plan, quite apart from the enormous amount of time and labour involved in it, would in any case have been the height of folly. In the first place there would have been the danger that the ciphers might have been read immediately they appeared in print; that is, at a time when, since he did not announce his authorship, Bacon clearly still required to preserve the secret; and in the second place they might never have been read at all, thus depriving Bacon of the credit with posterity we are assured he so ardently desired, for not even the Baconian Bacon could have known that in the nineteenth and twentieth centuries there would arise a galaxy of genius to make all things plain.

This concludes our examination of the evidence peculiar to the case for Francis Bacon. In fairness it ought to be added that it does not quite do this case justice. As pioneers in the enterprise of finding a substitute for Shakspere the Baconians are responsible for the discovery of much other evidence that has since been adopted and adapted by the other schools of thought. This common evidence, as already stated, is dealt with in the later chapters of this book, and the full strength, or weakness, of the Baconian theory cannot be properly assessed until it has all been examined.

CHAPTER IV

The Case for the Oxford Syndicate

In this chapter we shall examine the evidence peculiar to the Oxford theory. This theory, as we have seen (p. 18) underwent a considerable change as it developed. When first put forward by Looney in 1920 Oxford was claimed to be the sole author of the Shakespearean plays and poems, but by 1931 the groupist modification was generally accepted by the whole school. Slater, in *Seven Shakespeares*, thus describes the accepted view:

'The Oxford theory in its moderate form, is not that the Earl of Oxford was the sole author of the Shakespearean plays, but that he was the principal member of a group of collaborators. That in 1573 he began his dramatic career as an amateur actor, playwright, and manager. In the second stage, in receipt of a grant of £1000 a year from the Queen, he is said to have continued his work in some form of recognition by the State. Subsequently he threw more of his emotions and personality into his final revision.'

The theory, of which this is a summary, makes four assertions, upon the truth or falsity of which the Oxfordian case very largely depends. They are:

(1) That Oxford was a recognized dramatist.

(2) That he was the leader and inspirer of a group of amateur dramatists who wrote the Shakespearean plays with varying combinations of collaborators.

(3) That this group became a kind of Official Propaganda Department.

(4) That before the First Folio was published Oxford had personally made a final revision of the plays written by the group.

The fourth item must wait for consideration until we reach Chapter XVI, where the special problem of the First Folio is examined in detail; the other three may be dealt with at once.

The case of Oxford differs in one important respect from that of Bacon. There is no direct evidence of any sort that the latter ever wrote a play; for Oxford there is Meres' statement in *Palladis Tamia* that he wrote comedies and that they were among the best. We may therefore regard it as certain that Oxford was a dramatist and probably a good one, though Meres does not mention the titles of any plays he wrote, and none bearing his name as author have survived.

Palladis Tamia is, however, a double-edged weapon for the Oxfordians to handle, for in it Meres mentions Shakespeare as well as Oxford, and also the titles of a number of his plays. From this it follows that the comedies written by Oxford which Meres had in mind were not the Shakespearean plays, and that he certainly did not regard Oxford as the author of these. Meres is therefore actually a hostile witness; though there is an escape route open to the Oxfordians from this dilemma. It is that Oxford had written some early plays under his own name, and then retired with his collaborators behind the Shakespearean pseudonym, and that Meres was deceived, like everyone else not in the secret, and believed that he was dealing with two totally distinct authors. This of course is pure surmise, but it is no more improbable than the similar surmises of all the other theorists.

The evidence that the Oxfordians offer for the second item – the group of courtly collaborators writing the Shakespearean plays under the leadership of Oxford – is a passage in the *Arte of English Poesie* (1589),[1] which they quote, not quite accurately, as follows:

A crew of Courtly makers (Poets), Noblemen, and Gentlemen, who have written excellently well as it would appear if their doings could be found out and made public with the rest, of which number is first that noble Gentleman, the Earl of Oxford.

Now, quite apart from the fact that this was published before any of the Shakespearean plays were known to be written, it is immediately apparent that the passage does *not* give the mean-

[1] Montagu Douglas, *Lord Oxford and the Shakespeare Group*, p. 46. Col. Douglas ascribes the *Arte of English Poesie* to Lord Lumley. The generally accepted author by English scholars is George Puttenham.

ing the Oxfordians claim for it. All it says is that there were a number of anonymous poets at the Court who were producing work of a very high quality, and that Oxford was the chief of these. It does not even suggest that they were working as a group, there is not the faintest hint that it was plays they were writing, and Oxford is designated leader in no other sense than that he was the highest in rank ('first'). Everyone knew that the Court was full of 'concealed poets' at the time, and the writer, dealing with the poetry of the day, merely says that their work is very good. He no doubt mentions Oxford by name while preserving the anonymity of the others because Oxford, before inheriting the title, had published his poems openly. He was therefore hardly a concealed poet.

Thus the one piece of direct external evidence for the group theory that the Oxfordians have been able to discover proves on examination to be no such thing. If there is any truth in the theory it must be inferred from the plays themselves, and here the main trend of scholarship is against it. The majority of recent scholars, while not denying a certain amount of collaboration and working over old scripts in a few plays, insist on the essential unity of authorship in all the great canonical works. Of course this does not rule out the theory completely – a consensus of even scholarly opinion may be mistaken, and it is not so long ago that the ranks of the orthodox Stratfordians included a strong body of 'Disintegrators' – but it leaves it in a rather precarious position.

When we turn to the third item on the list we are at once confronted by a puzzle. Why did the Oxfordians put forward the theory of a Propaganda Department? Of course if it could be established that there was actually such an organization as they postulate, it would constitute evidence for the existence of the group. But there is no real evidence for it; they have merely built up the idea on the flimsiest of grounds, and it creates a host of insuperable difficulties for them.

The facts are simply these. In 1586 Oxford was granted under Privy Seal Warrant a special annuity of £1000. This annuity was continued throughout Elizabeth's reign and confirmed by James I when he came to the throne. And that is all that is known about the matter. Now it is quite true, as the Oxfordians

74

claim, that neither Elizabeth nor James was in the habit of paying out money for nothing. Oxford must have done something to earn it; but there were innumerable services that he might have performed, and, as we are not told, we simply do not know what this particular service was.

It is, however, on this ignorance that the Oxfordians base their Propaganda Department theory.[1] Oxford, according to them, was paid this sum to get together a band of dramatists to write patriotic plays, and thus stir up feelings of loyalty to the Crown and Government among the populace.

In reply to this it must be pointed out that, while the Shakespearean plays do show a great love of England, a hatred of disorder, and the need for a strong Government, only a few of them are 'patriotic' in the popular sense. Where such ideas occur they are usually introduced far too subtly to make much impression on the general public, and in many of the plays they do not occur at all; the plots are not concerned with such matters. Even if nothing untoward had occurred Queen Elizabeth would have quickly tired of paying out good money to support an organization that displayed such small interest in the purpose for which it had been created.

Something untoward, however, did occur. As we have already seen (p. 20), and the matter will be dealt with much more fully in Chapter X, the one occasion on which we know a Shakespearean play to have been deliberately used for propaganda was when the Essex faction produced *Richard II* to stir up popular feeling *against* the Queen and her Government; that is, the work of the alleged Propaganda Department was used against the very people who paid for it. Queen Elizabeth was furious about the affair. Yet Oxford was not summoned to the Inquiry that followed, his name was never mentioned in connection with the matter, and, what is more, the annuity continued to be paid. This would be an impossible situation if he had had any responsibility, no matter of what kind, for *Richard II*. In such circumstances the very least that could have happened to his Propaganda Department, had it ever existed, would have been the withdrawal of the Government subsidy.

Even this does not exhaust the absurdity of the Oxfordian

[1] M. Douglas, *Lord Oxford and the Shakespeare Group*, p. 48 f.

position. Its supporters give the same two reasons for the Shakespearean pseudonym as the Baconians and the Derbyites – (1) that it was *infra dig* for a courtier to make his work public under his own name, and (2) that it was dangerous for a man in an exalted position to express any opinion in plays or other works, as it might be construed as hostile to the Government with dire consequences. The Oxfordians emphasize this second point very strongly indeed, quoting a passage from Johnson's *Rise of English Culture* on the harshness of Tudor Law towards such offenders to demonstrate the risks the Oxford group ran.[1]

Now this is a perfectly reasonable line for the other schools to take. It would apply in the case of Bacon and in the case of Derby. It would apply also in the case of Oxford and his collaborators *if they had been writing in a private capacity*; but for an official Propaganda Department it makes utter nonsense. Is it possible to imagine that the Government paid out £1000 a year, a very large sum in those days, without knowing into whose pockets it was going? It certainly knew Oxford himself, for he is named in the warrant, and if the money were paid to him to run a Propaganda Department, then the Government would undoubtedly require to know all about its personnel. The pseudonym might be regarded as useful where the general public was concerned, but there could be no secrets from the Queen and her Ministers, and these are the people the Oxfordians clearly have in mind since they mention the Tudor Law. Moreover, why should the Government's own Public Relations Officers, for that, according to the theory, is what the Oxford group was, want to express opinions hostile to that Government? Their whole *raison d'être* was surely to do the opposite.

The truth is that we are here confronted with just another example of the confusion of thought that perpetually dogs all these theorists. They blunder through Elizabethan history and literature, snatching at every little detail they think they can turn to account, and in their eagerness to swell the body of evidence for their own particular theory overlook the fact that these bits and pieces not only do not fit together, but often flatly contradict one another, and thus reduce their whole argument to chaos.

[1] Douglas, *Lord Oxford and the Shakespeare Group*, pp. 59 f.

Our analysis of the first three items in the Oxfordian claims shows that only one thing can be considered established. This is that Oxford wrote some comedies, which were considered good in his own day, but have not come down to us, a fact which has always been known to students of English literature, and which no one has ever wished to deny. It throws no light whatever on the authorship of the Shakespearean plays.

The next type of evidence we have to consider is that upon which Looney chiefly relied – references in the plays which he considered reminiscent of incidents in Oxford's life. Much of this evidence consists of nothing more than identifying some character in one of the plays with a relative of Oxford's on no other grounds than that their names possess some similarity. Thus the pages of Oxfordian works abound with such items as 'Horatio (Sir Horace de Vere, Oxford's cousin) etc', which of course mean absolutely nothing. Relatives have names and so have characters in plays, and if enough of both are taken – and the de Veres and their collaterals were very numerous – there are bound to be similarities and even coincidences.

Sometimes these statements are considerably elaborated, probably on the same principle as that of Pooh-Bah in *The Mikado* – 'to give a touch of verisimilitude to an otherwise bald and unconvincing narrative'. The following is an example dealing with the opening scene of *Hamlet*. I give it in Colonel M. Douglas' own words:[1]

'Francisco is suggested by Sir Francis de Vere, who had recently returned from the Netherlands after twenty years service; and to whom Edward de Vere left the custody and stewardship of the forest of Essex. Francisco in the Quarto of 1604 says in one of his speeches –

> For this *relief* much thanks. 'Tis bitter cold
> And I am *sick at heart*.

(The italics are Douglas's.) Thus expressing, indirectly, his feelings after his return, depressed and wounded, and thankful to be relieved of his command.'

[1] M. Douglas, *Lord Oxford and the Shakespeare Group*, pp. 83 f.

Until I read this gem of interpretation I must confess that I had thought the words merely meant that Francisco was glad that his spell of sentry-duty was over, and that owing to the inclement weather he was thoroughly 'browned off'. I was also interested to note that the term 'relief', still in use in the Army for the man who takes over one's sentry-duty, was in use in Tudor times. In fact I foolishly thought the speech was part of the play, and had no idea that it was actually the means of giving to the world some intimate details of the de Vere family history.[1]

Of course authors do sometimes draw their characters from life, and there are satiric plays which deliberately mock or slander public figures thinly disguised; but whoever heard of an author dramatizing in the way just described some trivial family episode? Francisco is an utterly unimportant member of the *dramatis personae*, with only eight speeches to make, the longest being the one-and-a-half lines just quoted. He makes his exit a moment later, and does not appear again in the play. If this is how Oxford really wrote plays, Shakespeare's or any others, it is a matter of surprise that he ever completed one; the time involved in hunting through the family archives for material suitable to each and every trivial occasion and then working it into plot and dialogue must have been endless.

The next example comes from *Romeo and Juliet* (I, iv). Douglas quotes the following extract:[2]

> ROMEO. For I am proverb'd with *a grandsire phrase*;
> I 'll be a *candle-holder*, and look on.
> The game was ne'er so fair, and I am *done*.
> MERC. Tut! *dun 's the mouse*, the constable's own word.
> *If thou art dun*, we 'll draw thee from the mire
> Of – save your reverence – love, wherein thou stick'st
> Up to the ears.

On this Colonel Douglas comments, 'Holland shows that Oxford's grandmother's name was Elizabeth Trussell, an old

---

[1] I should like to ask the Oxfordians if they honestly believe that, had there been no Sir Francis de Vere to return from the Netherlands, the opening scene of the play of *Hamlet* would have been any different.

[2] *Lord Oxford and the Shakespeare Group*, p. 109.

way of spelling "Trestle"; and an old meaning of the word is a stand or frame for candles in religious worship. The crest of the Trussells was such a trestle; the design appears on her husband's arms and in that of the Earl of Oxford. Mr. Kennedy Skipton points out that Elizabeth Trussell's father (Oxford's great-grandfather) was Sir John Dun. Oxford's "grandsire" was thus a Trussell by name and *he himself literally a "candle-holder"*, while both Romeo and Mercutio play on the connection with Sir John Dun. Juliet is Ann Vavasour, Oxford's mistress; there is an obvious reference to her in Mercutio's reply.'

This interpretation is almost as extravagant as the Baconian cryptograms. The plain meaning of Romeo's speech, intro-duced by two lines omitted from the quotation – 'A torch for me, let wantons light of heart, Tickle the senseless rushes with their heels', is that, owing to the melancholy induced by un-requited love, he feels too old to dance; like other aged folk he will stand by the wall and hold a light for the dancers. It is a perfectly straightforward speech, perfectly suited to the con-text. The secondary meanings, forcibly read into it by the Oxfordians, are, as we shall see before we reach the end of our analysis, like the cryptograms, incapable of surviving close examination.

We may begin our criticism by asking the Oxfordians by what principle they identify Juliet, the faithful child-wife who kills herself for love of her husband, with Ann Vavasour, Oxford's mistress? There is not here even their usual stand-by – some similarity in the name. Moreover, it is *not* to Juliet that Mercutio is referring. Romeo had not yet met her at this stage in the play; their first meeting takes place in the following scene. Mercutio's reference is to Rosaline, the lady whose rejection of his love causes Romeo to sink into the 'mire' of melancholy, and who incidentally never appears in the play. The Oxfordians really ought to know the Shakespearean plays before assigning them to any author.

Now let us turn to Sir John Dun, Oxford's great-grandfather, who is, the Oxfordians assure us, intended by Mercutio's ex-pression 'Dun 's the mouse'. I would begin by directing the Oxfordians' attention to the following extract from the play *Westward Ho* by Dekker and Webster:

79

HONEYSUCKLE. Sergeant Ambush, as thou 'rt an honest fellow, scout in some back-room till the watch-word be given for sallying forth.
AMBUSH. *Dun 's the mouse.*

And to this from *Oldcastle* by Drayton, Munday, Wilson, and Hathwaye:

MURLEY. . . . Follow your master, your captain, your knight that shall be, for the honour of meal-men, millers, and malt-men. *Dun is the mouse.*

And this from *Two Merry Milkmaids:*

JULIA. If my consent wil do 't, 't is.
DORIGENE. Why then 't is *done, and Dun 's the mouse.*

This last containing the identical pun – 'done' and 'dun' – that is found in *Romeo and Juliet.*

If 'Dun' really stands for Oxford's great-grandfather, then the old gentleman shows surprising agility in popping in and out of various plays, for those I have quoted by no means exhaust the list. And by the same token the Oxfordians ought to claim all these plays for Oxford; what is evidence in one case must surely be so in another.

But of course 'Dun' does not stand for anyone's great-grandfather. The Oxfordians, like the Baconians, are not Elizabethan scholars. They find a phrase in a Shakespearean play which looks as if it might be twisted to their purpose, and they at once proceed to do the twisting without ever thinking of tracing the history of the phrase or ascertaining if it will bear the interpretation they plan to place upon it. The fact is that the three phrases in the R. & J. scene – 'Dun 's the mouse', 'Candle-holder', and 'Draw thee from the mire' – are all connected with Tudor proverbs, which is why they can be repeated, as I have shown they are in the first case, by so many authors. They can all be found, with notes on their origin and use, in M. P. Tilley's *Dictionary of Proverbs in England in Sixteenth and Seventeenth Centuries.* They have nothing whatever to do with the de Vere family tree.

To continue with such examples would be mere waste of

2 EDWARD DE VERE, SEVENTEENTH EARL OF OXFORD
Painting by Marcus Gheeraedts at Cranborne Manor

time, though they constitute the main evidence for the Oxfordian case. Quite apart from the fact that they usually collapse as
soon as they are analysed, they would be equally worthless if
there were no fault to be found with their details. In the whole
range of the Shakespearean plays there are innumerable names,
references, and episodes, which, with a little manipulation, can
be made to fit the circumstances of almost anyone; they are in
fact freely used by the supporters of all the theories, which in
itself is enough to condemn them.

The next type of evidence the Oxfordians offer is of an in-
direct rather than a direct nature. It consists of an attempt to
establish a much earlier dating for the Shakespearean plays
than that generally accepted. This could not of course prove
Oxford's authorship, but he was an older man than any of the
other candidates, and consequently if the dates of writing could
be pushed back far enough it would rule out the other claimants, and leave him at least the most probable author. The
first to put forward this view was an American, Mrs Eva Clark.
In her *Shakespeare's Plays in their Order of Writing* she contends
that they were nearly all written between 1576 and 1590. She
admits that none of them appeared at these early dates under
its present title, but postulates that new titles were given to
them later.

Her method, according to her own description, was to study
the titles of the plays contained in the Records of the Court
Revels for the selected period, and when she found one suggestive of one of the Shakespearean plays, she read carefully
both the Shakespearean play and the history of the period
around the date given in the Records. If she found in the play
any references that would seem to apply to the events in the
history, then she felt that her theory was in course of being
proved, and it does not surprise us to learn, having already
had some experience of the Oxfordians' powers of recognizing
references, that before long she became convinced that it had
been proved.

Colonel Douglas gives us an example of her method in
action,[1] which I reproduce here. It concerns *The Merchant of
Venice*, the accepted date of which is 1596.

[1] *Lord Oxford and the Shakespeare Group*, pp. 82 and 83.

Colonel Douglas writes, 'In 1580 the *History of Portio and Demorantes* was shown at White Hall. The play was *The Merchant of Venice*, and support is found in Gosson's *School of Abuse* (1579), in which he praises a play seen at "The Bull" called *The Jew*, representing "the greediness of worldly chusers, and bloody minds of usurers". Plays were given at small theatres like "The Bull" preparatory to presentation at Court.[1] The literary sources on which *The Merchant of Venice* was based were familiar to Oxford; and to them he added episodes of contemporary history, which tends to confirm that *The Jew, Portio and Demorantes* (a mistake in transcription for *the Merchants*), and *The Merchant of Venice* are different titles for the same play.

'The two episodes were – the proposed marriage between the Duke of Alençon and Queen Elizabeth and the third Frobisher Expedition of 1578. In order to weave into the drama the vision of various envoys as suitors for the Queen's hand, Oxford made use of the caskets, suggested by the possession by the sovereign of the time of three crowns of iron, silver, and gold, signifying the three countries of England, France, and Ireland. Oxford was in close touch with the Queen at the time (1578–79) and puts into Portia's mouth these words.

> But this reasoning is not in the fashion to choose me a husband – O me, the word choose. I may neither choose whom I would, nor refuse whom I dislike; so is the will of a living daughter curbed by the will of a dead father.

'This is a direct reference by Oxford to the will of Henry VIII, which provided that the Queen should not marry anyone without the consent of the Privy Councillors.'

In reply I would first point out that there is no recognizable reference in this play to the third Frobisher Expedition, though Mrs Clark tries to manufacture one by claiming that Shylock's name and the sum of three thousand ducats which Bassanio borrows were chosen because Oxford was cheated by a man named Lock out of £3000 invested in this expedition.

---

[1] This is a very misleading remark. 'The Bull' was not a theatre, small or otherwise; it was merely an inn yard where open-air performances sometimes took place. In 1579 there were only two theatres in existence – 'The Curtain' and 'The Theatre'.

This is surely more far-fetched than the 'Francisco' and 'Dun' arguments we have just reviewed, since it is founded on a single syllable of a perfectly good Hebrew name and a very commonplace round figure, with no s milarity whatever in the circumstances in which they are employed. Moreover the argument is a logical monstrosity; for the play's connection with the Frobisher Expedition is thus made to depend on Oxford's authorship, and Oxford's authorship on the play's connection with the Frobisher Expedition; that is, Mrs Clark first uses the conclusion to prove the premise, and then uses the premise to prove the conclusion. We will leave it at that and turn our attention to the other points in the argument.

Mrs Clark's suggestion that *Portio and Demorantes* is a mistake in transcription for *Portia and the Merchants* is ingenious, and I should have been willing to accept it as a possibility, but I am informed that such a mistake is virtually out of the question in the Old English Secretary hand, the script in use at the time. In this the 'ch' is most distinctive, and could hardly be mistaken for anything else. But even if there had been such a play, and if it had dealt with the pound of flesh story, this would not be evidence for its identity with *The Merchant of Venice*, still less of Oxford's authorship. The pound of flesh story had been known in England for more than 200 years, having first appeared in the Northumbrian poem *Cursor Mundi* in 1320, and may well have been used in a number of works now lost.

The next step, that of identifying Portia and her host of suitors with Queen Elizabeth's marriage arrangements, is very dubious indeed. There is no similarity between the two cases. Portia was obliged to marry whoever chose the right casket; Queen Elizabeth was not obliged to marry anyone, and in point of fact did not. She was also perfectly free to choose a husband if she so wished, and only needed to have her choice ratified by the Ministers of State, a restriction that has often been imposed on Royal ladies in all periods of history, and with such a character as Queen Elizabeth (who would certainly not have looked with favour on Oxford or anyone else who dared to hint that she was curbed by anything) her Ministers would hardly have dared to do other than ratify any choice she cared to make.

This, as a matter of fact, is proved by the very case Mrs Clark uses to support her theory – Elizabeth's proposed marriage with Alençon. Her Ministers, who were opposed to the union, were so certain that she intended to carry it through in spite of them that they appealed to Sir Philip Sidney to use his eloquent pen in an attempt to dissuade her. Sidney had little hope of success, but he made the attempt, pointing out what a blow it would be both to the Protestant religion and the desires of her people, and either his persuasive arguments or her own good sense in the end deterred her. This incident shows how much binding power the will of a dead father had on a living daughter in her case, and certainly makes nonsense of any parallel with Portia.

As for the casket story – this also is an ancient literary device. Varied occasionally by the substitution of vats or chests, it is found in many languages, appearing in mediaeval Romance as early as 800. There are variants in Boccaccio's *Decameron* and Gower's *Confessio Amantis*. The version closest to that in M. of V. appeared in Latin in *Gesta Romanorum* about the year 1300, and this was so popular in Elizabethan England that a translation of it ran through six editions between 1577 and 1601. It certainly did not need the three crowns of the English sovereign to suggest the idea to the author, even if one of those crowns had been lead, as the casket was, instead of iron.

So much for Mrs Clark's examples; they completely fail to establish themselves. If, however, the Oxfordians really desire an historical incident to which M. of V. may well refer I will supply them with one. A certain Doctor Lopez, a Portuguese Jew and one of the Royal physicians, was charged with attempting to poison Queen Elizabeth, found guilty, and executed. The affair caused a wave of anti-Semitic feeling among the populace of London. This was in 1594, just about eighteen months before the accepted date (1596) for the production of M. of V., and therefore not far from the time when the play might well have been first drafted. Moreover there are two additional circumstances which tend to confirm this view. The Elizabethan spelling of 'Lopez' was 'Lopus', which suggests the wolf that Gratiano calls Shylock in the trial scene; and the chief undoer of Lopez was a certain *Antonio* Perez.

In addition to this, in 1596, the accepted date, there appeared an English translation by L. P. (?Lazarus Piot, a pen name of Munday) from the French of Alexander Silvayn's *The Orator*, the 95th 'declamation' of which contains the story 'of a Jew who would for his debt have a pound of the flesh of a Christian'. Shylock's speeches in the Court scene bear a strong resemblance to the arguments of the Jew in this story. I do not claim that these instances I have just quoted provide positive proof of the play's date, but I do claim that as evidence for this they are much more plausible than Mrs Clark's far-fetched ideas.

Admiral Holland is another exponent of pushing back the dating of the plays by reference to external events with the same object — that of establishing Oxford's authorship — in view. I will quote one example from his pen.[1] It is based on two lines from *King Lear*:

> These late eclipses of the sun and moon
> Portend no good.

Now it would appear that Holland's contention is that the author could not have written these lines unless there had recently been a double eclipse to bring such a phenomenon to his notice.[2] He then states that the only total eclipse of the sun throughout the reigns of Elizabeth and James occurred in 1598, and that it was preceded by a nearly total eclipse of the moon. From this he deduces that K. L. was written in 1598 and not in 1606, the accepted date.

I cannot agree with Holland that an author of fiction is doomed to immobility over the details of his work until some external event happens to give him the required idea. Eclipses in Tudor times, as in the Middle Ages, were popularly regarded as evil omens, and if Shakespeare, whoever he was, required evil omens, I am convinced that he was quite capable of imagining a couple of eclipses without any outside help. How-

---

[1] Douglas, *Lord Oxford and the Shakespeare Group*, pp. 91 ff.

[2] In fairness to the Admiral it must be recorded that the Stratfordian, E. K. Chambers, appears to agree with him, though he, of course, finds another pair of eclipses closer to the traditional date. The Admiral, however, declares that Chambers' eclipses were not visible in England.

ever, if the Oxfordians are wedded to the idea of an external event, I can provide them in this case also with one associated with the accepted date. On February 11th, 1606, there was published in London a pamphlet bearing the legend, 'Strange, fearful and true news which happened at Carlstadt in the Kingdom of Croatia', which contained a lurid account of some terrifying eclipses. Here is at least as likely a source for the eclipses in K. L., if there must be one apart from the invention of the author, as that advanced by Admiral Holland.

This must not be taken to imply that I condemn the use of external factors altogether as evidence for dating. Shakespeare undoubtedly has some oblique references in his plays to external events, and sometimes these may provide evidence for dating; but pushed to the Oxfordian extremes the method is, to say the least, a very dubious one. The fact that I have been able to produce external events favouring the traditional dates for the same two examples as the Oxfordians have produced external events favouring earlier dates is a proof of the inherent weakness of such a method. It is the same kind of fallacy as the Oxfordian claim to recognize family allusions in the plays. With a large number of literary references and a large number of external events to juggle with, it is perfectly easy to make any play fit any date. Moreover, there is another point that the Oxfordians seem to have overlooked; that is, an event may be referred to long after it is passed, and therefore be of no use for dating. In Webster's *The White Devil* (III, ii) occurs the phrase, 'Better than tribute of wolves paid in England'. This is a reference to the tribute imposed by the Saxon King Eadgar about the middle of the tenth century in order to rid the country of wolves. But surely not even the Oxfordians would deduce from this that Webster's play was written long before the Norman Conquest. Thus their 'proof' from earlier dating goes the way of their other arguments. It proves nothing.

Their next piece of evidence, however, is more worthy of attention. It was first put forward by Canon Rendall, who, in his *Personal Clues in Shakespeare's Poems*, drew attention to certain similarities between lines 829 to 836 of *Venus and Adonis* and a stanza of a poem entitled *A Vision of a Fair Maid*, which, as far as is known, was never published, but has survived in manuscript form over the name of Oxford.[1] The two extracts are as follows:

> And now she beats her heart, whereat it groans,
> That all the neighbour caves, as seeming troubled,
> Make verbal repetition of her moans;
> Passion on passion deeply is redoubled;
>   'Ay me!' she cries and twenty times 'Woe, woe!'
>   And twenty echoes twenty times cry so.
>
> She, marking them, begins a wailing note,
> And sings extemporally a woeful ditty.

from *Venus and Adonis*, and:

> Three times with her soft hand, full hard on her left side she knocks,
> And sighed so sore as might have moved some pity in the rocks;
> From sighs and shedding amber tears, into sweet song she broke,
> When thus the echo answered her to every word she spoke

from *A Vision of a Fair Maid.*

Canon Rendall claims that the likeness between the two is so striking that they must have been written by the same hand, and that hand for him is of course Oxford's. According to his theory Oxford wrote *A Vision of a Fair Maid* as a young man, and then repeated a sequence of ideas he had used in it in V. & A., which he wrote many years later.

In reply it may be pointed out that this is going far beyond the limits of legitimate deduction, which can establish at the most only some vague connection between the two works. Canon Rendall's theory depends solely and entirely on the similarities; apart from them there is nothing to suggest a common authorship, and the two poems are completely dissimilar in style and language. Consequently, if any equally plausible means can be suggested to account for the similarities, then the theory at once loses all its evidential support.

There are in fact two other means by which the similarities can be explained, both of them at least equally as plausible as the common authorship view, in the opinion of many much more plausible.

---

[1] Douglas, *Lord Oxford and the Shakespeare Group*, pp. 63 f.

First, as we shall see in Chapter VII, where the whole question of parallelisms is fully discussed, the borrowing of ideas and even the expression of them from other writers was a very common practice among Elizabethan men of letters, and Shakespeare, whoever he may have been, was certainly guilty of it on occasion. A good example of this is his sonnet beginning 'Two loves have I of comfort and despair' (144). If this is compared with one – 'An evil Spirit (your Beauty) haunts me still' – written by Drayton shortly before, it will at once be seen that there are similarities in the two much more striking than those in *A Vision of a Fair Maid* and V. & A., for they are not confined to a few ideas, but extend to verbal expressions. Yet the two Sonnets are known to be by different authors. Of course the Oxfordians might say that Drayton's Sonnet had been published, and was therefore well-known, while *A Vision of a Fair Maid* never appeared in print, so that the author of V. & A., unless he were Oxford, was very unlikely to have had access to it. Such an answer, however, would not meet the case. It may be true that Oxford's poem was never published – though we cannot be certain about this, since a vast number of Elizabethan works have perished completely during the lapse of the centuries – but, as we know from Meres and other sources, poets frequently circulated their works in manuscript, and there might well have been many chances for the author of V. & A. to see and borrow from Oxford's poem.

The second explanation that I have to advance is an even more probable one. If we examine the similarities in the two poems in question, we notice immediately how utterly commonplace and conventional they are. All they amount to is that the lady in each case beats her breast, sighs, and then bursts into song, while the sound of these activities is echoed by the surrounding heights. The first two – beating the breast and sighing – are, as an expression of grief, so closely connected and so frequently accompany one another, that they almost count as one. The converting of sighs into song is a little less usual, but by no means uncommon. In poetic fiction in all ages, at least before the present one of robust females, distraught ladies have been given to expressing their woes in song; even as recently as the nineteenth century Tennyson's

Lady of Shallott, as she floated down to Camelot after the curse had come upon her, acted in precisely this way. The echo motif is even more common, and there can be few poets who have not made use of it at one time or another. Therefore, since in all other respects the two poems are so unlike, there may well be no more in these similarities than the chance coincidence of three or four very commonplace ideas.

So much then for Canon Rendall's theory of a common authorship for the two poems. At its very best, and without the introduction of Oxford's name, it is nothing more than one among several explanations of their possible relationship, and as such cannot be regarded as *proof* of anything. This, however, does not end the matter, for against the claim of Oxford's authorship of V. & A. there exists a completely convincing piece of evidence. This is the dedication of that poem and of its companion-piece, *Lucrece*, to the Earl of Southampton.

At the time V. & A. was published Southampton was still in his teens and Oxford was a man of forty-four. Moreover the Southampton earldom was of comparatively recent creation, while Oxford's was one of the most ancient, and, as the Oxfordians themselves repeatedly remind us, Oxford was a proud, sensitive man, somewhat touchy about points of honour. Now would such a man, this senior earl in the very prime of his life, write in the strain of these two dedications to one who was little more than a boy? I invite my readers to open their copies of Shakespeare's works and to study those dedications carefully. They may be less fulsome than some Elizabethan dedications, but if one fact stands out clearly, it is that they were addressed by an inferior to his social superior. Either Shakspere or Marlowe might have written them, but it is impossible that any of the other claimants could have done so, Oxford least of all.

Moreover, if for sake of argument we were to ignore this insuperable objection, what in Oxford's case is to be made of the phrase 'the first heir of my invention', which is used to describe V. & A. in the dedication? The Stratfordians can, and do, point out that this was the first poem Shakspere had published, and suggest that he probably did not regard the plays – in which at that date there had been some collaboration and a certain amount of working over old scripts, and which in any case ranked as a lower level of literature than poetry – as original work; but for the Oxfordians there is no such escape from the dilemma, as Oxford had already written a number of poems.

We can therefore only conclude that Canon Rendall's evidence carries no more weight than any of the other Oxfordian arguments that we have examined. Of course there remains the evidence – still to be reviewed — which this school of thought uses in common with the other schools, but I am afraid it does not do much to strengthen the case. I write this somewhat regretfully, for, as I have said more than once, I like the courteous Oxfordians and I find their theory very attractive. The idea of the immortal works emerging at the hands of a group of brilliant amateurs, throwing them off in intervals of leisure snatched from the Council Chamber and the battlefield, is in perfect accord with my romantic picture of merry England in the spacious days of the Virgin Queen. Unfortunately, however, romantic pictures cannot be allowed to play any part in a critical survey, and I am bound to record that on analysis the Oxfordian case appears to me a very weak one.

CHAPTER V

The Case for Lord Derby

The case for the Earl of Derby differs in one very important respect from that of any of the other candidates with whom we are dealing. Apart from a few short letters of a business nature, written during the latter part of his life, no acknowledged work of his, if he ever wrote any, has survived. In his case therefore there can be no literary comparisons with the Shakespearean works in the hope of discovering similarities of style and ideas. The whole theory has to be built up on external evidence only.

On the other hand there is what the Derbyites claim to be contemporary documentary evidence that he not only wrote plays, but wrote them for the professional theatre. This evidence is contained in two letters of a Jesuit spy named Fenner, an assistant of the notorious Father Parsons. Both letters were intercepted, and are preserved at the Records Office. Both of them bear the same date, 30 June, 1599. In one is the statement, 'Therle of Derby is busyed only in penning comedies for the commoun players', and in the other, 'Our Earle of Derby is busye in penning commedyes for the commoun players'.[1]

This seems at first glance very definite evidence that Derby did write plays, and the Derbyites naturally make it the starting point of their theory; but we must not overlook the fact that its source can scarcely be regarded as a trustworthy one, and there is certainly a suspicious element about the statement itself. If it means no more than it says, then it seems a very trivial piece of information for a spy to include in a letter, and it is still more strange that he should repeat it in a second letter written on the same day. One cannot help wondering if it might be some sort of code actually giving other and more important information about the Earl.

At that time the Roman Catholics, having recovered from the blow dealt to their cause by the defeat of the Spanish

[1] Titherley, *Shakespeare's Identity*, p. 30.

91

Armada, were becoming very active in various ways, and there were a number of plots hatched against the Queen. Derby was not a Catholic, but he was a man of very liberal outlook and was known to be favourably disposed towards the Catholics. Moreover the blood of the Royal House of Lancaster ran in his veins, and it was not impossible, with the question of the succession so uncertain, that he might be invited to ascend the throne on the death of the Queen. The Catholics might therefore have hoped to involve him in their schemes as a way of making sure of this. I am inclined to believe that Fenner's remark, repeated in both letters, was a guarded way of informing his addressees that nothing was to be looked for from Derby; his mind was elsewhere than on thoughts of the throne. At the same time the statement, even if used for this purpose, might have some truth in it, and while the evidence cannot be regarded as by any means conclusive, I am not prepared to deny that Derby may possibly have tried his hand at playwriting.

Titherley, however, goes much further than this, and weaves a romantic story into the episode.[1] According to this, Derby, who was in love with Elizabeth de Vere, Lord Oxford's daughter, was prevailed upon by the Ministers of State to become secretly engaged to the Queen in order to placate the Catholics. After a few months, however, the danger of a rebellion having receded, the Queen herself broke off the engagement, leaving Derby free to return to his first love.

Now, quite apart from the fact that there is no historical evidence whatever for it, this theory is manifestly absurd. How could a *secret* engagement placate the Catholics or anyone else? If they knew nothing about it, then it might just as well not be. To produce any effect it would have to be publicly announced, and of course nothing of the sort ever was publicly announced, though Elizabeth's real proposed engagements were all well known. The engagement is therefore nothing more than the merest surmise on the part of the Derbyites; yet it is constantly used by Titherley to support various deductions he makes. The following is an example.[2]

A certain minor poet, John Davies of Hereford, published a

[1] *Shakespeare's Identity*, pp. 72–73.   [2] Ibid., pp. 43–46.

collection of epigrams, one of which was addressed – 'To our English Terence, Mr. Will. Shakespeare'. It runs as follows:

> Some say good *Will* (which I in sport do sing)
> Hadst thou not played some Kingly parts in sport,
> Thou hadst bin a companion for a *King*;
> And beene a King among the meaner sort.
> Some others raile; but raile as they think fit,
> Thou hast no rayling, but a raigning Wit.
> *And* honesty *thou sow'st which they do reape*
> *So to increase their* Stocke *which they do keepe.*

Titherley interprets this as pointing to Derby as the author of the Shakespearean plays. He points out that Terence, generally considered to be the leading writer of comedies in ancient Rome, had been thought by some critics to be merely a mask for the patrician Scipio. He takes the first 'King' to stand for ruler in general, and thus to mean Queen Elizabeth; and 'of the meaner sort' to refer to a claimant of the throne through the female line, as Derby would be if he had made such a claim. He then gives a paraphrase of the epigram, with interpolations in brackets to bring out the desired meaning.

'To our English Terence (a second Scipio whose literary pseudonym is) Mr. Will. Shakespeare. Some say, good Will, that which I say sportingly; had you not played some Kingly parts in sport (as an amateur actor, and thereby mocked Royal dignity in the Queen's severe judgement) you might have become her companion (or consort and so *ipso facto* on her demise) a King (William III) of the meaner sort (by your descent from Mary Tudor through your mother). (Like a Royal Prince) you have a *reigning*, not a railing wit, but sow for others to reap.'

Now with all due respect to Dr Titherley, I can only say that this simply will not do. It is a perfect example of what Chapman has described as making 'anything mean anything'. By such a method any interpretation can be forced upon any statement. To demonstrate this I will use the same epigram, and, by applying Titherley's method, make it point directly to Shakspere, the Stratford actor.

For this I take Terence's name at its face value, that of a

famous dramatist. I take 'King' figuratively to stand for 'Poet' as the highest rank in the kingdom of letters, and 'of the meaner sort' to represent a dramatist, inferior in the general view to the pure poet as being mixed up with the professional stage. Shakspere had still further degraded himself by being an actor. But as dramatist and actor, instead of a Court poet producing romantic or satiric trifles for a limited circle of readers, his wit reigned over vast public audiences, who thus gained by his loss. My paraphrase then reads:

'To our famous English playwright, Mr. Will. Shakespeare. Some say, good Will, what I now say jokingly, that if you had not been an actor, you might have ranked as a companion of Poets, and a Poet yourself, even if only a dramatic one. But as it is, instead of your wit wasting itself on satiric trifles for courtiers, it reigns over much larger numbers in the public theatres, who thus gain by your loss.'

I could with equal ease make the same epigram point to Francis Bacon by taking over Titherley's suggestion of Terence as a mask for Scipio, and interpreting 'King' and 'of the meaner sort' in the light of the claim that some of the extreme Baconians make, that Bacon was a Tudor Prince, the illegitimate son of Queen Elizabeth.

Of course I do not advance either of these interpretations as proof of Shakspere's or Bacon's authorship, though I do claim that they have as much validity as Titherley's. My object is merely to expose the utter worthlessness of such a method in a problem like the present one. I would add that Titherley's idea of Queen Elizabeth's being shocked at Derby for engaging in amateur acting, if he ever did so, is very improbable. Her own father, Henry VIII, had taken part in masques and had also engaged in wrestling contests with professionals, while she herself sometimes gave displays of dancing to foreign ambassadors.

Moreover if we were to accept Titherley's claim, we should at once be involved in the confusion in which we so often found the Baconians, that between 'secret' and 'no secret'. If Davies meant what Titherley says he did, then he must have known the secret of Derby's authorship; and, since he put it into a published work, he must have felt confident that his readers had a pretty good idea of it too. In other words, it was no secret. But in that case, what was the use of Derby's having a mask, and how did Shakspere come to be credited with the authorship? The only reasonable interpretation of the epigram is that it was really addressed to the Stratford actor, whom Davies, rightly or wrongly, believed to be the author of the plays.

For his next argument Titherley invokes the aid of the science of genetics. He says:[1] 'According to the modern theory of genetics it is the hypothetical ultra-microscopic "genes" of the microscopically visible chromosome threads (in the nucleus of the germ cells) which transmit all hereditary dispositions. When 23 or 24 chromosomes of the single (male) spermatozoon pair with the normal 24 chromosomes of the (female) ovum to give the zygote, i.e. fertilized egg cell, to be respectively a boy (47 equally paired chromosomes) or a girl (48) the corresponding genes in each pairing thread themselves pair. This means of course pairing of the genes for any particular quality (such, for example, as musical talent), but in so pairing one gene ('recessive') may be suppressed by its fellow ('dominant') of the other thread. In such a case the resulting offspring will externally display only the dominant character, though invisibly or latently containing the recessive gene, the character for which may come out in the next or in subsequent generations. The child is thus not merely the product of his parents, but the sum of both visible and latent qualities derived from his ancestors.'

Titherley then proceeds to argue from this that Derby received a specially favourable inheritance from his ancestors that enabled him to become the genius who could produce the Shakespearean works. He instances all the families famous in history – Howards, Percies, Seymours, Nevilles, etc., etc. – to which the Stanleys were related, and claims that the inheritance that would come from them obviously points to Derby as the true Shakespeare, and that his undistinguished ancestry completely rules out the Stratford actor.

One might reply that if every word written by Titherley were literally true, it would not prove Derby's authorship. Oxford had a similar heredity, and Bacon, on his recognized works alone, is undeniably one of the world's greatest men of genius.

[1] *Shakespeare's Identity*, pp. 100–102.

There is, however, a much stronger counter to Titherley's argument than this. His genetics, if not positively incorrect, are greatly over-simplified.

In the first place he writes as if all inherited characters were single-factor ones; that is, one gene pair for every character. They are not. A few minor ones may be, but even such a simple character as coat-colour in the lower animals depends on several genes situated in more than one chromosome, and all the higher qualities of human beings are so amazingly complex that no detailed study of them has yet proved possible. Titherley is therefore basing his argument on the unknown, which may turn out to be very different from what he imagines.

Secondly, his statement on ancestral inheritance and his recital of the families connected with the Stanleys give a false impression. Every individual human being, whether the Earl of Derby, the Stratford actor, or anyone else, has two parents, four grandparents, eight great-grandparents, and so on, giving in the twentieth generation back an ancestry of 2,097,150 persons.[1] It is from these direct ancestors, and from no one else, that his inherited characters come. Uncles and aunts by marriage and second cousins twice removed have nothing to do with the case. To say, as Titherley does, that Derby's mother was related to 'black-faced Clifford' and 'Harry Hotspur' means nothing, unless these two famous men came in the direct line of his descent. To follow up the direct ancestral lines for any distance is of course impossible; the number of ancestors normally doubles in each generation as we work backwards, and even allowing for the reduction due to a certain amount of in-breeding, the very number of the various trails would soon cause most of them to become hopelessly lost; yet each has an .equal chance of being important in the final inheritance of an individual. Moreover, with such a vast host of ancestors from whom to inherit, it is always possible for anyone to acquire by random selection, which is the way in which genes are passed on, a highly favourable complement of characters. This no doubt explains why, as is the case, two mental defectives may

[1] Of course marriages between close relations, such as first cousins, would reduce this total considerably, but even so the number of ancestors would remain enormous.

3 SIXTH EARL OF DERBY

Drawing by Silvester Harding in the Sutherland Collection

produce a quite normal offspring, and most men of genius have sprung from ordinary normal parents.

Again an individual may inherit a character, which, owing to his circumstances, he may never have the opportunity to develop. There must have been many 'mute inglorious Miltons', born in the years before popular education, who never wrote a line because they had never learnt to write, but whose talent could be transmitted to their descendants. Titherley cannot legitimately rule out the Stratford actor because of the lack of known literary ability in any of his ancestors.

Finally, many Eugenists would say that genius was much more likely to appear in the new and vigorous middle class which came into such prominence in Tudor times, and to which Shakspere belonged, than in the worn-out aristocracy that had all but committed suicide in the Wars of the Roses. Sir Thomas More, Cardinal Wolsey, the Cecils, Drake, Ralegh, and Hawkins, as well as many famous London merchants such as Gresham, may be cited as examples of these new men, and some historians ascribe the Tudor genius itself to the fact that a certain quantity of this new blood ran in their royal veins.

This analysis should make it perfectly clear that the science of genetics, at least in the present state of our knowledge, can throw no light on the question of the authorship of the Shakespearean plays. Titherley's attempt to use it for such a purpose is quite unwarranted; the problem is not susceptible to such treatment.

We now come to what may be termed Titherley's *pièce de résistance*, which is nothing less than the claim that one of the 'Additions' to the play *Sir Thomas More*, an addition held by many leading critics,[1] most of them Stratfordians, to be the work of Shakespeare, is actually in the handwriting of Derby.[2] Such a claim, if true, would certainly be strong evidence in favour of the Derbyite theory. We must therefore subject it to a very careful examination.

The facts briefly are these. The play, which is the joint work

---

[1] But by no means all. Tannenbaum, the American expert on Elizabethan scripts, always disputed it, and Halliday, who would have liked to believe it, did not feel the evidence justified the claim.

[2] *Shakespeare's Identity* pp. 226 ff.

of several dramatists working for Henslowe, has survived in manuscript form, and is now in the British Museum. The manuscript is written in several hands, and W. W. Greg has labelled these respectively S, A, B, C, D, and E. It has been variously dated between the years 1587 and 1593, but an early date is, on the available evidence, the most probable. The main play is in the hand labelled S, and there are six additions to it in the other hands.

The second of these, in hand D and known as the 'Insurrection Scene', is the one ascribed to Shakespeare. It consists of three pages of writing, and the generally accepted view of its origin by those who believe it to be Shakespearean is that the authors were in trouble with the censor over the 'Insurrection Scene', which he had banned and is now lost, and that they then invited Shakespeare to help them out of their difficulty by rewriting it for them. A number of critics believe that the manuscript of this scene is not a scrivener's copy, but a genuine autograph; that is – written by the hand of Shakespeare himself. Titherley leaps on to this point, and claims that not only hand D, which wrote this particular scene, but also hand E, which was responsible for another of the additions, are both Derby's.

The position therefore may be summed up as follows:

(1) If the addition is Shakespeare's work,
(2) If the manuscript of this addition is an autograph, and
(3) If the handwriting of the addition is Lord Derby's,
    Then Lord Derby is Shakespeare.

'Much virtue in *If*', as Shakspere, Bacon, Oxford, Derby, Marlowe, or someone else made Touchstone say. Titherley, however, has no doubts that all these 'ifs' are facts, and we must turn our attention to the grounds on which his confidence is based.

First, that the addition is Shakespeare's work. It *could* be. It is very inferior to most of his work, but there are scenes in his plays, especially the 'Jack Cade' scenes in 2 Hen. VI, to which it is usually compared, that are no better, some perhaps even worse. On the other hand there are scenes in the plays of other dramatists that resemble the genuine Shakespeare quite as much as this does. To take the first that occurs to me, Cornelia's madness over her slaughtered son in Webster's *The White Devil* (V, iv) is at least as near in language and treatment to Ophelia's madness over her slaughtered father in *Hamlet* (IV, v) as the addition is to the 'Jack Cade' scenes, and if Webster could be influenced by *Hamlet* the author of the addition could be influenced by *Henry VI*. Titherley instances the similarity of Surrey's mode of addressing the mob, 'Friends, Masters, and Countrymen', to Mark Antony's mode to the Roman citizens in *Julius Caesar*, 'Friends, Romans, and Countrymen', and also appeals to Shakespeare's well-known hatred of mob rule. With regard to the former, quite apart from the fact that it could be imitated, the general pattern of the phrase was a conventional formula for addressing a crowd, and as a means of identifying an author is about as valuable as 'Ladies and Gentlemen' would be today. And does Titherley really imagine that Shakespeare (Derby) was the only person who hated mob rule? Apart from the mob itself, everyone did, and not least those connected with the theatre, who not infrequently suffered loss and damage from it. Moreover the author of the addition, whoever he might be, was only rewriting the dialogue of one scene to improve it and avoid dangerous political references; not providing a new plot. Presumably the original was also concerned with More's quelling of the mob. In the light of these considerations the most we can legitimately conclude is that, while the addition *may* be by Shakespeare, this is very far from proved.

Second, that the addition is an autograph, not a scrivener's copy. For this view Titherley has the support of some, though by no means all,[1] orthodox Stratfordians, who like to believe that at last they have found a specimen of Shakespeare's handwriting. The evidence Titherley offers for his contention is the high frequency of y-spellings the manuscript contains and the large number of alterations to be found in so short a passage. Both these items require a little explanation in order to reveal why they can be considered as evidence.

---

[1] Professor A. Feuillerat, the Franco-American authority, states categorically that the manuscript bears all the marks of a professional penman, who was interested in the calligraphy, not in the sense of what he was writing. See *The Composition of Shakespeare's Plays*, p. 48, footnote 9.

Up to the year 1550 'y' was used in the spelling of many words where 'i' is used today, e.g. 'tyger' for 'tiger'. After that date 'i' began to replace the 'y'. The change was, however, very gradual, and was very far indeed from complete in Elizabethan times. During her reign and subsequently all writers used both forms indiscriminately, though in general the older people tended to retain the 'y' and the younger people to adopt the 'i'. To this Titherley adds the by no means certain corollary that an author in the throes of composition would tend to revert to y-spellings, which would thus be plentiful in an autograph, while a scrivener, merely making a copy with no such pre-occupation, would tend to follow the new fashion, and his work would show many more i-spellings. Now it is true that the addition does have a fairly large number of y-spellings, and accordingly Titherley deduces that it is an autograph. This does not, however, follow as a matter of course. It might have been copied by an elderly scrivener to whom it was natural to use y-spellings, or by one with a personal preference for the old style, in both of which cases the copy might actually contain more y-spellings than the autograph. Titherley, the physical scientist, tends to overlook the unpredictability of human nature. He cannot possibly calculate, as he pretends to do here, what an unknown individual scrivener would do in any particular case, even if it were possible to establish a general average for the whole Tudor period, which is open to doubt.

The number of corrections in the manuscript is no more to the point. It is true that an author, having drafted a passage, naturally sets himself to improve it, with the result that his work accumulates a number of alterations; but neither is a scrivener's work free from corrections. Anyone who has attempted to make a copy of a lengthy passage knows how easy it is, when transferring the gaze from the original to the copy and then back to the original, to pick up the wrong place in the latter or make some other similar mistake. This is true even when working from a perfect original. Still more would it be the case when working from a much-altered manuscript with interlinings, marginal additions, etc. Nothing could be more likely than that the scrivener should make a number of mistakes, and these of course would have to be corrected. The addition to *Sir Thomas More* has forty-eight words that have been subject to correction, the majority of them consecutive words in two and a half lines, a condition that is by no means incompatible with a scrivener's copy.

Our conclusion must therefore be the same as the one to which we came in the matter of Shakespeare's authorship of the addition; that the case cannot be proved either way. The manuscript may be an autograph, but it is equally possible that it is only a copy.

Third, that hand D, the one that penned the 'Insurrection Scene' addition, and also hand E, are both actually the handwriting of Lord Derby. For comparison in his attempt to prove this claim Titherley had several letters written by Derby. At the very outset, however, he found himself faced by a difficulty. The letters all belonged to the later part of Derby's life, the earliest of them to the year 1597, while the addition was almost certainly considerably earlier than this, and it is a well-established fact that a person's handwriting changes as he grows older. The problem in this case is further complicated by the fact that not only did Derby's handwriting undergo this natural change, but simultaneously an artificial one. He evidently began by writing the old English Secretary hand, but later endeavoured to adopt the new Italianate script. He never wholly succeeded in this as far as we know, and his extant writing always shows a mixture of the two, with the Italianate becoming increasingly prominent. What Titherley has to do therefore is to demonstrate beyond all reasonable doubt that the letters represent truly what the writing of hands D and E in the additions would have developed into in the course of roughly ten years under the influence of the two factors, one natural and one artificial, mentioned in this paragraph,[1] obviously an exceedingly difficult task.

Titherley makes the attempt in the only possible way; that is, by taking a number of letters from the two hands in ques-

[1] There are some critics who argue for a date as late as 1600 for the addition. In this case, of course, there could not be even a pretence that Titherley's theory was correct, for this is later than the earliest letter, yet shows none of the developments of the latter. I agree, however, with Titherley that this late date is improbable.

tion, and pointing to their similarities with the same letters in Derby's acknowledged correspondence, illustrating his points with facsimiles of the documents and with enlargements of certain portions of them.

Of course there are resemblances; the matter could scarcely have been raised at all without some; but I personally failed to see many of the points Titherley claims are present. He himself, when criticizing the Baconian Cryptologists, remarks that in their interpretation of the alleged ciphers they seem to have been the victims of auto-suggestion. I wonder if the same might not be said of him when engaged in his pet hobby of recognizing Derby's handwriting in all sorts of improbable places, as we shall see he does (pp. 229 and 234). But even if all his points were correct, it would not prove the identity of the hands. There are persons whose writing is amazingly similar to that of another person. I have two correspondents who write to me several times a year, and I can never tell from which a particular letter has come until I have opened it and looked at the signature. Handwriting experts often differ from one another in their conclusions.[1] There have been cases of the condemnation of innocent men in the Law Courts – that of Adolf Beck is perhaps the best known – in part at least on the mistakes of such experts; and in these cases it has been a simple comparison of two documents; there have been none of the additional difficulties caused by natural and artificial changes in style such as occur in that of Lord Derby. In the light of these facts it is quite impossible to regard Titherley's contention as coming within measurable distance of proof.

There is, however, another kind of evidence which would appear to provide positive disproof. We must remember that according to the Derbyite theory Derby's authorship was a closely guarded secret. His supporters, no less than the Baconians and Oxfordians, emphasize the danger he would have incurred if any of the opinions expressed in the plays had happened to give offence in official quarters.[2] The addition was concerned with a most delicate topic – insurrection – and had

---

[1] As most experts see a difference between hands D and E, which appear the same to Titherley.

[2] Titherley himself does so. *Shakespeare's Identity*, pp. 48–50.

already occasioned trouble with the Censor, a Court official to whom the new version would have to be submitted, and Derby's handwriting would naturally be familiar to many of the important personages in the State. In these circumstances he would never, unless he were literally mad, let loose such a dangerous document without first ensuring, by having it copied by another hand, that it could not be traced to him. Titherley here falls into the common error of all the theorists, that of forgetting one half of his argument while developing the other half. The only conclusion that emerges from an analysis of his claim is that if the addition is an autograph, then Derby did not write it, and if it is not an autograph, then it is evidence of nothing.[1]

Titherley also makes use of the conventional types of evidence such as we have already encountered in the Baconian and Oxfordian cases, but he treats these in a rather perfunctory way, his main interest naturally being with the more scientific aspect of handwriting tests, spelling deviations, and similar factors. We shall have to consider his views again in some of the later chapters in connection with the evidence common to two or more theories; but for the conventional type of argument for the Derby case we will go over to Evans' *Shakespeare's Magic Circle*, where such arguments are treated more fully, and where some new 'discoveries', made since Titherley's book was published, are included.

Evans begins by claiming that the author of the Shakespearean works must have undergone certain specific personal experiences, and that Derby exactly fulfils this condition, while the Stratford actor most emphatically does not. He mentions a number of such experiences, and it would afford me great pleasure to work through the entire list with appropriate comments, but reasons of space absolutely preclude this. I must therefore content myself with reviewing one example.

[1] While it is not my purpose here to advocate the Stratford actor's claims, I may mention that a case at least as good as Titherley's can be made out for his writing of the hand D document. A summary of the evidence for this is contained in A. W. Pollard's article on 'Shakespeare's Text' in *A Companion to Shakespeare Studies*, ed. by H. Granville-Barker and G. B. Harrison, pp. 271–275.

Evans writes,[1] 'The author had an unusually intimate knowledge of ships and storms at sea (*Twelfth Night*, *The Tempest*,
Pericles).'

I can only assume, on reading this, that Evans did not
trouble to refresh his memory about the plays he mentions or
he would scarcely have committed himself to such an obviously
absurd statement. Let us see what this 'unusually intimate
knowledge' of ships and storms possessed by the author of these
three plays actually amounts to. We will begin with *Twelfth
Night*, at Act I, Scene ii, which is set on the sea-coast. Viola, a
Ship's Captain, and several sailors enter, having just escaped
from a wreck, and the following dialogue takes place:

VIOLA. What country, friends, is this?
CAPTAIN. This is Illyria, lady.
VIOLA. And what should I do in Illyria?
My brother he is in Elysium.
Perchance he is drown'd – what think you, sailors?
CAPTAIN. It is perchance that you yourself were saved.
VIOLA. O my poor brother! And so perchance may he be.
CAPTAIN. True, madam, and to comfort you with chance,
Assure yourself, after our ship did split,
When you, and those poor number sav'd with you,
Hung on our driving boat, I saw your brother,
Most provident in peril, bind himself –
Courage and hope both teaching him the practice –
To a strong mast that liv'd upon the sea;
Where, like Arion on the dolphin's back,
I saw him hold acquaintance with the waves
As long as I could see.
VIOLA. For saying so, there 's gold;
My own escape unfoldeth to my hope,
Whereto thy speech serveth for authority,
The like for him.

And that, with nine lines in the last act in which the Duke
praises the courage and skill shown by Antonio in a sea fight,
is positively all there is about ships and storms in *Twelfth Night*.
Comment would be superfluous.

The Tempest offers a little more. The first scene is actually the

[1] *Shakespeare's Magic Circle*, p. 15.

deck of a ship, with the crew struggling to avoid being driven on to the rocks by the fury of a storm. Some rapid entrances and exits give a sense of bustle and hurry, while the sailors' sudden dropping of respect for the high rank of their passengers when danger calls them to desperately urgent action is realistic, though of course such instances are not limited to the sea. In addition several nautical orders are given in the course of the dialogue in the correct sequence to carry out the required manoeuvres. They are – 'What cheer . . . Fall to 't yarely, or we run aground', 'Heigh, my hearts, cheerly', 'Yare, Take in the topsail', 'Down with the topmast', 'Bring her to try with main course', and 'We split'.[1]

In Scene ii, Miranda gives a fine but very short description of the storm and the wreck as she saw it *from the shore*, and Ariel gives an account of his behaviour under the guise of St Elmo's Fire. The rest that concerns the ship is Ariel's story of how, while creating the illusion of disaster, he has magically preserved both the ship and its company, so that not a hair of the latter has perished, nor have their garments received a blemish, which is scarcely so realistic that an 'unusually intimate knowledge' of ships and storms is required to write it.

Pericles has both more and less of the sea in it; more in that the sea is the setting for three scenes, one on the coast (II, i), and two (III, i and V, i) on board ship; less in that nothing much is said in any of these scenes about either ships or the sea. In the first, the coastal scene, Pericles enters and, in a short soliloquy, states that he has been cast ashore from a wreck. He then appeals for help to some fishermen, who reply by giving him some useful information about the country and its ruler. The second scene is certainly set in a storm at sea, but apart from one nautical order, 'Slack the bolins there!' the whole scene is taken up with the placing of the supposedly dead Thaisa in a chest, which is thrown into the sea and later washed ashore, where Thaisa is discovered to be still alive, and is ultimately restored to her husband, a fairy-tale episode that certainly did not require any great nautical expertise on the

---

[1] There is also 'Lay her a-hold', but no such term ever existed in nautical language. Shakespeare, whoever he was, tripped up here, as he did in some of his seafaring images in other plays.

part of the author. In the third the ship is in harbour, and, as far as dialogue and action are concerned, the scene might just as well have been set on land.

Such are the fruits of Evans' three examples of the 'unusually intimate knowledge' of ships and storms possessed by the author. The amount of accurate maritime information they contain is greatly exceeded in dozens of third-rate stories for children published every year. There is in fact nothing in any of them that a landsman of ordinary intelligence could not pick up quite easily without ever setting his foot on the deck of a ship. Miranda's short description is of a storm seen from the land, not experienced on the sea, and there was nothing to prevent even a humble actor from so seeing one – there is documentary evidence that Shakspere's company visited Dover in 1604, where such might easily have been the case. Ariel's speech about St Elmo's Fire is based on a recognizable passage in Hakluyt's *Voyages* (Vol. iii, published in 1598); and as for the eight nautical terms – seven in *The Tempest* and one in *Pericles* – the most lubberly of authors could have done what his modern successors do when they want information – ask those who have it. The age was one of maritime adventure, the interest of the whole population had been kindled by the voyages of discovery and the defeat of the Spanish Armada, while London was a port and therefore full of sailors, men who had sailed with Drake and the other great sea-captains. The author, even if – or rather especially if – he were a humble actor, could not help meeting these in the various taverns, and, if they were true to type, they would be as ready to tell their stories as he to hear them.[1]

As a matter of fact ships and the sea, or the mention of them, occur in other plays as well as in the three quoted by Evans – M. of V., A. & C., W. T., for example – but there is nothing in any of them that could not be fully accounted for in the way just described.

Evans attempts to extract further evidence in favour of his theory from *The Tempest*, which was produced at Court in 1611.

[1] There were also on sale in the London bookshops, as we shall see later (p. 174), books on navigation for amateur mariners, from which the author could have picked up a good deal of information if he had required to do so.

He says,[1] 'It is very remarkable that a play dealing with magic as the basis of the plot, should have been played before King James I. . . . James's abhorrence of all forms of magic and witchcraft is well known and the most severe laws were passed for the discovery and punishment of anyone suspected of practising those dangerous arts. Hatred of witchcraft became an obsession with James and those who mentioned it in their writing treated it as an unmitigated evil. *The Tempest* was the exception, for in it we see that there can be good as well as bad magic. At all events the production of *The Tempest* at Court was an extremely bold act and one likely to incur the grave displeasure of the King. No one but an author of high rank, greatly respected by the King and of known loyalty, would have dared to preach, as Shakespeare does, a lesson of moderation so contrary to the King's policy in the matter of magic.'

This paragraph is as full of errors and misconceptions concerning both Folklore and Literature as one of its length could possibly be. It is, of course, true that James I was obsessed by fear and hatred of witchcraft. He wrote against it, he tightened up the comparatively lax laws of Elizabeth for dealing with it, and he instituted a regular persecution of witches. He did not, however, need Lord Derby or anyone else to teach him the traditional belief, of which he was a past-master, that magic might be used for good as well as evil purposes.

According to this belief there was a marked difference between the witch and the magician. The former was a person who had sold his or her soul to the devil and was under control of evil spirits. The witch's magic was therefore always evil. The magician on the other hand was a person who, by his study of magic, had gained control over evil spirits, and could compel them to do his will. His magic might therefore be good or bad according to his personal character.[2] King James may

---

[1] *Shakespeare's Magic Circle*, pp. 115–116.

[2] It must be admitted that the magician ran considerable occupational risks, both real and imaginary. Evil spirits are dangerous material to meddle with, and might contrive to turn the tables and get the magician into their power, as happened in the case of Faustus. Moreover, if any public disaster occurred, the magician became suspect almost as easily as the witch. These factors, however, do not obliterate the essential distinction between the two.

have been a fool, but he was a learned fool, and could scarcely be unaware of the story of Merlin, the wise and benevolent magician on whose good offices King Arthur and the Knights of the Round Table so greatly depended. He could also find benevolent magic in Chaucer's *Canterbury Tales*, in Spenser's *Faerie Queene*, in Greene's *Friar Bacon and Friar Bungay*, and, written in his own reign, in *The Faithful Shepherdess* of Beaumont and Fletcher, as well as in many other works. Consequently he would see nothing strange or contrary to his own views in Prospero, who was simply a benevolent magician exercising his powers for good. Evans' statement therefore is quite incorrect – *The Tempest* is far from being an exception in this respect.

Again it required no special courage to bring an 'unorthodox view' of magic into the royal palace. On various occasions during James' reign Ben Jonson was commissioned to write a masque for private performance at Whitehall. Among those he wrote were *Love Restored*, produced for the Christmas festivities of 1610, that is the year before *The Tempest* was produced, in which magic was treated most frivolously and used for the purpose of satire, and *Prince Oberon* for the celebration of Prince Henry's elevation to the rank of Prince of Wales, in which the young Prince himself played the title rôle. This is much to the point, for, although many of the Elizabethan men of letters had taken to treating the fairies light-heartedly and suppressing their more unpleasant characteristics, according to the orthodox view, which was King James' view, the fairies were evil spirits and associated with witchcraft, and the Church exorcized them in exactly the same way as it did other evil spirits. Ben Jonson, who began his career as a bricklayer, was thus treating magic in a most unorthodox way apparently at the King's request, certainly with his approval, which suggests that His Majesty's bigotry did not extend to entertainments. In the face of this what becomes of Evans' statement that only a peer of the realm who, like Derby, enjoyed the full confidence of the King, would dare to do such a thing?

But of course such a statement is absurd in any case. Whoever actually wrote *The Tempest*, as far as King James and his Court were aware the author was the Stratford actor. This is just another instance of the theorists' ever-recurring confusion of thought about 'secret' and 'no secret'. No one has emphasized his candidate's determination to keep his authorship perpetually hidden more strongly than Evans has done that of Derby, as we shall see when we come to deal with the First Folio. Yet here, in order to make what he considers a favourable point, he forgets all about this, and writes as if there were no secret at all and that everyone knew Derby was the author.

We must now turn to what is certainly the most interesting feature in Evans' book, his account of Professor Lambin's claim to have made some new discoveries concerning the origin of *Measure for Measure* which favour Derby's authorship. These 'discoveries' were first published in *Les Langues Modernes*, 1951 to 1953, under the title of *'Sur la Trace d'un Shakespeare Inconnu'*, and Evans thus summarizes them:[1]

'No one knows the year in which *Measure for Measure* was originally composed. It was published for the first time in the 1623 Folio, and there are reasons (Titherley) for believing that it was probably taken from a copy of a copy after having been several times revised.

'The usual sources given are Cinthio's *Hecatommithi* of 1565, translated into French in 1584, and *Promos and Cassandra* by George Whetstone, published in 1578. But Shakespeare introduced numerous modifications and additions to these versions of the story; besides new names and new characters. For instance, in the play the scene is Vienna instead of Innsbruck. Coronius, King of Hungary, becomes Duke of Vienna, and remains incognito near his capital. Claudius' (?) crime is much attenuated. Isabella is about to enter a convent of nuns of the "Clare" Order. Angelo has a cast-off fiancée. Bernadine, Lucio, and Escalus are new characters. But the real scene of Shakespeare's play is laid in Paris in 1582, and not in Vienna, as we shall see.

'Professor Lambin's discoveries are of outstanding interest to our quest, because William Stanley arrived in Paris on July 25th, 1582, with his tutor, Richard Lloyd, as will be recalled. These two waited in Paris for their "permit to travel abroad". The permit having arrived on 12th September, Stanley and his tutor moved on (exact date not known) to the

[1] *Shakespeare's Magic Circle*, pp. 116–121.

neighbourhood of Angers, whence Lloyd on October 6th wrote acknowledging the receipt of the permit.

'Now Lambin has proved that Henri III left Paris, for a private journey in France, on August 11th, 1582. In his absence a certain Claude Tonart was condemned to death on September 8th, but rescued from execution on September 22nd. The King returned to Paris on October 7th.

'If it can be shown that the living drama enacted in Paris between August 11th and October 7th and the personalities in Paris are identifiable with the plot and characters of the play, we shall have taken a very long step towards identifying Stanley, who was there at the critical time, as the only possible author of *Measure for Measure*. The closer the details are studied the more certain it becomes that the play could only have been written by an eyewitness of these events.

'In the play we find that Isabella is about to enter a convent of the Order of St. Clare and that Francesca is the Mother Superior who initiates her. Her instructions conform exactly to the actual rules of the Order.

> You must not speak with men
> But in the presence of the Prioress;
> Then if you speak you must not show your face,
> Or if you show your face you must not speak.

There were no Clare nunneries in England at the end of the sixteenth century. There had been, but all were dissolved in 1538. Once more we note the astonishing accuracy and detail of Shakespeare's information.

'Even the names Francesca and Isabella were not chosen by Shakespeare by chance, since the Clares were of the order of Franciscans, and it was Isabella of France, sister of Saint-Louis, who founded, in 1256, the Clarissa nunnery at Long-champs which Isabella herself entered, died there, and was canonized later. In 1582 Longchamps had become one of the interesting places to visit from Paris, but not always on religious grounds. The severe rules of the order at Longchamps had previously been relaxed and it seems a village had grown up round the nunnery where the attractions were far from inno-cent; all resulting from a papal "Bull" of "Mitigation" (1263) which ameliorated the strict rules of the order. In the play, Lucio says, "Behold, behold, where Madam Mitigation comes!" (I, ii, 45) when speaking of the prostitute Mrs. Overdone; and Isabella also wishes that the rules were stricter. In 1583 Henri III installed the monkish order of Hieronomites in quarters near Longchamps, whose principal founders were Thomas de Suna and Pierre (Peter) de Pire – the names of the two monks in *Measure for Measure*. The Duke, as a Friar in the play, took the name of Lodowick, a most suitable name for a descendant of Saint-Louis. It was also a habit of Henri III to go frequently into "retreat" at Vincennes, presumably for prayer and meditation, but not everyone in Paris was convinced that his "retreats" were for religious purposes. In the play, Lucio, that incorrigible scandalmonger, hints this to the Duke (disguised), much to the Duke's indignation (III, ii, 127). When reporting Henri's disappearance to Vincennes, Lord Cobham always, even after living three years in Paris, spelt it Vincent, so that the reason why Shakespeare called the Duke Vincentio is easily explained. It was also Henri III's habit from time to time to disguise himself and behave as a monk.

'Lucio is a clever skit on a courtier of Henri III, called Saint-Luc (Francois d'Espiney), who was compelled by the King (as was Lucio in the play) to marry a repulsive and vicious woman. M'elle de B. Saint-Luc appears to have been an incorrigible practical joker and dropper of bricks – in fact Lucio in the play is rather a portrait than a caricature.

'We now come to some names introduced by the author into the play quite gratuitously, because they have nothing to do with the plot – Flavius, Valentinus, Roland, Crassus, and Varrius. Professor Lambin has discovered without the least doubt the real names of these and demonstrated their standing in Paris in 1582–84. Surely only an eyewitness, resident in Paris at the correct date, could have brought them so unnecessarily into his play. Two other names, however, are even more significant. First Bernadin Mendoza, lately the Italian[1] ambassador to England, but now ambassador in Paris, was frequently referred to by Walsingham, Stafford, and Derby in

[1] So Evans. Mendoza was of course the Spanish, *not* the Italian, ambassador.

their letters, as Bernadino. Mendoza had been nine years in England and boasted of his crimes there, but Henri turned a blind eye to his villainy, just as the Duke in the play postponed punishing the criminal Bernadine. As for the second, Ragosoni, the Papal Legate, who had been a bitter enemy of Elizabeth, there can be little doubt that in the play the pirate Ragozine was called after him.

'In the play the morals of Vienna were so bad (as they were in Paris in 1582) that the Duke deemed it necessary to revive some old rigorous laws against immorality. He leaves to Angelo this unpleasant task and departs dressed as a monk. Claudio is arrested for seducing Julietta (?) and condemned to death though he pleads that they were really married and Julietta agrees that her union with Claudio was by consent. It is agreed by the characters in the play that this judgement is cruel and unjust, but Angelo will not retreat. When, however, Isabella pleads with Angelo for her brother's life, Angelo agrees to pardon Claudio if Isabella consents to sleep with him (Angelo). The disguised Duke in the meantime makes private inquiries and concocts a highly complicated plan to save Claudio, confront Angelo with his villainy, and marry off everyone whether they like it or not – Lucio to a whore (i.e. M'elle B.) and Angelo to his cast-off fiancée.

'Now let us see what actually happened in Paris in 1582 as reported from two sources, viz, 1. The *Registre-Journal de l'Estoile*, for the reign of Henri III, of which the only publication was (in French) in 1621, five years after the Stratford actor's death, and 2. *L'Histoire Universelle*, which de Thou published in Latin in 1733.

'Soon after the departure (on August 11th, 1582) of the King from Paris, Claude Tonart seduced the daughter of Jean Bailly, President of the Council. As a result of the complaints of the girl's parents and as an example Tonart was arrested and thrown into the prison whose governor was the Prévot. Hence, probably, the name "Provost" used by Shakespeare for the man who combined the office of both chief of the police and gaoler; a combination of offices only known in France and the Netherlands. Claude Tonart, like Claudio, pleaded that he was really married to the girl, and that by mutual consent she was his wife, and she agreed that she was not only a willing party to the union but that the major responsibility was hers.

'Nevertheless Tonart was condemned to death but was rescued amid scenes of great indignation at the injustice of the sentence. Shortly afterwards (October 7th) the King returned from his retreat – as Cobham writes, "the king has said openly that he has long lived in private sort". Claude Tonart was pardoned but La Roche-Flavin (Flavius in the play) seems to have been blamed for having some responsibility for the condemnation of Tonart. Obviously Claude Tonart is the Claudio of the play, but Angelo appears to be a composite mixture of a number of unpleasant people in positions of importance in Paris at that time. Jean Poisle, for instance, a councillor of Paris, was denounced for many crimes by a colleague and everyone expected to see him hung, but as a result of the pleadings of his wife he got off with a light sentence. Malevaulte who succeeded him was no better. Another original of Angelo was councillor Jerome Angenoust, who had the appearance of a saint, but was "*un rigorist*", not unlike Angelo, in character.'

Such is Evans' exposition of Lambin's 'discovery', and any reader familiar with the literary history of *Measure for Measure* will recognize at once that it is nothing but a mare's nest. However, it is a comparatively new mare's nest, and, since it is used to propagate the Derby theory, we must analyse it point by point even at the risk of being a little tedious. It falls naturally into three parts:

(1) Argument from the knowledge shown by the author concerning the Orders of the Clares and the Hieronomites.

(2) Argument from the identification, through their names, of persons in the play with actual persons living in Paris.

(3) Argument from the similarity between events that actually occurred in Paris and those in the play.

With regard to the first, Evans writes as if it were absolutely necessary for the author to go to Paris to pick up details about the two Orders in question, or rather about the Clares, for, though Evans drags the Hieronomites into his argument, there is not a single reference to this Order in the play. The necessity for the Paris visit is simply nonsense. Quite apart from the fact that England was still swarming with Catholics and had been a Catholic country in the previous reign, so that the details of Catholic organizations were perfectly familiar there, Professor Muir[1] has shown that one of the sources of M. for M. was Erasmus' *Colloquia*, which could provide the author with virtually all the information on the subject he needed for the play. It contains not only an account of a young girl's initiation into the Order of the Clares, but also three of the names which occur in the cast of M. for M. – Francesca, Bernadine (once misspelt as *Barnadine*, the form Shakespeare actually adopted, and a detail Messrs Evans and Lambin seem strangely to have overlooked), and Vincentius. So their pretty theories about these names collapse completely, since it is obvious that the author took them ready-made from one of his sources.

As for Isabella, the name has nothing to do with the canonized sister of the martyr King of France. If Evans and Lambin had done a little research into contemporary English literature they would have discovered that in 1582 Whetstone, the author of *Promos and Cassandra*, Shakespeare's main source, rehandled the same story as narrative in his *Heptameron of Civil Discourses*, which there is ample proof in the text of M. for M. was also used by the author. Now in the *Heptameron* Whetstone adopts the device of having the story told by a lady, and gives her the name of Isabella. With this obvious explanation at hand for the name of the heroine, why should anyone go rummaging back through the centuries in search of another? The theory of Evans and Lambin is far-fetched in every sense of that phrase.

The reference to the Bull of Mitigation, if it is such a reference – and it must be admitted that it is difficult to see what other interpretation could be placed upon it – is something of a puzzle whoever the author might be. The Bull was promulgated about 300 years before the play was written, and after such a lapse of time even a Catholic audience might well miss the point of the 'Madam Mitigation' joke. I can only suggest that the author, having decided, with the help of Erasmus, on the Order which his heroine was to join, found stray scraps of information about the Franciscans floating about in his mind,

---

[1] *Shakespeare's Sources*, footnote pp. 108 f.

one of these being the Bull, and the joke then occurred to him. Whatever the explanation, the reference neither throws any light on the authorship nor necessitates a visit to Paris. At the time the Bull was promulgated it was as well known in this country as in France, though, as I have pointed out, by the time the play was written it had become very ancient history in both.

The claim that the names of the two friars in the play, Peter and Thomas, are derived from two early members of the Hieronomites, a House of which Order Henri III established near Longchamps, is a manifest absurdity. To begin with, Henri did not establish the House until 1583, a year later than the Paris episode and Derby's visit, so, even if he were the author, Derby could not have picked up this piece of information on the spot. Secondly, if the names had such an origin, the author could scarcely have failed to drive home his point by making his friars members of the Order of Hieronomites, but he does nothing of the sort; indeed he never mentions that Order in the play. Thirdly, and by far the most important, is the fact that these are two of the commonest names for monks and friars in both fiction and real life. It was the custom for persons entering a Religious Order to take a new name, that of some saint, to signify that they were beginning a new life, and the names of the Apostles were naturally prime favourites, especially Peter. In Shaw's St Joan, where the dramatis personae are all historical personages, no less than three of the ecclesiastics have the name of Peter. Moreover, if the names of the friars in M. for M. had been John and James, or any of a number of other pairs, instead of Peter and Thomas, Lambin and Evans could just as easily have found two real persons associated with the Order bearing those names, and made use of the fact in exactly the same way. The similarity of the names in the play and in the Order results, not from the fact that the former are copied from the latter, but that both are derived from a common source – the Calendar of the Saints.

Lambin and Evans also attempt to identify Henri III with the Duke in the play, and in support of this assert that the name Lodowick, which the Duke took when disguised as a friar, was 'a most suitable name' for a descendant of Saint-Louis. Perhaps it was, but it is certainly not evidence of the identity of Henri and the Duke. It was quite a common name in Germany and Austria, in the latter of which the scene of the play is laid, and it also occurs in a number of Elizabethan and Jacobean dramas. One of these is Marlowe's *Jew of Malta*, where, by a curious coincidence there is also a Bernadine in the cast. Evans adds, apparently as a corroborative detail, that Henri III sometimes wore a monk's habit. He may have done, but this is not why the Duke in M. for M. did so; there was a much more practical reason. A monk's habit has always been a favourite disguise on the stage because, with its hood, it forms a complete covering for the wearer, while at the same time it allows him to wear another costume underneath, and it can be flung off in an instant, revealing him in his true colours, as actually happens in M. for M. In addition to this there is the not unimportant fact that the plot demands the Duke should adopt the rôle of a friar, and that, no matter what Henri wore or did not wear, he would have to dress for the part if the play were to run its intended course.

So much for the first section of the argument. Now let us turn to the second, the claim that the names used in the play stand for real persons living in Paris at the material time. We will begin with the five – Flavius, Valentinus, Roland, Crassus, and Varrius – upon which Evans lays so much stress. He assures us that Professor Lambin has discovered 'without the least doubt' the real persons for whom they stand, Flavius, for example, being a certain La Roche-Flavin, a man of some importance, resident in Paris in 1582–84. This is truly a very remarkable achievement on the part of the Professor. He has made the identification on the bare names alone, without the slightest hint of character, age, appearance, or anything else to assist him, for these names do not represent *dramatis personae* at all. The first four are merely the addressees of a summons to a meeting, they never appear in the flesh at all – the meeting taking place off-stage, and are only mentioned the once when the list is read out: while the fifth is that of a messenger who is thanked by the Duke for running some errand, but never utters a word throughout the play. I am afraid I lack the credulity to accept the Professor's deductions from such meagre data; they are even less convincing than those of the Oxfordians we reviewed in the preceding chapter.

It may, however, be contended that if Lambin has found five names of contemporary Parisians corresponding to names in the play it could hardly be just coincidence. The contention is valid. It is not coincidence; it is something much simpler. If Lambin had used any sizable list of names from any source of any date, he would have found five to correspond just as closely to those in the play as do his five Parisians. We have to remember that they are not identical names, merely something more or less similar, and such approximations are bound to occur if the list taken is of a fair size. To test the truth of this I carried out the experiment with my local Telephone Directory, and in a few minutes had produced the following list:

Flavius =Flavell, Flather
Valentinus=Valentine, Vallender
Roland =Rowlands, Rowley
Crassus =Crashaw, Craze
Varrius =Varey, Verity

I maintain that if I wrote 'Alderman Flavell (Flavius in the play)', it appears quite as convincing as Evans' phrase 'La Roche-Flavin (Flavius in the play)', and incidentally has exactly the same evidence to support it. I may add that I could have added a number of other approximating names to my list if any purpose would have been served by so doing. In the face of such facts it is obvious that the method is worthless as evidence of anything.

The next two names on Evans' list are Bernadine and Ragozine, the former a criminal in the play and the latter a pirate, which Lambin claims were derived from Bernadin Mendoza, formerly Spanish Ambassador in London and occupying the same position in Paris in 1582, and Ragosini, the Papal Legate and a bitter enemy of Queen Elizabeth. I have already pointed out (see p. 114) that the first, which is Barnadine in the play not Bernadine, as Evans persists in spelling it, occurs in one of the author's sources, and so requires no other

117

derivation. Evans, however, to bolster up Lambin's view resorts – quite unconsciously, I am sure – to a *suggestio falsi*. He says that Bernadin Mendoza 'had been nine years in England and boasted of his crimes there, *but Henri turned a blind eye to his villainy, just as the Duke in the play postponed punishing the criminal Bernadine.*' (The italics are mine.) The suggestion here is that Henri acted in a certain way towards Bernadin Mendoza, and Derby, noting this, made the Duke in the play act in a similar way towards the criminal Barnadine. Its falsity lies in the fact that the circumstances in the two cases are entirely different. The Duke *could* punish the criminal, Barnadine, if he so wished, but Henri could *not* punish Bernadin Mendoza. The latter was a foreigner enjoying diplomatic immunity; what he had done in England was not Henri's business, and if he got up to any mischief in France the most Henri could have done would be to ask for his recall on the grounds that he was no longer *persona grata*, which was in fact what Elizabeth had done. There is not the slightest parallel between the two cases. Moreover, the plot of M. for M. required the postponement of Barnadine's punishment, and this would have happened whatever Henri could or could not do, did or did not do, to Bernadin Mendoza. As for Ragosini, he may have given his name to Ragozine the pirate, but as he had nothing to do with the Paris episode the matter has no significance. In any case both he and Mendoza were as well known in England as in France.

As we are here dealing with minor details, we may as well glance at the similarity which, as Evans points out, exists between 'Provost' and 'Prévot'. I have no wish to deny it; in fact I go further and insist, not on similarity, but on identity. They are merely two spellings, English and French, of the same word. That word, however, is not a personal name, but the very common designation of a supervisory office. It had been in use in England for centuries; there is even an O.E. form of it – 'profost'. In both the play and the account of the Paris episode it is equivalent to Prison Governor, and has just as much – or rather, just as little – significance as that term would have today. Moreover, Evans' remark about combining 'the duties of chief of the police and gaolor' has nothing to do with the case. In the play the Provost deals only with the prisoners actually in his charge, which is his proper function, and if some of his tasks seem incompatible with the dignity of a Governor, we must remember that the number of actors was limited and the prison could not be shown swarming with subordinates.

A more important matter is that of Lucio, whom Lambin identifies with a certain courtier named Saint-Luc. We may neglect the mere similarity of the name, for we have had ample proof of how little such similarities mean; but in this case Lambin brings forward a supporting factor. Apparently in real life Saint-Luc was compelled to marry an undesirable lady (a M'elle B.) just as Lucio was in the play, which is undoubtedly a stronger point in favour of his theory than any other we have come across. It is, however, very far indeed from being conclusive, for this form of punishment for an unpleasant, but not actually villainous, character was not uncommon in fiction at the time, and Henri is just as likely to have borrowed it from some tale or play as vice versa.[1] As a matter of fact this identical punishment occurs in the first part of Dekker's *Honest Whore* (V, ii), written shortly *before* the accepted date (1604) of *Measure for Measure*, where a young gentleman of position named Matheo is compelled by the Duke of Milan to marry the prostitute Bellafront. It is interesting to note that if Lucio stands for Luke, which is the name of one of the four Evangelists, then Matheo stands for Matthew, which is the name of another. Surely the identical idea, supported by this parallelism of the scriptural names, occurring in a slightly earlier contemporary play is a much more probable source than a trivial incident that happened in Paris years before.

We now come to the crucial point in this business of extracting evidence from names. Let us therefore pause for a moment to make sure that we follow its drift. Derby was in the region of Paris when the episode described took place, and Lambin and Evans, desiring to establish his authorship of *Measure for Measure*, attempt to do so by claiming that the names of the

---

[1] As a gang of confidence tricksters, the Wests and their associates, who were tried and sentenced at the Old Bailey in 1613, borrowed ideas from Jonson' play *The Alchemist*.

dramatis personae are pseudonyms for actual persons living in Paris at the time. I have demonstrated the fallacy of this contention by showing that the so-called pseudonyms would apply equally well to any sizable group of persons anywhere at any time. The method is therefore worthless as evidence. In the person of the hero-victim of the Paris episode, however, we are confronted with a different situation. He is a very particular person placed in very particular circumstances, not just a resident of Paris only loosely, if at all, connected with the episode. We cannot in his case apply the same criticism that we have used in the case of the others. It requires an altogether different approach.

His name was Claude Tonart, and the corresponding name in the play is Claudio. The resemblance therefore is undeniably close. It is of course legitimate to point out that the name Claudio occurs in an earlier play, M. Ado, and that Shakespeare, whoever he was, did in fact often repeat his names exactly or closely, in A.Y.L.I. actually giving the name Jaques to two distinct characters. This, however, in the face of the similarity of situation in episode and drama, does not greatly weaken the theorists' case, and we are left with the choice between two conclusions – either Lambin and Evans have got hold of a genuine favourable point or the matter is one of coincidence. Have we any means of deciding which of these is correct?

I think we have. If the author really were duplicating, thinly disguised, the names of the Parisian personnel, and if Claudio really stood for Claude Tonart, then there is one other character in the play whose name he was literally bound to derive in exactly the same way – that is the heroine of the Paris episode. Failure to match Claude's partner, when not only he himself is matched but also quite minor characters, is inconceivable if there were any deliberate system about it. Now the name of the lady in the play is Juliet, so we ought to find that Claude's partner possessed some such name as Julie. We can imagine the eagerness with which Lambin and Evans would have leapt at such a name and thrust it upon us as the keystone of the arch they had erected. But this does not happen. The lady's name is discreetly suppressed, and we are merely informed that she was 'the daughter of Jean Bailly, President of the Council'. I began this part of the discussion by saying that the point was crucial. I leave it at that.

The third section of Lambin's and Evans' argument consists in the claim that the events of the Paris episode were the principal influence in shaping *Measure for Measure*, and it is on this that they mainly base their case for Derby's authorship. Evans says: 'The play could only have been written by an eye-witness of these events.' In reply I assert categorically that not only is this statement not true, but that it is in the highest degree improbable that the Paris episode exercised any influence at all, and that the play could, and would, be exactly what it is if the Paris episode had never taken place.

Let us examine the facts. In 1578, that is four years before the Paris episode occurred, the English dramatist, George Whetstone, published a play – based on a still older work – entitled *Promos and Cassandra*, which even Evans is obliged to admit was one of Shakespeare's sources. Now in this play there is every single detail of importance used in the composition of *Measure for Measure*. There is the story of the guilty lovers, corresponding to the Claudio–Juliet story; there is the story of the suppliant sister and the corrupt judge, corresponding to the Angelo–Isabella story; and there is the story of the disguised ruler who rights the wrong in the end, corresponding to the disguised Duke story.[1] In the Paris episode there is only one of these – the case of Claude Tonart and his paramour, corresponding to the Claudio–Juliet story. No persons remotely resembling Angelo and Isabella appear in it; Claude Tonart's sister, if he had one, did not plead for his life, and consequently the judge had no opportunity to propose to her an infamous bargain; and the French King did not contrive Tonart's rescue; he was in fact absent when it was effected. There was consequently nothing that *Measure for Measure* needed to borrow from the Paris episode, and most of its material it could not so borrow, for it is not to be found in that episode.

It is true that Shakespeare modified some of the details he

---

[1] In *Promos and Cassandra* the ruler figures less prominently than in M. for M. in bringing about the happy ending, and in this respect it is the closer of the two to the Paris episode.

derived from *Promos and Cassandra*, as he generally did modify his sources, but the modifications were not in the direction of the Paris episode; they nearly all concerned the Angelo–Isabella story, which, as already stated, has no counterpart in the Paris episode.[1] The only resemblance between the latter and *Measure for Measure* is the story of the guilty lovers, and there is exactly the same resemblance between it and *Promos and Cassandra*. If it was essential for Shakespeare to have been an eyewitness of the events in Paris then it was equally essential for Whetstone, even if he had to witness them four years before they happened. In the face of these facts it is impossible to regard the Paris episode as a factor of any significance in the composition of *Measure for Measure*, still less as evidence that Derby wrote it.[2]

And here, if this book is to be kept within the limits necessary for its purpose, I must close my survey of the specific arguments in support of the Derby theory. I have already devoted considerably more space to them than I gave to those of the preceding theories. This is because they contain some unusual features that seemed to me to require fuller analysis. Titherley's scientific approach is something quite new, at least in this particular literary controversy, while Evans' exposition of Lambin's views, though on more conventional lines, does introduce some new material. We shall encounter both these authors again in

[1] The modifications mentioned by Evans are that the scene is changed from Innsbruck to Vienna, that the King of Hungary becomes the Duke of Vienna, that Angelo has a cast-off fiancée, and that Isabella is about to enter a nunnery. As Angelo and Isabella have no counterparts in the Paris episode, the two last named merely confirm my point. As for the other two, how calling Innsbruck Vienna proves that it is really Paris, and why reducing the King of Hungary to the rank of Duke of Vienna should prove that he is intended to represent King Henri III, are subtleties beyond my comprehension.

[2] Since the Paris episode had no counterpart to the Angelo story, I have omitted from my survey any analysis of Evans' statement that Angelo is a composite portrait of various unpleasant people in Paris, one at least of whom deserved to be hanged. I should like, however, to remark here that even the most cursory examination of Angelo will show that he is very far from the 'thing of shreds and patches' suggested by this comment. He is in fact a closely-knit and well-drawn character of an individual – a Puritan with a repressed sex complex.

subsequent chapters when we come to consider the evidence common to all theories. Meanwhile I can only state that, in spite of their novelties, I do not find them in any way more convincing than the other theorists; certainly they fail to produce anything that could be called proof of Derby's authorship of the Shakespearean plays.

CHAPTER VI

The Case for Christopher Marlowe

The case for Christopher Marlowe's authorship of the Shakespearean plays differs from all the others in that its supporters have not only to produce proof that he wrote them, but also that he was alive at the time in order to do so. Most of the plays belong to a period subsequent to the year 1593, and in the May of that year, according to the findings of a Coroner's Court, Marlowe was murdered in Deptford. His body was identified, and was afterwards buried in the churchyard of Deptford Parish Church, where the entry to this effect can still be read in the Parish Register. Marlowe's claims therefore cannot even merit consideration unless these awkward official records are first proved to be false. This is the task which Calvin Hoffman, the originator of the Marlowe theory, sets himself in the earlier part of his book, *The Man Who Was Shakespeare,* and it is to his efforts to perform it that we must first turn our attention.

In order to follow Hoffman's argument it is necessary to bear in mind certain details of Marlowe's career, and for the convenience of the reader I will give a short summary of these. Marlowe was born in 1564, the son of a cobbler in Canterbury. He was an unusually brilliant boy, and gained first a scholarship at King's School, Canterbury, and later one at Corpus Christi College, Cambridge, where he took in turn his B.A. and M.A. degrees.

Between taking these degrees he absented himself from the University for a period, and paid a visit to Rheims, a town at that time full of English Roman Catholic conspirators. On his return the University authorities made difficulties about conferring his Master's degree. They were, however, informed by no less an august body than the Privy Council itself that Marlowe's visit to France had been in the interests of his country, and were instructed to confer the degree without further delay. The generally accepted explanation of this incident is that

Marlowe had gone abroad as a Government spy in the employ of Sir Francis Walsingham, who was at that time at the head of a very efficient Secret Service, an explanation which certainly fits the facts, and is in all probability the correct one.

On leaving the University Marlowe went to London and began to write plays, which were an immediate success, and brought him fame though not fortune. Later he gained the patronage of Sir Thomas Walsingham, a Kentish landowner and a cousin of Sir Francis, who was famous as a patron of the arts and always ready to assist a brilliant young writer. Hoffman, however, suggests that there was more in this relationship than that of patron and artist; he claims that Sir Thomas was a homosexual and that Marlowe satisfied this side of his nature as well as his artistic leanings. There is of course no evidence for such a view,[1] but Hoffman needs the point to supply an incentive for the action that later he claims Sir Thomas took when Marlowe was in trouble with the authorities.

Marlowe also became involved with a group of intellectuals known as 'The School of Night'. Its leader was Sir Walter Ralegh, and it seems to have been remarkable for its free-thinking and outspokenness. No doubt the reports of its tenets were exaggerated – Ralegh's own writings certainly suggest this – but it was believed, among other things, to have propagated Atheism, and this, at a time when even heresy was still a capital offence, was a very serious charge, and naturally the circle came under official suspicion. It had, however, strong Court influence, and for a time no action was taken against any of its members.

What eventually touched off the train and brought about the explosion was quite a different matter. A number of Flemish Protestant refugees had, with the approval of the Government, settled in London. Their presence, however, was resented by

[1] Hoffman (*The Man Who Was Shakespeare*, p. 139) naturally attempts to produce some evidence. One or two of the Shakespearean sonnets, which, according to his theory, Marlowe wrote, are capable of a homosexual interpretation, and he makes considerable play with these. Even if they really were so, and most critics, both orthodox and unorthodox, reject such a view, it would in no way prove his point. He must first place it beyond all doubt that Marlowe wrote the sonnets before he can make the sonnets bear witness to Marlowe's character.

the citizens, who feared them as business rivals, and various forms of protest were made. Among these was the placarding of public places with slogans designed to stir up the populace against the intruders, and the Privy Council ordered the Lord Mayor to seek out and punish the authors of these.

Among those arrested was Thomas Kyd, the dramatist, and when his rooms were searched a document of an Atheistical character was found. Kyd denied that he was the author of this, and declared that it was left behind by Marlowe, who had at one time shared the rooms with him. The members of the Privy Council thereupon summoned Marlowe, who was staying with Sir Thomas Walsingham in Kent, to appear before them. The entry in the Registry of the Privy Council for May 20th, 1593, which records this event, reads as follows:

> This day Christopher Marlowe of London, Gentleman, being sent for by warrant from their Lordships, hath entered his appearance accordingly for his indemnity therein, and is commanded to give his daily attendance on their Lordships till he shall be licensed to the contrary.

It is important to note that Marlowe was not imprisoned, but merely required to report to the Council every day until the Lords decided what action should be taken in his case.

The decision, whatever it might have been, was never taken, for ten days later Marlowe was officially dead. At this juncture, however, an event occurred which is somewhat obscure. The Privy Council, evidently making further inquiries into the matter, received from Richard Baines, one of its agents, a report on Marlowe which contained some very serious charges indeed, so serious in fact that a copy of it was sent to the Queen; and it is here that the obscurity begins. The report itself is not dated, but the copy states that.it was received by the Council on Whitsun Eve, and that three days later its subject, Marlowe, was dead. Now Whitsun Eve in 1593 fell on June 2nd, when Marlowe had already been officially dead for two days, so clearly the scrivener who did the copying made a mistake somewhere. It is most probable that this was in the date of Marlowe's alleged death as three days later than Whitsun Eve, for if the latter were still alive when Baines' report was received the Lords could scarcely have done other, in view of the charges, than order him to be placed immediately under close arrest, and this was clearly not done.

There is one other point to be mentioned about the report. In it Baines coupled the names of Sir Walter Ralegh and Harriot, the mathematician, with that of Marlowe, and announced that there were other persons in high positions who were also involved, and that he would produce their names in due course. In the copy of the report sent to the Queen Ralegh's name was omitted.

Owing to the fact that there were no newspapers in those days few people apparently heard the news of Marlowe's death at the time, and those who did seem to have received very garbled versions of the incident, for the contemporary accounts vary greatly. The plague was raging in London, and some persons believed that Marlowe had been one of its victims. Gabriel Harvey accepted this view, and recorded it as a fact in a poem published the same year. Another report, chronicled by Thomas Beard in 1597, said that Marlowe was assassinated in a London street by one who bore him a grudge, and in 1600 William Vaughan stated that he was killed in a tavern brawl at Deptford.

These contradictory accounts were all that was known of the matter until 1820. In that year the scholar, James Broughton, having come across Vaughan's statement about the Deptford brawl, wrote to the Vicar of that place to ask if there were any record of Marlowe in the church registers. He received an affirmative reply, together with the following brief statement, which purported to be a true copy of the entry:

1st June 1593, Christopher Marlowe, slain by Francis Archer.

Nothing further came to light until 1925, when that indefatiguable literary detective, Dr Leslie Hotson, discovered among the archives of the London Record Office the actual report of Danby, the Crown Coroner, on the finding of the inquest. Its verdict was that Christopher Marlowe, having attacked a certain Ingram Frizer in a house in Deptford, was killed by the latter in self-defence on May 30th, 1593.

Such is the perfectly straightforward, consistent, and, for the

127

times, unusually well-documented story of the tragic career of Christopher Marlowe. It is this story which, in order to clear the way for Marlowe's claim to the authorship of the Shakespearean works, Calvin Hoffman attempts to demolish, and to substitute another of his own devising. His theory falls naturally into two parts – (i) his own version of the events leading up to the alleged tragedy, and (ii) his criticisms of the Coroner's report; and it is in this order that we shall examine them.

Hoffman[1] accepts without question the orthodox account up to and including Marlowe's summons to appear before the Privy Council. From this point, however, his reconstruction is entirely imaginative, except for the *dramatis personae* and the setting, which are derived from information provided by the Coroner's report. He pictures Marlowe, compelled by the Privy Council's order to remain in plague-stricken London, occupying a lonely lodging, and plunged in the depths of despair, for he knows that 'he is only a step from torture and execution, and that the blow may fall at any moment'.

In these depressing circumstances he is found by Sir Thomas Walsingham, a man bound to him 'not only by friendship but by a romantic if abnormal tie', who through official friends has heard of Marlowe's danger, and has already concocted a plan to save him. Marlowe is to fly the country, and take up his abode on the Continent under an assumed name. Meanwhile Walsingham will stage a faked murder. He has in his employ three men, Frizer, Skeres, and Poley, stout fellows who would kill anyone without question provided they were well paid for doing so. They will kill some man, any man, preferably a foreign sailor about whose disappearance few questions are likely to be asked. They will not run away after the killing, but will swear it was done in self-defence. Walsingham will bribe the Coroner to accept this plea and also the identification of the body as that of Marlowe.

Deptford is the place selected for the deed. It is a rather disreputable port into which a certain amount of foreign shipping comes, and it is unusually crowded at the present time, for Drake's ship, *The Golden Hind*, is at anchor there, and is attract-

[1] *The Man Who Was Shakespeare*, pp. 56–122.

4 CAMBRIDGE PORTRAIT

Painting discovered at Corpus Christi College and claimed by
Hoffman to be a portrait of Christopher Marlowe

ing many sight-seers,[1] all of which makes it specially favourable for the deed. Moreover, it is less than eleven miles from Greenwich, where the Queen is at present in residence. This brings it officially 'within the verge', and means that the Queen's Coroner, Danby, not a local man, will hold the inquest, and Danby, having taken a bribe, will never dare to betray the secret, for to do so would mean confessing his own guilt.

Marlowe naturally jumps at such a chance, and the plot is put into action at once. Marlowe starts for Dover that same night, for he must not risk being recognized after the murder has taken place. The next morning, May 30th, Frizer, Skeres, and Poley hurry to Deptford. They soon find a suitable victim, a foreign sailor as Walsingham had suggested. They stand him a few drinks, and then lure him into a house of which Frizer knows, kept by a certain Eleanor Bull, who is always ready to let a room for some disreputable purpose. There they murder him.

The Coroner's inquest follows, and all goes according to plan. Frizer's plea of self-defence is accepted, and the body is identified as that of Marlowe, and, by the Coroner's order, is hastily buried at the Parish Church, with the entry in the register that he was 'slain by Francis Archer', a name Hoffman suggests Danby 'picked out of the blue' in order to avoid attracting attention to Ingram Frizer when he should be released and return to Walsingham's service, as he did soon after.

Meanwhile Marlowe has safely reached the Continent, and settles in North Italy. He will continue to write, and send his plays to Walsingham for disposal. Of course they cannot be produced under his own name, so Walsingham looks around for a substitute, and finds William Shakespeare, 'a steady, not too imaginative fellow . . . who did not mind lending his name to anything as long as . . . gold flowed freely', and who has the advantage of already being connected with the theatre. The business is quickly arranged, and Walsingham sets the ball rolling by causing the poem, *Venus and Adonis*, the manuscript of which Marlowe has left behind him, to be published under

---

[1] If Hoffman is correct in his statement the excitement over Drake's ship seems to have lasted an unusually long time, for it was fifteen years since it had returned from its famous voyage. Clearly it proved more than a nine days' wonder.

the name of William Shakespeare, the first work to be printed with this name attached.[1]

Such is Hoffman's reconstruction of the events that led up to Marlowe's disappearance. My summary of it, though of necessity omitting the trappings with which he adorns it, includes every one of his significant points and provides all the information necessary to make a fair examination of it. To this examination we will now turn.

I would first call in question what I consider to be Hoffman's exaggeration of Marlowe's danger. He states that he was 'only a step from torture and execution'. Of course, if the Baines report had been in the hands of the Privy Council from the first the situation would have been different; but we have seen that there is good reason to suppose that it did not arrive until after Marlowe was officially dead. In any case its arrival must have been very late in the proceedings or the Lords would certainly have ordered Marlowe's close arrest, and not merely invited him to drop in daily until further orders. Even in these milder times, when a man is presumed innocent until he is proved guilty, bail is never allowed in the case of a capital offence or one serious enough to make it worth while for the accused to abscond; and in those harsher days when, owing to lack of communications and an organized police force, it was so much easier to abscond, the Privy Council would never have left Marlowe at liberty if it had believed that there was any very serious charge for him to answer.

Still I do not wish to lay too much stress on this point. The astute mind of Walsingham and the guilty knowledge of Marlowe might well have foreseen the possibility of the case turning serious at any moment, and so decided that it was better for the

---

[1] This part of Hoffman's case can be disposed of at once. *Venus and Adonis* was entered in the Stationers' Register, with Shakespeare's name as author, on April 18th, 1593 – that is, nearly five weeks before Marlowe was arrested, and therefore before there could be any plot to rescue him. Moreover Field, the publisher who was responsible for the registration and eventually published the poem, was a Stratford man and a friend, or at least an acquaintance, of Shakspere's. This would entail his being let into the 'secret', and thus more danger and expenditure in bribery for the poor Sir Thomas Walsingham. In the light of such facts this purely suppositious plot becomes absolutely incredible.

latter to remove himself while the way was open. But even so there would be no need for the murder, and overwhelming reasons against it. Why did not Walsingham just supply Marlowe with the necessary money and let him abscond? According to Hoffman's theory he was at least as far as Dover on his journey before the murder was committed.[1] The murder therefore could not facilitate his actual flight in any way. There was no extradition in those days, and once on the Continent under an assumed name Marlowe would have been safe enough, and no one would have known that Walsingham had had anything to do with his escape. Why then have the murder? Its only effect was to cause Walsingham to spend large sums of money in bribes, and to run the considerable risk of letting a number of people, wholly or in part, into the secret. Hoffman says that Danby, the Coroner, could not betray Walsingham without at the same time condemning himself.[2] But this would only be the case if he first agreed to the plot, took the bribe, and did not confess until after Marlowe had made good his escape. If he had rejected the whole scheme from the start and betrayed it at once, as he might well have done, then he would certainly have won approbation from the authorities and possibly a substantial reward, while Marlowe would not have escaped and Walsingham would have paid the penalty of his treason.

As a matter of fact the presence of Danby in the case is a strong argument against the truth of the theory. There is of course indisputable documentary evidence that he was the coroner concerned, so Hoffman is obliged to work him into the story, but from every point of view he is the wrong person for it. As the Queen's Coroner he was an important official with a great deal to lose, and thus hardly likely to lend himself to such a dangerous scheme. If Walsingham had really plotted a murder, as Hoffman says he did, he would have seen to it that the crime took place, *not* 'within the verge' where the Queen's Coroner would be in charge of the investigation, but in the jurisdiction of some local coroner near his own home, a man who would be already under the influence of the powerful landowner and much easier to bribe.

[1] Hoffman, *The Man Who Was Shakespeare*, p. 119.
[2] Ibid., p. 118.

So far then, even if the circumstances had been precisely as Hoffman describes them, there was no need whatever for any murder to be committed in order to secure Marlowe's escape; on the contrary the preliminaries for such a murder might well have prevented that escape, while they would certainly have involved Walsingham in considerable danger and enormous expense. Even if it were felt that Marlowe would be safer if he were supposed to be dead there was still no need for the murder of anyone else. The plague was raging in London, multitudes were dying and being buried in haste, and it would have been very much simpler and easier to arrange for Marlowe to appear as one of its victims than to carry out the complicated plot Hoffman imagines. As a matter of fact there was a rumour that Marlowe had perished in this way (see p. 127), which was believed by many who had not heard of the Coroner's inquest. Had this not taken place there is no doubt that the story would have been generally accepted, and not even the Privy Council would have wanted to go around London digging up the plague pits just to make sure of the truth.

There is one other point that must be mentioned before we leave this section. It is a case of suppressed evidence. We have seen (p. 127) that the copy of the entry in the church register sent by the Vicar of Deptford to James Broughton in 1820 stated that the name of Marlowe's slayer was 'Francis Archer', whereas the coroner's report shows it to have been Ingram Frizer. Hoffman suggests that the false name was deliberately concocted by the Coroner at Walsingham's instigation in order to confuse the issue. He says:[1] 'And who caused the name "Francis Archer" to appear in the Deptford Church Register instead of the name of the actual murderer, Ingram Frizer? Is it not possible that Danby was acting under instructions?'

The actual facts are very different. It is true that the Vicar, probably because he was unfamiliar with the Elizabethan script and the writing was very small, copied the name as 'Francis Archer'; and since nothing was known about Danby's report at the time, scholars never troubled to verify this. When, however, in 1925, Dr Hotson discovered the report and noted the discrepancy of the names, he at once visited Deptford

[1] *The Man Who Was Shakespeare*, p. 107.

and examined the entry for himself. He found the name given was not 'Francis Archer' but 'ffrancis ffrizer'. The Christian name is incorrect,[1] but the surname is the same as in Danby's report. There was thus no attempt to confuse the issue by Danby or anyone else. Hotson says that the Vicar's mistake arose from the common Elizabethan use of a small initial double 'f', which does in fact in the very small writing in which the entry is made bear some resemblance to a capital 'A', though he maintains that the similar formation at the beginning of the previous word 'ffrancis' should have guided the reader to the correct interpretation. The name 'Archer' is therefore just a guess on the part of the Vicar, misled by the supposed capital 'A' and unable to decipher the other diminutive letters except perhaps the final 'r'.[2]

Now Hoffman has clearly read Dr Hotson's book, for he refers to it frequently and quotes freely and at length from it; yet he never gives the faintest hint of this important discovery, but, as we have seen, uses the 'Francis Archer' episode to throw doubts on the honesty of Danby. Of course he might claim that he does not agree with Dr Hotson's finding; but even so he ought to inform his readers of it and give his reasons for rejecting it, though he would certainly find the latter a difficult task. Hotson gives a facsimile of the Register entry, and one glance at it through an ordinary magnifying glass reveals that the surname is indisputably 'ffrizer'. In the light of such facts it is obvious that the deductions Hoffman makes from the Register cannot be accepted.

So much for the first part of Hoffman's argument. The second part comprises his attack on the report of the inquest on Marlowe. He does not deny that the document discovered by Hotson is the actual one drawn up by Danby – that would be impossible in any case – but he maintains that its contents are of such a suspicious nature that it must have been designed to

[1] Inaccurate entries are a common feature of Elizabethan registers owing to the fact that parish clerks were often only semi-literate and not very intelligent men. We have already encountered another probable example in the Hathaway–Whateley confusion in the Worcester Diocesan Register (see p. 42).

[2] Hotson, *The Death of Christopher Marlowe*, pp. 21 f.

conceal facts very different from those stated. In order to follow, and to refute, his arguments it is necessary to have the actual wording before us. The original is in Latin, but Dr Hotson has translated it into modern English. It is his translation that Hoffman uses, and I accordingly do the same.

Inquisition indented taken at Deptford Strand in the aforesaid County of Kent, within the verge, on the 1st day of June, 1593, in the presence of William Danby, Gent., Coroner of the Household of our said Lady the Queen, upon view of the body of Christopher Marlowe, there lying dead and slain upon the oath of . . .(*There follow the names of the sixteen members of the Jury.*) who say upon their oath that when a certain Ingram Frizer, late of London, Gentleman, and the aforesaid Christopher Marlowe and one Nicholas Skeres, Gentleman, and Robert Poley, Gentleman, on 30th day of May, at Deptford Strand, within the verge, about the tenth hour before noon of the same day, met together in a room in the house of a certain Eleanor Bull, widow, and there passed the time together and dined and after dinner were in quiet sort together, and walked in the garden belonging to the said house until the sixth hour after noon of the same day and then returned from the said garden to the room aforesaid and there together and in company supped; and after supper the said Ingram and Christopher Marlowe were in speech and uttered one to the other divers malicious words for the reason that they could not be at one nor agree about the payment of the sum of pence, that is, *le recknynge* there; and the said Christopher Marlowe then lying upon a bed in the room where they supped, and moved with anger against the said Ingram Frizer then and there sitting in the room aforesaid with his back toward the bed where the said Christopher Marlowe was then lying, sitting near the bed with the front part of his body towards the table and the aforesaid Nicholas Skeres and Robert Poley sitting on either side of the said Ingram in such a manner that the same Ingram Frizer in no wise could take flight; it so befell that the said Christopher Marlowe on a sudden and of his malice towards the said Ingram aforethought, then and there maliciously drew the dagger of the said Ingram which was at his back, and with the same dagger the said Christopher Marlowe then and there maliciously gave the aforesaid Ingram two wounds on the head of the length of two inches and of the depth of a quarter of an inch; whereupon the said Ingram, in fear of being slain, and sitting in the manner aforesaid between the said

Nicholas Skeres and Robert Poley so that he could not in any wise get away, in his own defence and for the saving of his life, then and there struggled with the said Christopher Marlowe to get back from him his dagger aforesaid; in which affray the same Ingram could not get away from the said Christopher Marlowe, and so it befell in that affray that the said Ingram, in defence of his life, with the dagger aforesaid, of the value of 12d, gave the said Christopher then and there a mortal wound over his right eye of the depth of two inches and the width of one inch; of which mortal wound the aforesaid Christopher Marlowe then and there instantly died.

This is the document which Hoffman maintains does not represent the truth of what happened, but is a false report designed to cover Marlowe's escape and also to secure Frizer's aquittal on the grounds of self-defence. I will deal with his points in the order in which he raises them.

First, he queries the set-up of the room and the positions occupied by the four men – a table with probably a bench alongside it and a bed behind the bench, Marlowe lying on the bed, and the other three seated on the bench with their backs towards him. He calls it a strange picture and a very odd setting for an acrimonious talk. Now, quite apart from the fact that, whether their story was true or false, Frizer, Skeres, and Poley would take good care to get the details of the room correct in case any juryman insisted on viewing the scene of the crime, what is there odd about it? The room was a small one, and was probably from the nature of the house usually let for amorous assignations – a meal followed by the use of the bed. It was the occupants of the room, not the room itself, that were a little unusual, and they would have to adapt themselves to the conditions. They had probably been drinking heavily – the three at the table possibly continuing to do so – and a quarrel in such circumstances was only too likely.

Second, Marlowe in a rage snatched Frizer's dagger, which was 'at his back'. Hoffman makes merry over 'this strange place for a man like Frizer to wear his dagger', and regards the statement as evidence of the unreliability of the report. He might have reflected that Danby, if he were really falsifying the main issue, would, for this very reason, have been particularly careful to make all the circumstantial details as plausible as possible, and would not have indulged in any palpable absurdities. As a matter of fact in Elizabethan times the dagger was usually worn *behind* the right hip, as Viscount Dillon states,[1] quoting the contemporary writer, Harrison, who in his *Description of England*, writes: 'Seldom shall you see any young countryman above eighteen or twenty years old to go without a dagger at least at his back.' At his back is therefore just the place where Frizer's dagger would be, and from whence, as he sat at the table, Marlowe, lying on the bed behind him, could easily snatch it out exactly as the report states. Hoffman, like most of the theorists, reveals some woeful gaps in his knowledge of the Elizabethan background, and accordingly sees points in favour of his theory where none exist. This is clearly the case here.

Third, Hoffman remarks that Frizer's two scalp wounds appear to be very insignificant to be made by a dagger 'wielded by an infuriated man, *who stabbed downward with all the power of his body*'. (The italics are mine.) Hoffman's sense of the dramatic has run away with him here. There is not a phrase in the report, as a reference to it will show, to suggest that anything of the sort happened. There we are told that, when the quarrel began, Marlowe was lying down. His first attack was therefore probably a clumsy one delivered from a half-reclining position, and by the time he had manoeuvred himself into a more advantageous one, Frizer had also turned, and was ready to defend himself.

Fourth, Hoffman derides the apparent immobility of Skeres and Poley, one on each side of Frizer, thus preventing him from getting away and leaving him no alternative but to kill Marlowe in self-defence. But this is just another dramatic flourish on Hoffman's part. The report does not say that they were immobile, though it does imply, what would undoubtedly be the case, that they were jammed in between the bench and the table, with the table-legs making it difficult to get out, and two men fighting desperately between them. Far from being immobile they would be fully occupied in dodging any random blows that came their way.

[1] Article on 'Armour and Weapons' in *Shakespeare's England*, Vol. i, p. 134.

Thus we see that all Hoffman's objections to the report are based on his own strained interpretation of it or on details he has read into it, not on anything it actually says. In fact, given such a room as it suggests, four men the worse for drink, and a sudden quarrel such as often blows up among men in that condition, and what is claimed in the report fits the situation perfectly.

Hoffman, however, has other points of a more general nature to make. He queries the likelihood of Marlowe's presence at such a meeting, and asks what he had in common with the other three, who were in every way his inferiors. The answer is that in any case they certainly had two things in common; they all were, or had been, spies, a profession that often brings about incongruous associations, and they were all in the service of Sir Thomas Walsingham. Moreover, whatever they may have been intellectually, the others were not Marlowe's social inferiors. Dr Hotson,[1] with his usual thoroughness, has uncovered the status of the three men in question. All are described in various documents as 'Gentlemen',[2] just as we have seen Marlowe was in the Privy Council's Register (p. 126), and they were agents in touch with Sir Francis Walsingham through his cousin, Sir Thomas. Poley indeed played an important part in the unmasking of the Babington Plot, and Frizer was certainly a man of some wealth. It is true that they were rather unsavoury characters, but in this respect Marlowe's own reputation was not of the highest, and there was no reason why he and they should not have spent the day at Deptford together.

This also explains another point raised by Hoffman, namely the fact that Walsingham retained the three men in his service after the killing of his friend. The reply to such an objection is that they were too useful to him and to his important cousin to allow a little matter like a murder, especially one which, officially at least, was not deliberate on their part, to interfere with their continued employment (see also p. 139).

Hoffman further sees something suspicious in the presence of

[1] *The Death of Christopher Marlowe*, pp. 41–55.
[2] All three are so described in Danby's report. Hoffman suppresses this detail in his reproduction of the document. I have restored it in mine (see p. 134).

the sixteen members of the jury, collected so quickly, he says, after the event. What was suspicious about it he does not explain, and the ordinary person finds it difficult to imagine. There was no mystery about the jurors themselves. Danby's report gives a full list of their names, and they have been identified. Two are described as gentlemen, and the rest were farmers and tradesmen; all belonged to Deptford or its immediate environs, and could have been summoned at short notice. I fail completely to understand Hoffman in this matter. Does he intend to imply that Walsingham selected the jury before the murder had been committed, and visited them all in person to tell them what was intended and bribe them to give the required verdict? Unless something like this ludicrous idea is what he does mean, there seems no point in his dark suggestions.

In regard to the report as a whole, it must be remembered that it is only a summary of the proceedings, not a verbatim account, and consequently many details must be omitted or inadequately explained. At the time it was written it had to be submitted to the Court of Chancery, and could be supplemented by a verbal report if that Court so desired. The modern investigator, however, has not this means of obtaining fuller information and so must find it unsatisfactory in some respects, and it is true, as Hoffman points out, that a number of scholars have frankly stated that it leaves a great deal unexplained. Not one of them, however, it must be noted, lends the least support to Hoffman's theory or considers anyone but Marlowe was the victim. What they are concerned about is whether the story at the inquest was true, or whether the three men deliberately murdered Marlowe and then invented the story to escape the penalty. The doubters all believe that Marlowe was killed to stop his mouth in case he should involve some highly-placed personage in his alleged crimes. Dr Tannenbaum, for instance, in his *Assassination of Christopher Marlowe*, maintains that Sir Walter Ralegh was the instigator of the murder. Some others[1] suggest that the Privy Council itself was responsible, preferring to get rid of Marlowe quietly, rather than be faced with any

[1] Philip Henderson, *Christopher Marlowe*, pp. 73 f., where some of these theories are described.

embarrassing accusations he might make; and in support of this view there is at least the fact that the Council had Ralegh's name omitted from the copy of Baines' report that it sent to the Queen (see p. 127).

To these theories I am prepared to add one other, one that should appeal to Hoffman. It is this. There was a Walsingham plot as he suggests, but it was a plot to *kill* Marlowe, not to *save* him. Since the arrest, which had taken place in his house, Sir Thomas had feared that Marlowe, if made to talk, might implicate him, and so took prompt steps to have the young dramatist eliminated. He could do it with less risk than anyone else, for the three assassins were already in his employ and had done dirty work for him before. It would be quite easy too. A message to Marlowe pretending to offer him a means of escape would be sufficient to lure him to Deptford; and, once they had killed him, they had only to tell the story they actually did for matters to arrange themselves as they actually did. Of course this is not my real view. I agree with Hotson that the official version is probably the correct one; but I do claim that my theory is a much simpler and more plausible one than Hoffman's, and it rests on exactly the same evidence, which is none at all.

This concludes our survey of the first part of Hoffman's theory, his attempt to prove that Marlowe was not killed in 1593. As we have seen, not one of the points he makes either in his reconstruction of the earlier events or in his criticism of Danby's report can stand up to analysis; they are all unnaturally strained or so trivial that they collapse at a touch, while his handling of some of the evidence, as in the case of the entry in the Deptford Church Register (see p. 133), is, to say the least, scarcely in accord with the best traditions of scholarship. If this were purely a controversial essay I should stop at this point, claiming that as he was undoubtedly dead when they were written, there could be no case for Marlowe's authorship of the Shakespearean plays. Since, however, my purpose is also to review his theory as a whole, it is necessary to examine the other arguments Hoffman puts forward.

Many of these are a mere rehash of those used by the other theorists – we shall deal with the more important in later chapters – but some are specific and have a certain novelty. The most interesting is the one to which Hoffman gives the grandiloquent title of 'Fingerprinting Authorship'. As it will facilitate criticism and the passage is not a long one, I will give the details in Hoffman's own words. He writes:[1]

'But there is a further proof for my thesis. Let us turn to Dr. Thomas Corwin Mendenhall, professor at the college that later became Ohio State University, who revealed more than fifty years ago that he had developed a plan of investigation whereby the identity of an author, through his writing, could be scientifically detected – that, from a mechanical point of view, a style of composition would be uniquely individual throughout:

> Nearly twenty years ago (i.e. about 1880) I devised a method for exhibiting graphically such peculiarities of style in literary composition as seemed to be almost purely mechanical, and of which the author would be absolutely unconscious.
> The chief merit of the method consisted in the fact that its application required no experience or judgement – accurate enumeration being all that was necessary. By displaying one or more phases of the mechanism of composition, characteristics might be revealed which the author could make no attempt to conceal, being himself unaware of their existence.
> It was further assumed that owing to the well-known persistence of unconscious habit, personal peculiarities in the construction of sentences, in the use of either short or long words, in the number of words in a sentence, etc., would in the long run manifest themselves with such regularity that their graphic representation would become a means of identification.

'Dr. Mendenhall undertook to experiment with the works of twenty noted poets and prose writers. The guinea pigs included such distinguished figures as Percy Shelley, John Keats, Sir Walter Scott, William Thackeray, John Stuart Mill, Lord Byron.

'The investigator set himself to the Herculean task of counting each letter of every word in the representative works of each writer being tested.

'He set up graphs of the characteristic curve of each author which would reflect a predisposition to use a vocabulary con-

[1] *The Man Who Was Shakespeare*, pp. 158–161.

taining anywhere from one- to fifteen-letter words. These graphs, when compared, revealed the fact that each author possessed his own characteristic peculiarities in the length of his words.

'The tests were then computed mathematically, down to the minutest decimal. No two were alike. The conclusion, therefore, was that no two authors will, mechanically, write identically.

'Dr. Mendenhall then laid aside his work. He had proved his theory.

'Towards the end of the century, Dr. Mendenhall received an urgent communication from a wealthy Shakespeare enthusiast requesting an appointment. After the meeting in Boston, Dr. Mendenhall was assigned a tremendous task.

'The wealthy·Bostonian, he was informed, was a champion of Francis Bacon as the author of Shakespeare's plays and poems. Hearing of Dr. Mendenhall's study, the Baconian wished to retain him to test his theory through the mechanical, graphological method to prove that Lord Bacon actually wrote the works of Shakespeare.

'Several women were hired for research. Their task was to assemble the works of various authors, and count the letters of more than two million words dredged from the works of Ben Jonson, Oliver Goldsmith, Francis Beaumont, John Fletcher, Christopher Marlowe, Lord Lytton, William Shakespeare, Joseph Addison, Francis Bacon and a group of then-modern authors as controls.

'After several months (the women could work only from three to five hours a day – had they sustained the count longer they would have been left in a state of collapse) the letters of more than two million words had been counted and tabulated; 200,000 from Bacon, from his *Advancement of Learning*, the prose history of Henry VII, and a number of shorter essays; 75,000 from the plays of Ben Jonson; all the words from the seven plays of Christopher Marlowe; 400,000 from the works of William Shakespeare, and well over a million words from the numerous other authors examined.

'Dr. Mendenhall started to plot the characteristic curves of Bacon and Shakespeare on to each other's finished sheets. He didn't have to finish the job. A single glance ruled out any possibility of similitude.

'Shakespeare's vocabulary, the diagram revealed, consisted of words averaging four letters in length. The words used with the greatest frequency also were four-letter words. This was, as Dr. Mendenhall told his employer, "a thing never met with before in the works of any other writer he had analysed".[1]

'Bacon's graph, on the other hand, showed constant use of much longer words. The graphs of the other writers were entirely different from one another. From Jonson to Beaumont to Addison to Lord Lytton – each writer disclosed his own peculiarity of style of composition.

'And then the professor diagnosed Christopher Marlowe's works. This is what he has to say:

> It was in the counting and plotting of the plays of Christopher Marlowe, however, that something akin to a sensation was produced among those actually engaged in the work. In the characteristic curve of his plays Christopher Marlowe agrees with Shakespeare as well as Shakespeare agrees with himself.

'The printed transcripts of these texts are available. It is incredible to observe how absolutely identical are the characteristic curves of these so-called "different" authors.'

I have given Hoffman's account in full, without a single cut or change of phrase. Now let us see what it all amounts to. When we strip it of the technical verbiage designed to give it a scientific flavour, we find that the Professor simply counted

[1] In order to ascertain if there were any significance in this statement I myself carried out a rough experiment. I found the average number of letters per word of fifty short passages of English prose, all of equal length, selected at random from various books on my bookshelves, copies of my daily newspaper, the *Radio Times*, and a school magazine. *In every case except two the average number of letters per word was 4 and a fraction.* The two exceptions were a children's story, where the average was just below 4, and a scientific article employing a technical vocabulary, where the average was just over 5. In most cases too the words of highest frequency were either 3- or 4-letter words. While agreeing that a much more elaborate experiment would be necessary to amount to proof, this does suggest that the figures that seem to have startled Professor Mendenhall were those produced by almost every writer in English.

the number of letters in a number of words in a number of works of certain authors, and then calculated the average number of letters per word. This average, together with a note on the number of letters in the words of highest frequency and one or two other similar details, he attached to the author in question as the 'fingerprint' of his style. Having found the average differed in all the authors selected for his experiment, he came to the conclusion that, as in the case of real fingerprints, no two were alike, and so if two works gave different averages they must be by different authors, and if they gave the same average they must be by the same author.

A more unsatisfactory theory could scarcely be imagined. In the first place it is built up on the logical fallacy of generalizing from insufficient data. Out of the many thousands of authors in all periods from, say, Chaucer onwards who have written in the English language, Professor Mendenhall examined the works of a mere twenty, a preposterously inadequate number for such a purpose. It is not surprising that, when a few more authors were added for the Bostonian test, he obtained a result that upset the conclusion he had drawn from the first. Had he further increased the number he would no doubt have discovered other duplications in addition to the alleged Shakespeare–Marlowe one. Moreover, as far as we are informed – and it is unlikely that Hoffman would have failed to emphasize such valuable evidence if it existed – the Professor never had his deductions checked by a second investigator working with another set of authors, the usual kind of check in scientific experiments; he relied entirely on his own single and very inadequate experiment for his so-called proof. He may have been a profound English scholar, but his knowledge of the scientific method was clearly defective.

Again there is the unsatisfactory way in which both experiments were carried out, without any check whatever. Anyone who has attempted to count the number of whole words in a fairly lengthy paragraph of print knows how easy it is to make mistakes. The possibility of error in the counting of individual letters in the complete works of twenty authors must therefore have been very great even in Professor Mendenhall's initial experiment, where he did the work himself with the incentive of testing his own theory. What would it then be in the case of the inexperienced women, with no such incentive, employed to make the count in the 'wealthy Bostonian's' test? Even if they were consistently conscientious their errors in dealing with all those millions of letters would certainly be enormous. But there is no guarantee that they were consistently conscientious. Their heads aching and their eyes smarting after some hours of this trying and monotonous work, they may well have yielded to the temptation to lighten their task by spells of guesswork; if they did, no one would have been any the wiser. It is obvious therefore that both from their inherent nature and from the way in which they were carried out, no reliance can be placed on Professor Mendenhall's experiments, particularly the second.

These, however, are mere generalities, and there is no need to rely on generalities to demolish this fantastic theory, which incidentally, to the best of my knowledge, no man of letters has ever invoked to aid in solving a literary problem since its inventor first put it forward more than half a century ago. Even if we were prepared to overlook the fact that in the period with which we are concerned there was (i) no standardized system of spelling, and consequently different authors, or the same author on different occasions, spelt the same word in different ways with a different number of letters in it; (ii) that the original spelling of an author underwent considerable changes at the hands of both the scrivener and the printer; and (iii) that in the texts that have come down to us there are many verbal corruptions; I say, even if we overlook all these supremely important matters and allow Professor Mendenhall to do his jugglery with editions printed with modern spelling[1] and containing all the guesses and emendations of modern scholars, the appeal to the average number of letters in a word and similar devices is still a manifest absurdity.

---

[1] In this connection it should be noted that if at any time a system of revised spelling were introduced into the English language, as some people desire, then many words would contain a different number of letters from the number they contain at the present time while others would retain the same, with the result that all the Mendenhall 'fingerprints' would undergo various catastrophic changes simultaneously, and any system built upon it would be plunged into confusion.

In the first place the major part of every writer's vocabulary consists of all the commonplace words – articles, pronouns, conjunctions, etc., which are always the same for all, while the longer and more unusual words, where differences are most likely to occur, are made up of a comparatively small number of letters, and though they differ in spelling and meaning, their letters are often identical in number. For instance, the scientific – *biology*, *analyse*, the poetic – *romance*, *lyrical*, and the commonplace – *railway*, *playful*, all contain seven letters. Thus variation in average is a distinctly limited character, and many writers, totally different in style, might well have a close or even an identical average. It is only because of the insignificant number of works examined by Mendenhall, to which reference has already been made, that this obvious fact failed to reveal itself in his first experiment.

Where the greater differences will mainly occur is in books of widely different genre. An author of my acquaintance distributes his literary output between stories for children and articles on folklore. In the former he uses the simplest and shortest of Anglo-Saxon words, in the latter long Latinized words and technical terms. Moreover the whole structure of his writing is totally different in the two forms. If his productions in each class were tested by the Mendenhall method he would certainly be written down as two distinct authors. Yet in each class his style is his natural one for that genre, and he writes each with the same fluency. I do not believe that Bacon was Shakespeare, but I do feel that the 'wealthy Bostonian' had a very raw deal when the Professor fobbed him off with a comparison between such works as Bacon's *Advancement of Learning* and *History of Henry VII* and Shakespeare's plays, mainly in verse. The vocabularies and style of such diverse genre were bound to be different.

As matter of fact dramatic literature is even less susceptible to tests of this kind than any other form, for in it an author is not using his own vocabulary as much as striving to put into the mouth of each of his *dramatis personae* the vocabulary and manner of speech such a person as he or she would use in real life. It is true that the poetic dramatists of Elizabethan times did not carry this technique as far as do the modern realistic writers, but it is by no means lacking in their work. We have only to compare the speeches of, say, Pistol, Dogberry, Hamlet, and Miranda, to realize the truth of this. The peculiarities of style therefore in dramatic works, including the average length of the words, depends at least as much on the types of character introduced as on the author's own idiosyncracies, and will vary from play to play.

When we come to consider the alleged near identity of the Shakespeare–Marlowe average there is another factor that must be taken into account. In Elizabethan times collaboration and the refurbishing of old plays was the ordinary custom of the theatre. The players usually bought a play outright and might alter it in any way they wished. Frequently they had it re-written by one or more dramatists for a revival, and additions by another hand were very common. It is generally agreed by scholars that some of Shakespeare's early work was of this nature; while some of Marlowe's plays, in the form in which we have them, are less than half his own work, a fact that greatly enhances his reputation. His plays were not printed until many years after they were written, and they were in a very bad state of corruption when at last they reached a publisher. Some authorities believe that the original last three acts of *The Jew of Malta* were lost and that the actors botched them together from memory for the printers. At least the first two acts are the work of a genius, while genius is totally lacking in the last three. Further most scholars are convinced that only about 825 lines in *Doctor Faustus* are by Marlowe; all the rest are by a tenth-rate dramatist.[1] It therefore follows that the similarity of average, if indeed it is genuine and not the result of errors on the part of the inexperienced women-counters, is just one of the duplications that we have seen would be bound to occur in a certain number of cases, but brought about by the joint styles not only of the two principal authors, but by all the other hands that had a part in their plays.

From these facts it is clear that there can be no such thing as 'a mechanical fingerprinting of authorship', and especially is this so in the case of the Elizabethan period. The free and easy method of spelling in vogue; the alterations made by scriveners

[1] F. P. Wilson, *Marlowe and the Early Shakespeare*, pp. 65–75.

and printers; the limited number of letters in words, rendering some duplication of averages inevitable; the diverse styles of even the same author in works of a different genre; the specialized nature of dramatic work in representing the speech of the *dramatis personae*; collaboration and the revision of plays by others; and the highly unsatisfactory nature of many of the texts that have come down to us; all render any data obtained by such devices completely unreliable. We may therefore dismiss the Mendenhall method from this discussion, and turn to a consideration of what Hoffman makes of the more conventional type of argument.

He does not include many examples, and most of those he does include are mere adaptations from the repertoire of the other theorists, as we shall see in the later chapters of this book. There is one, however, that is quite original, and we will examine it as an example of his method.

It is concerned with the Prologue to *The Jew of Malta*. This Prologue is spoken by a character named Machevil, which does not appear elsewhere in the play, and there are reasons for believing that it was not included in the first production of the play in 1594, though it may well have been added for some later production. It was printed in the first published edition in 1633. The following is an extract from it:

> Albeit the world thinks Machevil is dead,
> Yet was his soul but flown beyond the Alps,
> And now the Guize is dead, is come from France
> To view this land and frolic with his friends.
> To some perhaps my name is odious,
> But such as love me guard me from their tongues,
> And let them know that I am Machevil,
> And weigh not men, and therefore not men's words;
> Admired am I of those that hate me most.
> Though some speak openly against my books
> Yet will they read me, and thereby attain
> To Peter's chair . . .
> But . . . I come not, I
> To read a lecture here in Britain.

This appears to Hoffman as strong support for his theory, and he proceeds to develop it as such. His method is the same as that of Titherley in the case of the Davies epigram (see pp. 92–95), namely embellishing – with no intent to deceive, of course – the original document he quotes. In other words he makes a paraphrase of the lines, with interpolations of his own at various points, all designed to give it the sense he desires, as follows:

Although the world thinks, I, Marlowe, have died,
Yet I – my soul – had fled beyond the Alps, to Italy,
And now the Guize (symbolic reference to a high government
  authority in England, who, being alive, prevented my return)
  is dead,
I, Marlowe, can now come from France (to which country I had
  travelled from Italy)
To view my beloved England and visit once again my friends –
  Walsingham, Blount, and Thorpe, for example.
To some perhaps – my known enemies – the name Marlowe is
  odious;
But such as love me (and know of my being alive) guard (my
  name) from their tongues,
And let them – my enemies – know I am not Marlowe, but someone else (Machevil, or say, another name).
I, Marlowe, weigh not men – the multitudes – nor their words –
  and therefore do not care what the vulgar think.
I am admired (i.e. my creative superiority is both admired and
  envied) of those who hate me most;
Though some people will speak and have spoken against my
  writings because of my reputation,
Yet will they read my books – my poems and dramas – charmed
  by my ability to attain – as they in turn attain – the highest
  heaven of beauty's perfection.
But I have not returned to Britain to read you a lecture on my
  'rebirth'!

One could hardly hope to find a better example than this of the practice, common to all the theorists, of making anything mean anything. Hoffman seems to be completely unaware of how large the figure of the real Machiavelli loomed in the life of the Elizabethans. He even thinks it is necessary to seek for some explanation of the use of the name, thinly disguised, for the speaker of the Prologue, and suggests, of course without a shred of evidence, that it might have been applied to Marlowe as a

nickname by his friends. Machiavelli, as the symbol of ruthlessness and intrigue, was the bogyman of the Tudor period, as
Wyndham Lewis has pointed out.[1] There are no less than 395
references to him in Elizabethan literature, and apart from such
direct indications of his influence, he was the source of all
ruthless intriguing characters, such as Iago, Richard III,
Tamburlaine, and numerous others in the works of many
writers. Barabbas in *The Jew of Malta* was such a character,
and it was therefore quite in accordance with the attitude of
the times that, when a Prologue was added to this play, it
should be put into the mouth of a person representing Machiavelli; there is no need to look further for an explanation.

There are several details in Hoffman's paraphrase which call
for comment as illustrating his method of twisting the obvious
meaning of the words. For instance, in lines 2 and 3, the
obvious meaning is that the soul of Machiavelli flew across the
Alps from Italy, where he spent most of his life, into France,
and then came on to England, a journey progressively north-
ward; whereas Hoffman, in order to support his theory that
Marlowe fled to Italy (see p. 129), interprets the flight over the
Alps as southward. Again 'Guize', in line 3, most certainly does
not symbolize 'a high government authority in England'; it
obviously stands for the historical Guise, a Machiavellian if
ever there was one; that is, a man in whom the spirit of Machiavelli was active, and whose exploits incidentally Marlowe had
chronicled in his play *The Massacre of Paris*. The mention of him
therefore in another of Marlowe's plays was a most natural
thing. Finally the words 'Peter's chair', line 12, equally obviously do not mean 'the highest heaven of beauty's perfection'
and have nothing to do with poetry; they mean 'sovereign
power', which the Machiavellian precepts were designed to
obtain and maintain. The father of Caesar Borgia, on whom
Machiavelli founded the hero of his treatise *The Prince*, did
literally occupy St Peter's Chair as Pope of Rome. In short, the
Prologue means exactly what it says. Machiavelli's body may
be dead, but his spirit is still alive. It flew from Italy to France,
where it inspired the ruthless career of Guise. Now that he too
is dead, it has come to Britain, but only for a frolic (i.e. as

[1] *The Lion and the Fox*, p. 64.

Barabbas in the play), not for the real thing as on the Continent. Most people regard Machiavelli's principles as odious; though he has his friends and defenders. But he is Machiavelli, and cares not for men or what they may say about him. He is admired even by those who hate him and attack his books. They read them none the less, and by his precepts gain power. But he has not come to Britain to give a lecture on the subject.

This, put into straightforward prose, is exactly what the lines in the Prologue say. Its meaning is perfectly clear, true according to the opinion of the day, and quite appropriate to the occasion. There is a useful dictum of Science that Hoffman might well have remembered – never strain after a far-fetched and complicated explanation if there is a simple one that covers the facts equally well. In this case it is absurd to press and twist the words into an unnatural meaning when their face-value is fully adequate.

There is one thing at least which may be said in praise of Hoffman's theory. Unlike the exponents of the other schools of thought, he has certainly chosen a dramatist and poet of the first magnitude for the honour of displacing Shakspere. He sometimes blots his copy-book, however, by failing to give the full facts of the situations he describes, as in his handling of the Deptford Church Register entry (see pp. 132–133). To me it seems rather a pity that Hoffman did not write his book as a straightforward work of fiction; it has all the ingredients of a first-class 'thriller', and his imaginary reconstruction of the events leading up to the murder and the murder itself are excitingly and dramatically narrated. Offered as sober fact, however, it is a complete failure, and its arguments, if not as naïve as those of the Oxfordians, are even less convincing.

CHAPTER VII

Parallelisms and the 'Promus'

In this chapter we shall begin our examination of the evidence common to two or more of the theories, and the first we shall deal with is the argument from parallelisms. A literary parallelism, as its name implies, is a passage occurring in a work by one author which bears a marked resemblance in thought and expression to a passage occurring in a work by another author. When such a parallelism is discovered it naturally suggests some connection between the two works. This connection may result from any of the following causes:

(1) Deliberate plagiarism.
(2) Unconscious plagiarism.
(3) Derivation from a common source.
(4) The use of a commonplace expression.
(5) Coincidence.

All these terms are largely self-explanatory, and very little need be said about them. The first is simply barefaced stealing, though there is a less culpable form of it where the theft is acknowledged either explicitly or by implication. The second is very common and easily committed. In our general reading most of us absorb many ideas and turns of expression, the source of which is quickly forgotten even if we are aware of the process at the time, and we may produce these later quite honestly believing them to be original. The third is even more usual. All the great works of the past – for example, the Latin and Greek authors, the classics of our own language, or the Bible – are quarries out of which more recent authors have always dug many of their gems, and it is inevitable that two or more should sometimes strike the same vein. The fourth is only too well known today; the avenues that are explored, the stones that are turned, the smear campaigns that are waged, the witch hunts that are organized, and the statesmen who lean over backwards, must run into thousands if the number of times various writers and speakers use these phrases represents the actual facts.

The fifth requires a slightly more detailed examination. It may be coincidence pure and simple; that is, two authors by mere chance hitting on the same idea and expressing it in similar terms quite independently. This, however, though it may sometimes happen, is unlikely to be of frequent occurrence. A much more probable form is a similar situation in a play, poem, or novel, giving rise to similar ideas and expressions. After all the number of situations in which human beings can find themselves is limited, as is also what can be said in the circumstances. Even in poetic imagery, where pure coincidence is unlikely, a form of coincidence may occur. This is when the image is trite and obvious. For instance, even the most illiterate lover, who had never read or heard the expression, might well compare his mistress's eyes to twin stars, while it is in the highest degree improbable that two poets, however great their genius, would independently hit on Shelley's simile, 'Life, like a dome of many coloured glass, stains the white radiance of eternity'. In dealing with apparent coincidence in imagery the nature of the image must always be taken into consideration.

It is necessary that we should bear all these types of parallelism in mind as part of our critical armoury for dealing with the problems raised in this chapter. They are none of them, however, the type of parallelism beloved of the theorists. On the contrary the latter dislike them intensely, and never mention them unless obliged to do so in the course of controversy. This is only natural, for it does not help their cases to show how two different authors may produce a parallelism; what they desire to demonstrate is that the presence of a parallelism proves that the two works in question are by one and the same author.

Now it must be freely admitted that parallelisms of this kind do actually occur. Consciously or unconsciously an author, especially a poet, will occasionally repeat himself both in idea and expression, the latter not usually in exactly the same form, but close enough to be easily recognizable. It must also be conceded that there are many parallelisms between the various works of Shakespeare and those of three out of the four rival claimants, and the theorists have seized on this fact as an argument to support their respective theories. Our problem is to determine whether the parallelisms they produce as evidence are of the second kind, that is, those of an author repeating himself, in which case they would fulfil the purpose claimed for them; or whether they fall under the heading of one of the types belonging to the first kind, in which case they would have no evidential value.

As no acknowledged work of Derby is extant no parallelisms can be alleged in his case; the Derbyites are therefore not concerned in this matter. There are, however, a large number of parallelisms between Bacon and Shakespeare, almost as many between Marlowe and Shakespeare, and a few between Oxford, whose surviving work is decidedly limited in quantity, and Shakespeare. It might be thought that the very fact that parallelisms can be found in Shakespeare's work for three distinct writers would have made the theorists cautious about attaching much importance to such evidence, for all three could not very well be Shakespeare. This fact does in itself suggest very strongly that the parallelisms concerned belong to the class described in the opening paragraphs of this chapter and not to those produced by a single author. But perhaps one cannot blame the theorists for refusing to acknowledge this without a fight, so we must devote a little space to their arguments. We will begin with the Baconian case.

This was first put forward systematically by Ignatius Donnelly of cryptogram fame (see p. 67) in a work entitled *Shakespeare Studies*, three-fifths of which was devoted to parallelisms – unusual words, similes, opinions, and various expressions – between Bacon and Shakespeare. Donnelly claimed that these amounted to proof positive that Bacon and Shakespeare were one and the same person. He was immediately answered by a number of Stratfordians, who asserted that all his examples, when they really were parallelisms, were merely common expressions of the day used by almost every writer, as Donnelly could easily have discovered if he had read any Elizabethan literature other than the works of Bacon and Shakespeare.

This brought Dr R. M. Theobald into the field to defend Donnelly, whose views he reiterated in *Shakespeare Studies in Baconian Light* (1904). He began his defence with the decidedly

153

dubious statement[1] that 'Opponents of this method select one or two weak or doubtful cases, and smuggle in the assumption that the whole case rests on these, and is defeated by their overthrow.' I use the adjective 'dubious' because the 'one or two doubtful cases' Theobald says were selected included virtually the whole of Donnelly's list. Having committed himself to this misleading statement, Theobald next proceeded to defend the evidence of parallelisms by claiming that it was not like a chain, dependent on its weakest link, but like a cable composed of many strands, each one, however weak in itself, contributing to the strength of the whole; or, to change the metaphor, like the various items in circumstantial evidence, where no item is sufficient in itself to prove the case, but the cumulative effect of all of them establishes it completely. He then reproduced eighty of what he considered Donnelly's strongest instances, and maintained that they fully proved the Baconian claims.

Theobald was answered by Robertson in *The Baconian Heresy*.[2] Robertson began by pointing out the fallacy of Theobald's metaphors and the reasoning based on them. There are, or ought to be, no *weak* strands in a cable; each should be of the full strength required for its own particular purpose. If there are any *weak* strands, then the whole cable is to that extent weakened, and if they are all weak it will promptly snap as soon as any strain is put upon it. In the same way in circumstantial evidence, each item must be true and it must be relevant. If one item after another can be shown to be false or irrelevant, then they cease to have any value as evidence. This, said Robertson, turning Theobald's own metaphors against himself, is precisely the case with the parallelisms from Donnelly's book that Theobald had reproduced; they were either not parallelisms at all or they belonged to the type which might well occur in the works of different authors, being mainly common expressions in general use in Elizabethan times and many of them for a century or two earlier.

To prove his point Robertson subjected Theobald's selection to a detailed analysis. In order to avoid any accusation of picking and choosing he dealt with the first forty seriatim, omitting none. Of the second forty he selected eighteen, omitting

[1] *Shakespeare Studies in Baconian Light*, p. 204.   [2] Pp. 376–380.

for reasons of space those which were so trivial that their falsity would be obvious to anyone with a little knowledge of Elizabethan literature.

Obviously I cannot repeat the whole of Robertson's demonstration here. His examination of a single item sometimes occupies nearly two pages of small type. I can do no more than give one example by way of illustrating the thoroughness and meticulous care with which the analysis is carried out, and then recommend the interested reader to study the material section in *The Baconian Heresy* for himself.

I will take for my example the expression 'to be in, or within, a person's danger'. Theobald points out that Bacon in his *History of Henry VII* uses the phrase 'stand in his danger', and that Shakespeare in the trial scene of M. of V. makes Portia say to Antonio 'You stand within his danger, do you not?' This Theobald, following Donnelly, claims is one of the parallelisms proving identity of authorship.

Robertson replies that the expression comes from the Old French, and means 'to be in someone's power' or 'at his mercy'. It had been in common use at least from the time of Chaucer, and continued to be so throughout the Elizabethan era. To prove this, Robertson gives the following by no means exhaustive list of references:

> In daunger hadde he at his owne gyse
> The yonge girles of the diocyse.
> > Chaucer, *Prologue to the Canterbury Tales.*
> Narcisus was a bachelere
> That Love had caught in his daungere.
> > Chaucer, *Romaunt of the Rose.*
> The world is all in his daungere.
> > Chaucer, Ibid.
> Then said the knight unto Arthur, thou art in my danger, whether me list to save thee or slay thee.
> > Mallory, *Morte D'Arthur.*
> How they passed out of the Kynges danger, I finde not.
> > Fabyan, *Chronicle*, Hen. III, ann. 38.
> Out of his daunger will I be at lyberte.
> > *Interlude of Calisto and Melebea.* (circa. 1530)
> In sin, and in danger to death and hell.
> > Tyndale, *Pathway unto the Holy Scripture.*

What suppose ye that Luther would do, if he had the Pope's
holiness in his danger?
                                          Bishop Fisher.
Had brought herself in danger of lawe through ignorance.
          Brief Discourse of the Murder of Saunders. (1575)
                Betray his fame and safety
     To the law's danger and your father's justice.
              Chapman, *Revenge for Honour*, III, i.

In this full and detailed fashion, taking one item after
another, Robertson completely annihilated the Baconian claims
based on parallelisms, and also clearly proved his own contention that most of the supporters of that theory were profoundly
ignorant of Elizabethan literature, and had read little, if any,
apart from the works of Bacon and Shakespeare.

It is unnecessary to devote any time or space to the Oxfordian
parallelisms. As already stated, so little of Oxford's acknowledged work survives that less than a dozen examples have been
discovered. In any case what parallels there are between his
work and Shakespeare's are all open to the same criticisms as
those of the other claimants.

The case of Marlowe is very different. In an Appendix to
The Man Who Was Shakespeare Hoffman lists seventy parallelisms between his works and those of Shakespeare, and states
that they form the strongest link in the chain of evidence for
Marlowe's claims. Of course Hoffman's examples are also
susceptible to Robertson's method of criticism; indeed the name
of Marlowe appears frequently in Robertson's lists of other
writers who have made use of some expression supposed by the
Baconians to be exclusive to Bacon and Shakespeare. There
are, however, some additional points to be observed in the
case of Marlowe since he, like Shakespeare, was primarily a
poetic dramatist, while Bacon was a prose writer on philosophical, historical, and kindred subjects. We must therefore
turn our attention to these special points.

In the first place it is to be noted that many of the examples
Hoffman calls parallelisms scarcely merit the name. They are
merely expressions such as every writer of fiction, whether plays
or novels, is compelled to use by the exigencies of his plot. I
quote the following as examples:

(1) Did ever man see such a sudden storm,
Or day so clear so suddenly o'ercast.

Marlowe, *Dido*.

So foul and fair a day I have not seen.

Shakespeare, *Macbeth*.

(2) Shape we our course to Ireland, there to breathe.

Marlowe, *Edward II*.

To-morrow next
We will for Ireland, and 'tis time, I trow.

Shakespeare, *Richard II*.

(3) I arrest you of high treason.

Marlowe, *Edward II*.

I arrest thee of high treason.

Shakespeare, *Henry VIII*.

The first of these examples, in which there is not the slightest resemblance between the words used in the two quotations, merely means 'There has been a sudden change in the weather'. This is surely, in a climate such as ours, the most common of all commonplaces, and must have been used by most writers in the English language who have had occasion to remark on the weather. In the second again there is no resemblance whatever in the words used. Two kings, who historically did actually visit Ireland, and who are required by the plots of the two plays in which they respectively appear to state this fact, simply state it. It would be no more outrageous to claim a common authorship for all stories in which someone says that he, or she, is going to London, than to offer such passages as evidence of the common authorship of the two plays. In the third the words are virtually identical, but, since they constitute the official Tudor formula used in making an arrest, it would be strange if they were not. Hoffman will find their modern equivalent in almost every English detective story, and so, I suppose, will be convinced that all detective stories are written by one and the same author.

There are other so-called parallelisms offered by Hoffman for which there is even less excuse. I give three examples out of many:

(1) Ugly hell, gape not.

Marlowe, *Doctor Faustus*.

. . . though hell itself should gape.

Shakespeare, *Hamlet*.

157

(2) . . . breakers of the peace.

Marlowe, *Massacre of Paris.*

. . . disturbers of the peace.

Shakespeare, *Romeo and Juliet.*

(3) Here is my dagger.

Marlowe, *Tamburlaine.*

. . . there is my dagger.

Shakespeare, *Julius Caesar.*

In the first of these there is again no similarity in the wording, and the idea is the veriest commonplace used by numerous writers at least since the time of the Miracle Plays, when 'Hell's mouth' was an important stage property. 'Gaping' was, and still is, a common epithet for a wide-open mouth, as also for other menacing orifices such as caves, and so is naturally applied to hell's mouth. The second is merely two slightly different versions of another common phrase also still in use, and employed by numerous writers in all periods. As for the third, it is too absurd for any comment to be possible. I can only leave it to make its own impression on the reader.

Hoffman's next example is somewhat different. It is:

Hola, ye pampered jades of Asia.
What, can ye draw but twenty miles a day?

Marlowe, *Tamburlaine.*

And hollow pampered jades of Asia,
Which cannot go but thirty miles a day.

Shakespeare, *II Henry IV.*

Hoffman seems to be blissfully unaware that the rather bombastic lines he quotes from *Tamburlaine* shared with one or two speeches from Kyd's *Spanish Tragedy* the doubtful honour of being the most parodied in all Elizabethan literature. A number of satiric writers introduced them in various ways into their works. A good example is the comedy, *Eastward Ho,* produced jointly by Chapman, Jonson, and Marston, which contains among its *dramatis personae* a comic apprentice, Francis Quicksilver, who makes use of Marlowe's lines, without acknowledgement, more than once when addressing the serving-women. Shakespeare puts the lines into the mouth of that great comic exponent of bombast, Ancient Pistol, and this fact, together with the punning variation of 'hollow' for 'hola' and the verbiage of the rest of the speech in which they occur, makes it clear that he is ridiculing the lines, an unlikely thing if he were the original author.[1] In any case their presence in *Henry IV* is no more evidence for Marlowe's authorship of that play than their presence in *Eastward Ho* and other works is for his authorship of them.

The next example, though Hoffman's omission of an all-important line conceals the fact, is just a simple case of *acknowledged* quotation from another work. The alleged parallelism, as he gives it, is as follows:

> Whoever loved that loved not at first sight?
> > Marlowe, *Hero and Leander.*
> Whoever loved that loved not at first sight?
> > Shakespeare, *As You Like It.*

The line that Hoffman illegitimately suppresses in Shakespeare's play is the one that immediately precedes the quotation. It reads: 'Dead shepherd now I find thy saw of might.' 'Shepherd' was the traditional term for poet, and Marlowe's poem was well known. The omitted line is therefore the plainest of acknowledgements that the conceit is a borrowed one. As Marlowe is referred to as 'Dead shepherd' the quotation would appear to be a little tribute from Shakespeare to his great predecessor and to follow quite naturally if Marlowe's fate were what the orthodox account says it was. Hoffman of course disputes this conclusion, but as the question will have to be discussed fully in a later chapter (see pp. 218 f.), we will leave the matter for the present, merely emphasizing that in the light of the facts given this so-called parallelism is in no way evidence for Marlowe's authorship of A.Y.L.I.

Hoffman is much more to the point in the next example we shall consider, for here, though neither the thought nor the wording are identical in the two plays concerned, they are so similar and so unusual that there is no doubt about

---

[1] Marlowe is by no means the only dramatist whose lines appear parodied in the speeches of Ancient Pistol. There are several other victims, his favourite being Peele. If this is evidence of authorship, then Peele has much greater claims than Marlowe.

their forming a true parallelism. The quotations read as follows:

> Weep not for Mortimer
> That scorns the world, and as a traveller
> Goes to discover countries yet unknown.
>
> Marlowe, *Edward II.*
>
> The undiscovered country from whose bourn
> No traveller returns. Shakespeare, *Hamlet.*

A point of particular interest about this parallelism is that, long before Hoffman pointed it out, the Baconians appropriated the *Hamlet* quotation and utilized it for their own purpose. They showed that the idea on which the lines were based was to be found in Catullus, and argued that only a good Classical scholar, a qualification they of course denied to the Stratford actor, would be familiar with such an author. Replying to this, Robertson pointed out that Shakespeare probably got it from Sandford's translation of Cornelius Agrippa, made about 1570, where the same idea occurs. The basic idea therefore did not originate with either Shakespeare or Marlowe; it was derived from the Classics, and such being the case the parallelism in the two plays need be nothing more than one due to a common source.

From this last example it will be seen that, though no more valuable as evidence for his theory, all Hoffman's parallelisms are not as frivolous and far-fetched as those we examined earlier. We will now examine another and even more striking case. It is the following:

> By shallow rivers, to whose falls
> Melodious birds sing madrigals.
> And I will make thee beds of roses,
> And a thousand fragrant posies.
>
> Marlowe, *Passionate Shepherd.*
>
> To shallow rivers, to whose falls
> Melodious birds sing madrigals;
> There we will make our beds of roses
> And a thousand fragrant posies.
>
> Shakespeare, *Merry Wives of Windsor.*

Before making any comment on this apparently devastating example,[1] I should like to draw the reader's attention to another

[1] See Appendix.

parallelism of which Mr Hoffman is either ignorant or prefers
not to mention it in this connection. It is the following:

Like to an almond tree ymounted hye
On top of greene Selinis all alone,
With blossoms brave bedecked daintily;
Whose tender locks do tremble every one
At everie little breath that under heaven is blowne.
                    Spenser, *The Faerie Queene.*
                    (Describing a helmet plume.)
Like to an almond tree y-mounted high
Upon the lofty and celestial mount
Of ever-green Selinis quaintly decked
With blooms more white than Erycina's brows,
Whose tender blossoms tremble every one,
At every little breath through heaven is blown.
                    Marlowe, *Tamburlaine.*
                    (Describing a helmet plume.)

I should like to know whether, on this evidence, Mr Hoffman
believes that Spenser wrote *Tamburlaine* or that Marlowe wrote
The Faerie Queene. The correct answer is of course 'Neither',
and the true explanation that one stole from the other. It is a
simple case of plagiarism, and that brings us to the root-cause
of by far the greater number of parallelisms.

Plagiarism was rife in Elizabethan times. Almost every
writer, at least every professional writer, indulged in it, though
some of them squealed when it was practised against themselves. The main reason for this state of affairs was of course
the fact that in those days there was no copyright law to protect an author, and anyone might help himself freely to another
man's ideas and words. The dramatists were the worst offenders,
largely because speed was of supreme importance in the
theatre. When the actors wanted a new play they wanted it
quickly. The diary kept by Henslowe, who ran playhouses
purely as a business proposition, throws a great deal of light on
contemporary methods. A dramatist did not as a rule submit a
completed play to various managements, hoping for its acceptance; usually each theatrical company had a number of hack-
dramatists attached to it, who worked to order. Sometimes a
plot was purchased from one dramatist and, when haste was
specially urgent, some of the scenes were farmed out to one or

two other dramatists so that they could be written simultaneously. But whether he worked in collaboration or alone the hack-dramatist – and nearly all were hack-dramatists at least at the start of their career – almost always wrote under pressure of time. In such circumstances, with no leisure for prolonged thought, it is not surprising that the poor dramatists were often tempted to borrow from others when their own ideas refused to flow freely.

If the theorists had extended their studies to Elizabethan literature in general, they would have found plenty of parallelisms between Shakespeare and other dramatists besides their own particular candidate. I will give two examples, in the first of which Shakespeare is the borrower, and in the second he provides the material borrowed. They are as follows:

(1) In fayth, then fare well frost, more such haue we lost. . . .
I should haue but a colde sute with my wooing. But belyke you are betrothed already; and that makes you so dayntie, if you be tell me, that I loose no more labour.

Munday, Zelauto (1580).

Fare you well, your suite is cold. . . .
Cold indeede, and labour lost,
Then farewell heate, and welcome frost.

Shakespeare, Merchant of Venice.

(2) The lapwing runs with a shell on his head.

Shakespeare, Hamlet.

Forward, lapwing. He flies with a shell on 's head.

Webster, The White Devil (1612).

Naturally too there are plenty of parallelisms which do not involve Shakespeare at all, but occur between other dramatists, a fact that ought to have caused the theorists to pause in their facile deductions. There has of course been no deliberate and systematic search for parallelisms among these authors, for they have not been involved in any controversial claims, and consequently there are no lists in existence like those compiled by the Baconians and Hoffman. Editors of their works have drawn attention to such parallelisms when they have noticed them, and a considerable number has been brought to light in this perfunctory way, a circumstance that suggests there may well be hundreds more still awaiting recognition.[1] In any case there are quite enough to reveal how common the practice of all forms of plagiarism and imitation was throughout the Elizabethan era.

It was in the conditions just described that Shakespeare, whoever he was, developed his art and wrote his plays. It is therefore in no way remarkable that his work should contain many parallelisms of various kinds. In this it resembles exactly the works of nearly all other dramatists of his time. The lists put forward by the theorists, in spite of the many examples they contain which are not parallelisms at all and others that result from the use of a common source, do show that Shakespeare was guilty of plagiarism, both of the conscious and unconscious varieties, and of several other forms of borrowing and imitation. This, however, so far from ruling out the Stratford actor as the author of the plays, is on the contrary a point in his favour. It is the hall-mark of a man of the theatre, which is what *Shakspere* certainly was. Bacon, Oxford, and Derby, men of leisure and means, working in their quiet studies, would have no need to resort to such methods. The theorists, as we have seen (pp. 43–45), in their efforts to denigrate the Stratford actor, have quoted what they claim are references to him

[1] I myself discovered a very interesting example, involving no less than four writers and stretching across a century from the reign of James I to that of George I. It is a comment on the futility of attacking spirits with cutting weapons:

If their bodies be cut, with admirable celerity they come together again.

Burton, Anatomy of Melancholy (1621).

The gridling sword with discontinuous wound
Passed through him; but the etherial substance closed,
Not long divisible.

Milton, Paradise Lost, Bk. vi (1667).

Fate urged the sheers and cut the sylph in twain,
But airy substance soon unites again.

Pope, Rape of the Lock (1714).

But empyreal forms, howe'er in fight
Gash'd and dismember'd, easily unite.

Tickell, Kensington Gardens (1722).

I may add that so far I have succeeded in resisting the temptation to advance the theory that these four works were all written by one and the same author.

accusing him of plagiarism. Well, the plays themselves give some colour to this accusation, and the inference is that he was their author. The theorists cannot have it both ways.

To sum up, the following points emerge from our analysis of the argument from parallelisms:

(*a*) The number is not nearly as large as stated by the theorists, many of the examples listed not being parallelisms.

(*b*) Of those which are genuine, none necessarily implies a common authorship with that of its pair; all can be explained as one or other of the forms possible to two distinct authors.

(*c*) That similar parallelisms are found in the works of nearly all the other dramatists of the period; they result from a common practice.

(*d*) The presence of such parallelisms in the plays is favourable to the authorship of the Stratford actor, and certainly in no way counts against it.

There remains the problem of Bacon's 'Promus', which is a special case of this question of parallelisms, and it must now have our attention.

The original manuscript of the *Promus of Formularies and Elegancies*, as Spedding named it, is in the Harleian Collection in the British Museum. It was first published in 1883 by Mrs C. M. Pott, and again in 1910 by Sir Edwin Durning-Lawrence, who had a careful revision of the whole 'Promus' specially made by Mr F. B. Buckley of the British Museum for his *Bacon is Shakespeare*. It consists of fifty folio sheets, now numbered 83 to 132, but this numbering is quite modern and was added merely for convenience when the 'Promus' was bound up with other Baconian papers, which were numbered at the same time 1 to 82 and 133 onwards. Originally the sheets were unnumbered. The third sheet of the 'Promus', that numbered 85, is dated December 5th, 1594, and the thirty-second sheet, that numbered 114, is dated January 27th, 1595. The handwriting in which all the entries are made, with the exception of a group of French Proverbs, was declared by James Spedding to be undoubtedly that of Bacon.

The contents of this interesting document consist of texts from the Bible; metaphors; aphorisms; English, French, Spanish,

Italian, and Latin Proverbs – all taken from a collection published by John Heywood; forms of morning and evening saluta-
tion; and a large number of miscellaneous entries. They are
arranged in columns, sometimes single and sometimes double,
on each page. Most of the pages are fairly well filled, but others
have only a few entries and much blank space. Similarly some
of the sheets have entries on both sides; others on one side only.

The most important point about the 'Promus', however, is the
fact that many of its entries, or at least the thoughts they express, have been found in an expanded form in the Shakespearean plays. Naturally the Baconians have leapt upon this
as evidence for the truth of their theory. B. G. Theobald summarizes their arguments[1] in the following propositions:

(1) The Stratford actor could have had no access to what was
a private note-book of Bacon's, and so could not have borrowed
from the 'Promus'.

(2) The notes, as suggested by the two dated folios, would seem
to have been made between 1594 and 1596; that is, before most of
the plays had appeared, and so Bacon could not have borrowed
much from them.

(3) The notes were not made for reproduction in Bacon's
acknowledged works, for very few of them appear there.

(4) They occur only rarely in other authors of the time.

(5) They occur profusely in the Shakespearean plays.

From these propositions, Theobald claims, the only reasonable conclusion which can be drawn is that Bacon wrote the
Shakespearean plays.

Before subjecting this argument to analysis, we will just take
a glance at the attitude of the other theorists towards the evidence of the 'Promus', for their cases are of course affected by
its truth or otherwise to exactly the same extent as is the case
of the Stratfordians, and their reaction to a Baconian point will
certainly help us to evaluate their reactions in other respects.
The Oxfordians and Hoffman are easily dealt with, *since they
ignore it altogether.* The Derbyite, Evans, does not mention it
either; in fact the only author of any school, other than the
orthodox, that I have come across who really faces up to the
problem is Titherley.

[1] *Enter Francis Bacon*, p. 99.

165

Titherley's treatment of it is typical of his method of argument, but it requires a little preliminary explanation before it can be properly understood. Derby, like all young men of position in those days, apparently spent some time in the study of the Law. The Register of Lincoln's Inn shows that he was entered there in August 1594, his sponsor being Sir John Puckering. Titherley, however, discovered that Derby's father had put his name down in 1562, when he was still in his infancy, for admission to Gray's Inn when the time should arrive for him to begin his studies. From this Titherley concludes that Derby, before entering Lincoln's Inn, studied at Gray's, where he was a contemporary of Bacon, and that the two had long serious discussions on various topics, out of which the 'Promus' was born. He writes[1] as follows:

'Here were two youths of diametrically opposed temperaments; William, as yet untravelled, buoyant, high hearted, poetic, impulsive, and a brilliant wit in conversation; Francis, full of his multiple, if boyish experiences abroad, cynical, prosaic, analytical, philosophical, and critical. Both young men were deeply learned, and it is easy to conceive that some intellectual sparks must have flashed out between them at Gray's Inn. Viewed in this perspective it may well be that mental-penetration led to a veritable intellectual synthesis, and initiated the profound thought which runs like an endless thread through Shakespeare's drama. If so and if Stanley resumed his relations with Gray's Inn after the ripening years of experience abroad, Bacon must have played, if unconsciously, an inspiring part in the birth and development of this mighty dramatic art. Between them must have arisen many abstract conceptions in common, not only those reflecting contemporary thought, but culled from the sages of the past, comprising proverbs, similes, and metaphors, such as are found committed to writing in the "Promus"; as well as other brilliant ideas forged on the common anvil between them. Did (one wonders) Bacon with characteristic egotism regard such aphorisms or ideas as his own, and secretly resent this exploitation for poetic and dramatic purposes by Stanley? Such resentment might explain why he never had a word of praise for him either in the rôle of the Earl

[1] *Shakespeare's Identity*, pp. 149–150.

of Derby or of Shakespeare; or was it simply that he considered Play-writing an idle pastime not worthy of comment?'

I am no Baconian, but the Baconians have my full sympathy when their arguments are met with such stuff as this. The highest flights indulged in by the cryptologists rest on scarcely more flimsy foundations. There is not a single scrap of evidence that there was ever any intimacy between Derby and Bacon, or that Derby was ever at Gray's Inn. In our own day there have been many cases of a father putting down his son's name in infancy for some famous school, and then, when the time came for him to go to it, sending him to another. If Derby actually did enter Gray's Inn, why is there no record of the fact in the Register; and why did he later enter Lincoln's Inn, of which entry there is a record? Such evidence as does exist points to one conclusion, and one only: namely, that for some reason Derby was prevented from entering Gray's Inn at the time intended, and later went to Lincoln's Inn instead. But even if it could be proved that he was in residence at Gray's, this would not be evidence for Titherley's fantastic picture of the conversations between the two young men 'of diametrically opposed temperaments' whose 'mental-penetration' led to 'a veritable intellectual synthesis', eventually resulting in the production of the 'Promus'. The whole thing is pure fiction, and nothing else.

We may therefore dismiss Titherley from this part of the case, and resume our examination of the five propositions laid down by B. G. Theobald (see p. 165), or rather of the first four, for the fifth is substantially correct, and would not be disputed by anyone.

The reply to the first is simple. It is true, as Theobald says, that the Stratford actor could not have had access to Bacon's private note-book, but the sources from which much of that note-book was compiled were as readily available to him as to Bacon, and the same ideas that appear striking to one person frequently appear so to another, as the repetitions in numerous anthologies, collections of quotations, etc., demonstrate beyond dispute. Many of the Promus–Shakespeare parallelisms therefore may well be nothing more than derivations from a common source, and require no further explanation.

Nor need we accept Theobald's second proposition – that the reverse was also the case, and that the 'Promus' could have owed very little to the Shakespearean plays because most of these had not appeared when it was compiled. It will be remembered that the third sheet from the beginning bears the date December 5th, 1594, and the nineteenth from the end the date January 27th, 1595, and if these mark terminals, or approximate terminals, as Theobald claims, then the 'Promus' is certainly earlier than most of the plays. But do they mark terminals? There is no evidence that they do, and the fact that they are not on the first and last sheets counts against the idea. It is possible that Bacon, while not habitually dating the sheets, did so either by chance or for some specific reason with this particular pair, in which case it would be impossible to form any estimate of the time when the 'Promus' was completed. Its compilation may have been spread over a number of years, thus allowing many more Shakespearean plays than Theobald thinks to be available for Bacon to extract ideas from, exactly as he did from the other sources. Theobald's proposition cannot therefore be accepted as evidence. It is true that it cannot be disproved, but neither can it be proved. My suggestion is at least equally plausible, and there is no means of telling which is correct.

Theobald's third proposition, probably because he followed Mrs Pott without verifying her statements, is demonstrably false. Bacon made profuse use of the 'Promus' in his recognized works, as many Baconians, including Durning-Lawrence, have pointed out. It is not easy to understand why Theobald or anyone else should have troubled to deny this, for it makes little difference to the Baconian theory. If Bacon had really written the Shakespearean plays he could still have used the 'Promus' for his other works; and if he did not write the plays, such a fact would not oblige him to use the 'Promus' for his own works if he found no occasion to do so. The matter is of no real importance, and we need give no further attention to it.

The fourth proposition – that the 'Promus' entries do not occur in the works of other writers – is also untrue, though in this case the matter is very important to the Baconian argument, and Theobald has the support of his fellow-Baconians.

To refute their claims we may begin by pointing out that Robertson found so many of the 'Promus' items in Ben Jonson's works, particularly in his *Discoveries,* that he has suggested that Bacon employed Jonson to do some of his collecting for him, as he employed him in other ways, and that Jonson freely helped himself to what he brought in.[1] The best criticism of the Baconian contention, however, is contained in an Essay on 'The Bacon–Shakespeare Problem', by C. Crawford, published in *Collectanea,* second series, Stratford-on-Avon, 1907. Mr Crawford shows that a number of the expressions expanded from the 'Promus', which are common to both Bacon's and Shakespeare's works, are to be found in the works of many other writers, some of them written long before the 'Promus' was compiled. Since, like those of Robertson, Crawford's examples and their analysis are decidedly lengthy, I can afford space for only one here, and must refer the reader who wishes to pursue the matter further to Mr Crawford's essay.

Crawford writes, 'Bacon in the *Promus* quotes the proverb: "He that pardons his enemy, the amner (almoner) shall have his goods": and in *De Augmentis* remarks that "None of the virtues has so many crimes to answer for as clemency" (Antitheta on Cruelty; VI, iii, No. 18); repeating the idea more fully in another place (VIII, ii, No. 14). Again he writes to Buckingham, "Mercy in such a case, in a King, is true cruelty."
'So Shakespeare:

> Sparing justice feeds iniquity.
> > *Lucrece.*
> Pardon is still the nurse of second woe.
> > M. for M., II, i.
> Mercy but murders, pardoning those that kill.
> > R. & J. III, i.

'But this was an ancient commonplace, often found in Tudor literature:

> He that for every little occasion is moved with compassion . . . is called piteous, which is a sickness of the mind, wherewith at this day the more part of men be diseased.
> > Elyot, The *Governor,* B. ii, c. 7.

[1] *The Baconian Heresy,* p. 437.

For most oftentimes the omitting of correction redoubleth a
trespass.

Id., B. iii, c. 21.

We must wreak (revenge) our wrongs
So as we take not more.

Chapman, *Revenge of Bussy D'Ambois*, III, i.

Fathers, to spare these men, were to commit
A greater wickedness than you would revenge.

Jonson, *Catiline*, V, 6.

No worse a vice than lenity in Kings.
Remiss indulgence soon undoes a realm.

Hughes, *The Misfortunes of Arthur*, iii, i. 1587.

There must the rule to all disorders sink,
Where pardons more than punishments appear.

Fairfax, trans. of Tasso's *Jerusalem Delivered*, B. v.

Compassion here is cruelty, my lord,
Pity will cut our throats.

Daniel, *Civil Wars*, B. v.'

Thus Theobald's fourth proposition falls to the ground.
Crawford's demonstration makes it clear that expanded forms
of the 'Promus' entries do occur frequently in the works of
many writers besides Bacon and Shakespeare, and if other
writers could acquire them without the necessity of being
Bacon, so also could Shakespeare. Of course Crawford's list is
not exhaustive. He has not been able to show that *all* the
Bacon–Shakespeare parallelisms based on the 'Promus' have
been used by other writers. This was hardly to be expected.
Some may be genuinely absent for the reason that, though
available, they were not required. Others may well have been
lost in works that have not survived, and a study of the analysis
I have quoted from Crawford's essay will reveal the magnitude
of the labour involved in the search for examples, and how easily
a material passage might be overlooked by a searcher as he
read through work after work.[1] The point is that, in spite of all
difficulties, a very large number can be shown to have been

[1] It should be noted that Crawford only sought his examples among those
which had been used by both Bacon and Shakespeare as well as appearing
in the 'Promus', a Herculean task. If he had contented himself with examples
which merely occurred in the 'Promus' and in works by other writers, he
could greatly have lightened his labours and still refuted the Baconian
claims. But he chose the harder way as the more conclusive.

generally available, and this is sufficient to invalidate Theobald's argument.

To sum up then, there is nothing mysterious about the 'Promus'. It is simply a note-book containing phrases and sentences collected by or for Bacon from various sources. These sources were equally open to other writers, including Shakespeare, and are certainly responsible, as Crawford has proved, for many of the Bacon–Shakespeare parallelisms. For the rest, Shakespeare could certainly have borrowed some from Bacon's published works, and, as we have seen (pp. 167–168), it may well have been possible for Bacon to have borrowed some from him.

In the light of these considerations the 'Promus' cannot be regarded as evidence for the Baconian theory.

CHAPTER VIII

Shakespeare's Scholarship and Vocabulary

One of the principal arguments of all the theorists is that the Shakespearean plays could have been written only by a very learned man, and that Shakspere the actor was not a learned man; therefore Shakspere the actor could not have written them. The reply the orthodox Stratfordians make to this contention is that the plays are far less learned and the actor more learned than the theorists suppose, and therefore there need be no question about the authorship on these grounds. Our purpose in this chapter is to examine the evidence for both these views, and to determine as far as possible which is correct.

We may begin by dismissing the contention of the wilder Baconians, such as Durning-Lawrence, that Shakspere was completely illiterate (see p. 32). It is true that there is no known record of his attendance at any school, but in this his case is parallel with that of many famous men of letters of those days, including Lyly, Heywood, and Dekker. Yet, since the first two of these at least were University men, they must have attended some school; thus lack of record cannot be evidence for non-attendance. It is only to be expected that many school records should have been lost during the centuries that have elapsed between that time and the present, and since the art of biography did not develop until some time later, there was no alternative method of preserving the knowledge of such details. We do know, however, that education was more widespread in the Elizabethan era than at any time before or since until the nineteenth century.[1] William Shakspere's father was one of the most prominent citizens of Stratford, a man who held in succession a number of important municipal offices, includ-

[1] L. F. Salzman, *England in Tudor Times*, p. 9.

ing that of Mayor,[1] and it is inconceivable that the son of such a personage should not have attended the Free Grammar School there, as did the sons of all the other leading citizens. It is much more dubious to assume that he did not do so than to assume that he did, and to be quite fair it is only a small minority of the theorists who deny this fact.

On the other hand the theory put forward by some of the Bardolators that Shakspere was sent to one of the Universities by some benevolent nobleman, who early recognized his genius, has nothing to recommend it. The lack of all reference here cannot be discounted as completely as in the case of a school, for the Universities appear to have preserved their records with much more care, and there are a number of Elizabethan men of letters whose schools are unknown, but whose names are found in a University list. We may therefore dismiss such a view at once.

This, however, by no means rules out the possibility of Shakspere's becoming a very learned man. Ben Jonson also failed to get to a University, and when he left Westminster School served a seven-year apprenticeship as a bricklayer, where this monotonous toil employed him daily for twelve hours in the summer and from dawn to dusk in the winter, besides which he served as a soldier in Flanders, and then joined a company of touring actors. Yet in spite of this unpromising background he became one of the greatest scholars in the country, so that even the pre-eminent Francis Bacon sought his aid in translating his philosophical works into Latin, and both Universities conferred honorary degrees upon him. Nor was Ben Jonson the only Elizabethan non-graduate, though the greatest, to attain such success in learning. There were others as, for instance, R. Willis who, in his *Mount Tabor*, himself tells us that by his own efforts, without the advantage of a University degree, he eventually became secretary to the Lord Keeper Coventry. It is obvious therefore that the road to learning was not closed to Shakspere if he should be disposed to travel along it in spite of the fact

---

[1] Actually the title in use at Stratford-on-Avon was Bailiff, a survival from the days when the town formed part of a feudal estate, and its chief official was the overlord's agent. In Tudor times, however, the office of Bailiff was indistinguishable from that of Mayor, as is that of Vicar from Rector today.

that he lacked the advantages a University might have given him.

Let us now see what opportunities of a formal kind Shakspere, as a non-graduate, had at his disposal for acquiring knowledge, leaving the less formal to be considered when we deal with any specific items that occur in the plays. First of all his schooling would give him a thorough grounding in the elements of Latin, for not only was this the principal subject taught in every Grammar School, but all the instruction was given in that language, and the pupils had to speak it as well as read and write it. This was certainly sufficient to provide him with the 'small Latin' that Ben Jonson tells us the author of the plays possessed.

Then Shakspere went to London, a town which Chute calls 'the home of short cuts to knowledge'. Anyone who wishes to discover what the London of Elizabeth I had to offer the seeker after knowledge should consult Chute's *Shakespeare of London*, pp. 54 ff., where the subject is treated in detail. I have space for only two items. The first of these is foreign languages. There were in the city teachers of Arabic, Russian, Italian, Spanish, Dutch, Turkish, German, and Polish, and a whole colony who taught French. The latter charged a shilling a week, and gave a thorough training in colloquial French. Shakspere could have taken lessons from any of these foreign teachers, or got them to make translations for him in either direction if he ever needed to do so. With such aids so readily and cheaply available the use of any foreign language in the plays is no bar to his authorship.

The second item is books. Some of the theorists declare that these were scarce and expensive. On the contrary they were plentiful and cheap. Paper-backed quartos usually cost sixpence; that is, something between five and ten shillings in our post-war values. The Londoners were great readers, and eagerly devoured works on almost every conceivable subject. Among the books that have survived – and of course the greater part must have perished completely – either actually or in some record, are works on surveying land; how to play musical instruments without a teacher; how to ride, write, garden, and take spots out of velvet; first aid in the absence of a physician, navigation for amateur mariners, hunting, hawking, and other

174

outdoor sports. In addition to these were the chronicles of such historians as Holinshed, and many translations of the Classics and other foreign works. With all this on sale there was no lack of information for anyone who wanted it, even for Shakspere the actor.

While on the subject of books, we may as well treat of a favourite point of the theorists; namely the absence of all mention of books from Shakspere's will. By their reasoning this means that he never possessed any, and, by a deduction that appears logical to them, he could not therefore be the author of the plays. It never seems to dawn upon them that a person might own books without mentioning them in his will, or that he might have given them away before he died. In Shakspere's case a very likely recipient was on the spot in his intellectual son-in-law, Dr John Hall, for whom he bought a fine house in Stratford as a wedding present. The mere fact that none are mentioned in the will proves nothing. Among the extant wills of the period are those of Samuel Daniel, the poet; Reginald Scot, the author of *The Discoverie of Witchcraft*, a work for which he would need some very specialized reference books; and, above all, Richard Hooker, scholar and theologian, Cambridge University professor, and one-time Master of the Temple, who must have owned a very considerable library. Yet, like Shakspere, not one of these famous men of letters makes any reference to books in his will. The argument from silence on this topic therefore is surely one of the flimsiest ever put forward to support a theory.

This review makes it clear that Shakspere lacked neither the means nor the opportunity to acquire a great deal of learning, and there is no reason to suppose that he did not make use of them. We can now turn to the second part of our task, the examination of the alleged learning in the plays, with the purpose of discovering whether this amounts to anything that would necessarily be beyond his scope.

We will begin with the claim – one advanced by every school of thought, though most strongly urged by the Baconians – that the plays display such a familiarity with all the Latin and Greek authors that the dramatist must have been a profound Classical scholar; no knowledge acquired while at school could possibly have been so deep and so extensive. In support of this they instance the multitude of allusions to the sayings and teachings of ancient authorities that occur in the plays; the numerous references to mythological, legendary, and historical personages of the past that are found therein; and the accurate depicting of Roman history and its social background in the three great Roman plays.

As is usually the case where the Baconians are involved, there is a complete answer to this claim in J. M. Robertson's *The Baconian Heresy*. For nearly two hundred pages (178 to 375) he subjects their examples, one after another, to detailed examination and annihilating criticism, and anyone desirous of obtaining a full knowledge of this important question should consult the relevant section of his great work; here I can do no more than give the barest summary of his arguments.

He begins by pointing out that in making the claim to original Classical scholarship for the author of the Shakespearean plays, the theorists are once again betraying their own lack of Elizabethan scholarship. Because of their ignorance of Tudor literature and the Tudor background they failed completely to realize how great was the general interest in the Classics in those days when the impact of the Renaissance was still being felt in almost full force, and how this general interest was catered for in various ways. There were in fact several ways in which a vast amount of Classical lore was made available, not only to those who, like Shakspere, might desire it for some special purpose, but to the public in general.

First, there were the translations of the Classical works, such as Phaer's 'Aeneid', Golding's 'Ovid', and Halls' 'Homer's Iliads'. How rapidly these were sometimes turned out may be gathered from the fact that Horace's *Satires* were translated by Lucas Evans in 1564, again by a writer signing himself B. L. in 1567, and yet again in the same year by Thomas Drant, who added the *Art of Poetry* and the *Epistles* to his edition. A considerable number of these translations have survived, and there must have been many more that have been lost during the lapse of the centuries, for translation was an exercise that most young men with a literary bent attempted at some time in their career throughout this period.

Second, and more important because of their wider appeal and cheaper price, were the popular plays of the earlier Tudor period. No one who has not studied these plays would ever guess how much Classical lore was scattered about them. Some of the Interludes were especially abundant in their allusions. A single one, *The Trial of the Treasure*, has references to Diogenes, Alexander, Pegasus, Morpheus, Hydra, Hercules, Hector, Tully, Epicurus, Croesus, Æsop, Aristippus, Solon, Adrastia, Circe, Dionysius, Tarquin Superbus, Heliogabalus, Helen, Thales, and Cressida, as well as to numerous gods and goddesses. Nor were these mere passing references; they were often discursive and explanatory, as the following extracts will show:

The advice of Aristippus have in your mind
Which willeth me to speak such things as be permanent . . .
For treasures here gotten are uncertain and vain,
But treasures of the mind do continually remain.

Thou never remembering Thales his sentence,
Who willeth men in all things to keep a measure,
Especially in love to incertainty of treasure.

Another Interlude, *The Four Elements*, contains an elaborate argument to prove the roundness of the world and several discussions of natural phenomena, introduces the Scholastic 'Natura Naturata', and has frequent allusions to cosmography. In short the early Tudor drama was a source of popular education as well as of entertainment.

Third, there were the homiletic works, of which many were published and eagerly read in those days of religious controversy. These were regular storehouses of Classical information, most of which was adequately explained in the text or in notes. A good example is Tyndale's translation of the *Echiridion Militis Christiani* of Erasmus, first printed in 1533, and marginally 'glossed' by the translator with long elucidations. It contains a number of references to Plato's works, including the famous similitude of the cave; and accounts of Phocion, Apelles, Crates, Alcibiades, Hesiod, and Catullus, together with the stories of such mythical beings as Prometheus, Pandora, Proteus, Ajax, Achilles, Aeneas, Ixion, Tantalus, Hercules and the Hydra, Ulysses and the Sirens, and a number of others.

Armed with these facts and others like them, Robertson found it an easy task to demonstrate that the Classical information contained in the Shakespearean plays was no more than their author could readily have acquired without being a profound Classical scholar or possessing any first-hand acquaintance with Classical writers. Moreover he was able to show that this information was the common knowledge of the reading public, an exceedingly important piece of evidence against the Classical scholar claim. For some reason it never seems to dawn upon the theorists that if Shakespeare, whoever he might be, had insisted on filling his plays with allusions and references which his audiences could not understand, he would soon have ceased to have any audiences, as Ben Jonson, who really was a great Classical scholar and sometimes allowed his scholarship to overflow into his plays, discovered on more than one occasion.

The Baconian assertion concerning the 'marvellous accuracy, the real substantial learning of the three Roman plays'[1] Robertson rebuts by demonstrating that the claim is simply not true. Shakespeare's main source of information for these plays was an English translation by North of a French translation by Amyot of Plutarch's *Lives*. North falls into error on several occasions through following or misunderstanding Amyot, and on each occasion Shakespeare repeats North's errors, besides making several more through his own ignorance. The blunder of making Lartius speak of Cato (Cor., I, iv, 59) as a contemporary or a predecessor, when he was not born until nearly three centuries after the period represented in the play, is an example of the latter; while the blunder about 'the napless vesture of humility' (Cor., II, i, 224) results from his following North, who took Amyot's 'robbe simple' to mean a 'poor gown'.[2] Moreover, in *Julius Caesar* (II, i) Shakespeare is guilty of the anachronism of making the clocks of Rome strike the hour, and in the same play (I, i) he erroneously assumes that it was the custom in ancient Rome for the various trades to have a special dress, as it was in England in his own day. It is obvious

---

[1] Lord Penzance, *Biography of Shakespeare*, p. 61.

[2] The inaccuracies in the proper names, *Decius* Brutus and *Caius* Ligarius, also result from Shakespeare's following North.

178

then, both from his own mistakes and his repetition of North's, that Shakespeare's knowledge of the subject was neither accurate nor substantial.

To this specific criticism there are two points of considerable importance to be added. Stated very briefly, they are as follows:

(1) The Shakespearean plays were by no means the only works to contain this Classical lore. Many contemporary writers, dramatists and others, made equal or even greater use of it. A good example is John Taylor, known as the Water Poet. He was of humble parentage and little education. In his youth he was apprenticed to a Thames waterman. Later he was pressed for the Navy, and made several voyages, but ultimately returned to his old trade of plying for hire on the Thames. On his own confession his attempt to learn Latin had proved a failure, yet his works actually contain more Classical allusions and references than do those of Shakespeare. Moreover Taylor himself tells us that he had read *in English* Ovid, Homer, Plutarch, Marcus Aurelius, Seneca, Suetonius, and Cornelius Agrippa, as well as Fairfax's 'Tasso', Du Bartas, Montaigne, Guevara, Josephus, Chaucer, Sidney, Spenser, Daniel, Nashe, Purchas, Speed, Camden, Fox, and Holinshed. What a waterman could do in this way an actor could do also, and if a waterman could obtain the necessary books so could an actor.

(2) Ben Jonson who, as already remarked, was himself a great Classical scholar, wrote a commendatory poem for the First Folio of the Shakespearean plays when it was published in 1623. In this he definitely stated that their author had 'small Latin and less Greek'. Clearly he, a contemporary, did not consider that the plays showed any evidence of original Classical scholarship or he would not have risked his own reputation by committing himself to such an opinion. And he was supported in this view at a later date by Milton, another great Classical scholar, as his lines in *L'Allegro* on Jonson and Shakespeare make perfectly plain.

We can therefore, in the light of what has emerged from this discussion, reject as completely untenable the theorists' argument from Classical scholarship. It is no doubt true that Shakespeare, whoever he was, knew a great deal more about

Classical lore than is known by the average person today, but that is only because in Renaissance times the general interest in the subject was so great. There is no evidence in the plays to suggest that he knew any more than any other moderately well-educated man of his period, and consequently nothing to rule out the authorship of the Stratford actor.

Another claim of the theorists is that the plays show such a profound political insight and such accurate knowledge of State affairs that they could only have been written by a man possessing, as Titherley, who treats this matter most fully, puts it,[1] 'a statesman's intimacy with the intricate problems of government'.

When we are confronted with an assertion of this kind we can only gasp in astonishment, and plaintively ask where examples of this political insight and statesman's intimacy with the problems of government are to be found. It is true, as a number of authorities have pointed out, that Shakespeare was a careful student of the history of his native land. He had certainly read all the *Chronicles*, of which there was no lack, as well as the Homilitic literature setting forth the position of the monarchy and the duty of subjects in the Tudor scheme of things. But all these sources of information were equally available to and freely used by every contemporary historical dramatist, as Professor Ribner has clearly demonstrated in *The English History Play in the Age of Shakespeare*, where he lists over seventy such plays. There is nothing in Shakespeare's works to suggest that he derived his knowledge in any way different from that of his fellows; certainly not that they were penned by a man who had had practical experience in administrating the affairs of state.

When Titherley attempts, as he does, to find examples in support of his claims he can, of course, find none of a specific nature, and so is driven to seek refuge in generalities. He compiles a list of five general principles which he asserts are maintained and exemplified in the plays. His list is as follows:

(1) That pusillanimity leads to disaster no less than injustice.
(2) That weak rule is as dangerous as mob rule.

[1] *Shakespeare's Identity*, p. 61.

(3) That murder of Princes and foreign intervention in England, invited by rebellious subjects, is never justifiable.

(4) That the mob is fickle.

(5) That tyranny even in lawful authority is wrong.

Now I am perfectly willing to concede that all these principles are, as Titherley claims, maintained and exemplified in the Shakespearean plays; I could even add a few more of a similar nature to his list. What I deny is that such principles were the exclusive property of statesmen and those concerned with the intricate problems of government. They were the common-places of many others besides, and especially of that class of bourgeois merchants and traders to which the Stratford actor belonged. What Titherley overlooks is the history of the times. Shakespeare's generation and its immediate predecessors had lived through a period when the breach of these very principles had brought disaster or the threat of disaster on the land. There had been civil strife when Warwick had attempted to put Lady Jane Grey on the throne, to go back no further than the beginning of the previous reign; there had been Mary's persecution of Protestants, combined with her pusillanimity and vacillation as a ruler: there had been the numerous Catholic plots against Elizabeth, relying on foreign aid and culminating in the danger from Mary Queen of Scots; there had been the tyranny of Spain in the Netherlands, and the threat of it in this country; the mob supported Wyatt and Essex in their subversive acts, and had more than once created a disturbance over foreign refugees. The merchants and traders were as familiar with all these things as we are with the consequences of two World Wars and the threat of the hydrogen bomb. They knew the principles well enough and what the breach of them would mean to their new-found prosperity, and they rallied around the strong government of their lawful Queen and her Ministers as the one protection against such disasters.

There is therefore nothing surprising in the strong enforcement of these principles in the plays whoever their author might be. It certainly did not require a practising statesman to express what was the common opinion of the vast majority of Englishmen at the time. What was remarkable was, not the principles themselves, but the language in which they were clothed and the imagery by which they were reinforced. This is, however, the proper work of a poet, not of a politician, and if the Stratford actor were a poet there is nothing in this matter to exclude him from the authorship.

A third claim, advanced by all the theorists, is that the Shakespearean plays show a knowledge of European geography that could only have been gained by foreign travel. The point of this, of course, is that Bacon, Oxford, and Derby are all known to have travelled on the Continent, and according to Hoffman's theory Marlowe fled to Italy to escape the clutches of the Star Chamber, while there is no evidence that the Stratford actor ever left England. This, they contend, should rule him out as author.

The main answer to such a claim is a flat contradiction. In any general sense it is completely untrue. The Shakespearean plays show no close knowledge of European or any other geography, and any references to it that they contain are of the vaguest. The author in fact often treats the subject with complete disdain. His forest of Arden in A.Y.L.I., for instance, with its Warwickshire scenery, is dumped down in France, and then tropical lions and snakes are introduced into it to revel among the sheep of his very English peasants. This is typical of his method. Whatever he needed for his purpose he cheerfully introduced into his setting, regardless of probability or even possibility. Titherley, to do him justice, is aware of this, and remarks[1] that 'Shakespeare's geography, being ubiquitous in its range, is evidentially inconclusive'. He does, however, maintain that there are some minor details that suggest local knowledge, and when any of the theorists attempt to support their general statement with evidence it is always on such minor details that they have to rely. We must therefore turn our attention to these.

We will take as an example one on which Titherley lays great emphasis. It comes from *Love's Labour's Lost* (Act I, sc. i), and, according to Titherley, reveals a personal knowledge of the grounds of the Palace of Henri IV, King of Navarre, at Nerac. In the letter the fantastic Armado writes to the King, reporting the illicit assignation between Costard and Jaquenetta that took place in 'thy curious knotted garden', he states that he himself

---

[1] *Shakespeare's Identity*, p. 63.

witnessed the obscene incident while walking in the place 'ycleped thy park', which place lay 'north-north-east and east from the western corner' of the garden. This, Titherley points out, is the correct orientation, for a line drawn from the west corner of Henri's knot-garden in a north-easterly direction would actually cross the park.[1]

One might dismiss this particular example at once as an accident rather below the level of a coincidence. A knot-garden, that is a garden composed of rectangular flower-beds, and a park were common features of almost every great house in Elizabethan England. The compass bearing, though it may happen to fit Henri's park too, is virtually a confirmation of the native origin of the description, for in England it was the general custom to have trees to the north-east of the garden to protect the flowers from the most destructive of winds.[2] An author therefore with no inkling whatever of what the Palace grounds at Nerac were like, and drawing merely on what he had seen of the homes of the nobility in England, could well have written the three simple phrases that occur in Armado's letter. And this example is by far the most telling that any of the theorists have been able to advance in support of their views; most of the others are the merest trivialities.[3]

I have, however, no wish to settle this issue merely by pointing out the inadequacy of the theorists' arguments. There are at

[1] It is a little strange that this particular example should be quoted by a Derbyite, for there is no evidence that Derby ever was at Nerac. There is documentary evidence for his travels abroad, and on his journey to Spain he must have passed fairly close to Nerac, but the very fact that it is not mentioned is surely evidence against his having gone there. One would imagine that a visit to the famous Court of the King of Navarre, to which so many young Englishmen were flocking at that time, would be worthy of record if it had taken place, especially when other details of far less importance were duly set down.

[2] R. E. Prothero, Article on 'Agriculture and Gardening' in *Shakespeare's England*, Vol. I, p. 371.

[3] For instance, that the author must have known that Milan was connected with the port of Ticino by the Naviglio Grande Canal, since in *The Tempest* he makes Prospero tell Miranda that the conspirators 'bore us three leagues to sea', and that giving Bohemia a sea-coast, as he does in *The Winter's Tale*, and was laughed at by Ben Jonson for his pains, would have been quite correct three centuries earlier.

least three ways in which the Stratford actor could have acquired sufficient knowledge of Europe to introduce a great deal more local colour than the few vague suggestions of it that actually occur in the plays.

First, while it is true that there is no evidence that Shakspere ever travelled abroad, it is by no means impossible that he did so. Between his marriage in 1582 and when we next pick up his trail in 1594 there is a gap of nearly twelve years, during which we do not know how he spent his time. That he must have been associated with the players for most of it is certain, for the 1594 reference is the document naming him along with Kemp and Burbage as a payee for performances given by the Lord Chamberlain's Company before the Queen (see p. 36). He must therefore have been at least the third most important member of the company, and could only have gained such a position by considerable service in and to the theatre. Now there is ample documentary evidence[1] that several companies of English actors made extended tours on the Continent during this very period, playing at least in Germany, France, the Netherlands, and Denmark, where they were much admired and very popular. It is far from improbable that Shakspere was a member of one of these companies, and if so he would have had the opportunity of gaining some knowledge of Europe for himself.

Still, while there is nothing against this view, as I have shown that there is against Derby's alleged visit to Nerac (see p. 183, ftn.), it is, like the latter, only an assumption, and I am not prepared to base anything on an assumption, whatever the theorists may choose to do. I prefer to claim that Shakspere would be bound to meet the returned actors – Kempe, who had been in Denmark, was a fellow member of the Lord Chamberlain's Company – hear their experiences at first hand, and, if there should be any particular information he wanted, that he would ask one of them or some other traveller, for there were many at this time, to supply it.[2] After all that is the kind of

---

[1] See 'Shakespeare as a Man of the Theatre', by J. Isaccs, in *Shakespeare Criticism*, ed. Anne Ridler, pp. 295–297.

[2] As we shall see in Chapter XVII (p. 296) there was one period in Shakspere's career when he was in a particularly favourable position for picking up information about the Continent.

thing we have all done at one time or another. It is only a Durning-Lawrence who would deny that Shakspere had a tongue in his head or sufficient wit to wag it when occasion required.

Again the Shakespearean plays rarely, if ever, had original plots. Their author always made extensive use of sources, and his sources for plays with a foreign setting all came ultimately from the Continent. Moreover, the principal influence on English drama throughout the greater part of the Tudor period was Italian literature. What therefore appears to be local colour in the plays may well be derived from some foreign source either as quotation or reminiscence. There is little enough in any case, and I venture to think that I have shown that ample opportunity existed for the Stratford actor to have acquired it all and much more also.

To this may be added the fact that some of Marlowe's plays show a considerable knowledge of the geography of Northern Africa, including that of Negro states.[1] Yet not even Hoffman has desired to suggest that Marlowe must have made a grand tour of the Dark Continent. If therefore Marlowe is able to convey the impression of familiarity with Africa without having been there, it does not seem impossible for Shakspere, in the few cases where such appears in the plays, to achieve the same result for the much better known Continent of Europe.

These three items – knowledge of Classical authors, of Politics, and of European Geography and Local Colour, together with a knowledge of the Law already dealt with in a former chapter (see pp. 48–54) – constitute the main evidence for the learning alleged to be displayed in the Shakespearean plays. Certain other matters, such as beliefs about magic, are mentioned by some of the theorists, but these are minor details, and I have no space to deal with them here. I can only say that they refer to things which were common knowledge at the time. The theorists seem to imagine that if a topic of the past is known only to a few specialists today, it was necessarily known only to a similar minority in its own day, which of course is absurd. The time may well come when football pools, rock 'n' roll, the Teddy Boys, and other contemporary

[1] J. A. Symonds, 'Introduction' to his edition of *Marlowe's Works*.

185

commonplaces will be known only to a few specialists in twentieth-century Social History.

I cannot conclude this section better than by quoting a few sentences on this very matter from E. M. W. Tillyard's *The Elizabethan World Picture*, a book some of the theorists might read with advantage. He writes: 'The old truth that the greatest things in literature are the most commonplace is quite borne out. I hope that this book has shown to some people how much more commonplace than they thought is the substance of some of the writing that appears (and of course in a sense is) most novel and most characteristic of its author. . . . Divested of their literary form they (the author's ideas) are the common property of every third-rate mind of the age.'

There remains one other matter, rather different in its nature, to be considered. It is alleged, not only by the theorists, but by some Stratfordians as well, that Shakespeare's vocabulary is enormous, far greater than that of any other author. To bring the matter down to a form where comparisons can be made, it is asserted that while Milton makes use of about 7000 words, Shakespeare makes use of more than double or even treble that number, not counting inflections. The figures given by those responsible for the computations are as follows: Morgan 15,000, Craik 21,000, and Titherley 24,000.

All the theorists agree that this eliminates the Stratford actor; words, they argue, are acquired knowledge, and whether he could write better poetry or not, he could not possibly have a larger vocabulary than every single one of the University-trained writers. The Oxford groupists go even further, and hail this situation as conclusive evidence for the truth of their case. No one man, they claim, could possess such an immense vocabulary; but a group of writers might conceivably do so. And it must be acknowledged that, taken at their face value, both these arguments seem very plausible. Before, however, we concede the point, it would be wise to examine the matter a little more closely to determine whether they can be taken at their face value.

Any reader must be struck at once by the wide discrepancy between the results of the various computations. Between the lowest, that of Morgan, and the highest, that of Titherley, there is a difference of 9000 words; that is, 2000 words more than the whole of Milton's vocabulary; while the difference between Morgan's and Craik's is 6000, and the difference between Craik's and Titherley's is 3000. When such diverse results are reached by the 'experts' it is obvious that we cannot place complete faith in their methods. Their astronomical figures certainly suggest gross exaggeration, and the most we can safely accept is that Shakespeare made use of an exceedingly large vocabulary, larger than that of any other writer whose vocabulary has been computed.

This, however, raises another question. What do we really mean when we talk about a man's vocabulary? Having studied and lectured on Shakespeare's plays for a great many years I now know the meaning of almost every word he uses, and it is only on rare occasions that I have to resort to a glossary. I must therefore have a larger vocabulary than Shakespeare, for I not only have his 15,000, 21,000, 24,000, or whatever the number of words he uses really is, but a host of words in addition that have been coined since his day. Yet in spite of this I should be very much surprised to find that I have used more than 4000 or 5000 words in writing this book, or that I ever use more when speaking or writing, for the simple reason that I can call to mind when I need them only a small percentage of the words I actually know. The truth is that everyone of us has two vocabularies, as follows:

(1) A larger vocabulary consisting of all the words of which we know the meaning when we see them written or hear them pronounced. This depends entirely on acquired knowledge.

(2) A smaller vocabulary consisting of the proportion of the total number of words we know that we can call to mind at will when required to express some idea. This depends on some innate ability associated with memory.

When once the implication of this is grasped it will be realized that a man who appears to have a larger vocabulary than another may in fact have less knowledge of words, only a better memory for them; that is, Shakespeare may well have used considerably more words in his writings than Milton, while actually knowing fewer. No one will deny that the author of the Shakespearean plays was a supreme poetic genius, and an

187

abnormally good memory for words is a highly probable con-
comitant of supreme poetic genius.

Moreover, there is another point to be considered. Shakespeare's unusual words are not broadcast evenly throughout his
plays. His normal style consists in his perfect arrangement of
familiar terms, the ordinary speech of ordinary people used in
an extraordinary fashion; and this is as true of the great
soliloquies in the tragedies as in the lyric parts of the early plays
and of the comedies. His unusual words are limited to a few
plays, such as *Troilus and Cressida* and often to particular portions of these. Sometimes the reason for this is obvious, as for
the pedantic personages in *Love's Labour's Lost*, and one is
tempted to ask if he found the words in some source or deliberately collected them for his purpose.[1] At least it is clear that
they were not habitual with him, and if the few plays which
contain them were cut out of his repertoire, his vocabulary,
though still profuse, would not be phenomenal.

In the face of such facts as we have brought to light by our
analysis, the theorists' case, like Macbeth's witches, vanishes
into thin air. Once again they have failed to establish any insuperable barrier to the Stratford actor's authorship of the
plays.

---

[1] This can be taken as virtually proved. In his *Shakespeare's Sources*, Professor Muir shows over and over again how in the plays the author makes
use of a number of words taken direct from his sources, and that in some
cases it is the only occasion in his whole literary output that he makes use of
these particular words. (See, among many examples, pp. 161 f.)

CHAPTER IX

Metamorphoses of the Sonnets

The metamorphoses undergone by Ovid's heroes and heroines sink into insignificance beside those suffered by the Shakespearean sonnets at the hands of the various theorists. Often one and the same sonnet is given three or four different interpretations, all equally good, or equally bad, to make it refer to the diverse circumstances required by the different interpreters; a particular phrase is snatched from another and twisted into two or more completely incompatible meanings to bolster up two or more completely incompatible views; and the whole sequence is rearranged in several various ways in a desperate effort to make it tell the life-story of the several various candidates for the authorship. No other portion of English literature has ever been subjected to such a mad whirl of kaleidoscopic changes as these 154 little poems known as the sonnets of Shakespeare.

All this is of great importance for our purpose, for it illustrates and proves up to the hilt what I have iterated again and again in these pages – that if you take a sufficient amount of literary material, especially poetic material, you can extract from it references which, without any difficulty, can be made to apply to almost any desired person or event and to support any theory you may wish it to support. Read in isolation some of these interpretations may appear quite convincing; but the moment they are brought into touch and compared with one another the bubble bursts, and they stand revealed for the worthless fancies they really are.

In this chapter we shall bring together the various interpretations the theorists have advanced and compare them, allowing the result largely to speak for itself. Before doing so, however, it will perhaps be convenient for the reader if I give a brief sketch of what is known and what is conjectured about the sonnets as a whole.

The sequence, as already stated, consists of 154 little poems, not all of them true sonnets in form. The exact period when they were written is uncertain, the most generally accepted view being between the years 1592 and 1598, the latter the date of the publication of Meres' *Palladis Tamia* in which there is a reference to 'Shakespeare's sugared sonnets'. Half-a-dozen of them were printed in 1599 in *The Passionate Pilgrim*, but no complete version of them appeared until 1609, when a Quarto was published by Thomas Thorpe.

They fall naturally into two main groups. In the first, consisting of Nos. 1 to 126, most of the sonnets are addressed to a young man of almost feminine beauty, who would appear to be the friend and patron of the author, and many of them are couched in extravagantly complimentary terms. This group is subdivided as follows:

1–17. The author urges the young man to marry, and reproduce his personal beauty in a child.

40–42. These suggest that the young man has stolen the author's mistress. The author, however, bears him no grudge, and blames the woman for what has happened.

78–86. The author complains that a rival poet has supplanted him in the favour of his patron.

The intervening numbers are on miscellaneous topics, and may not all be addressed to the young man.

The second group, Nos. 127 to 152, is addressed to a dark-haired beauty, who is apparently the false mistress. Many of the sonnets in this group protest the author's love for her before the betrayal, but a number are of a 'vituperative nature', and clearly follow that betrayal.

Nos. 153 and 154 are two versions of a Greek epigram on Cupid, and are only doubtfully Shakespearean.

The sequence is preceded by a somewhat cryptic 'Dedication', which reads as follows:

To the Onlie Begetter of These Insving Sonnets Mr. W. H. All Happinesse and that Eternitie Promised by Ovr Ever-Living Poet Wisheth the Well-Wishing Adventurer in Setting Forth. T. T.

The main problem raised by this concerns the identity of the person to whom the work is dedicated, the person represented by the symbol 'Mr. W. H.' Originally it was assumed to be the Earl of Southampton, largely because V. & A. and R. of L. had been dedicated to him, and he was generally believed to be Shakespeare's patron. According to this view the word 'begetter' meant 'inspirer', and he was taken to be the addressee of most of the first 126 sonnets. Owing to the very personal nature of these it was of course impossible to name him recognizably; so his initials were reversed – his name was Henry Wriothesley – and his title dropped.

It is not impossible that this represents the truth of the matter, and there are still scholars who accept it as such. There is, however, one very strong objection to it, namely why the Dedication is signed with the initials 'T. T.', those of Thomas Thorpe, the publisher, and not with those of William Shakespeare, the ostensible author.

This has led a number of critics to come to quite a different conclusion. They take the word 'begetter' to mean simply 'getter', and claim that the sentence is not properly a Dedication at all, but merely the grateful publisher's way of saying 'thank you' to the person who obtained the copy of the sonnets for him. The person they identify as 'Mr. W. H.' is William Hall, himself a printer, and one who certainly had associations with Eld, the man who printed the Sonnet Quarto for Thorpe. It has recently been discovered that this William Hall got married just about the time the sonnets were published, and might therefore fittingly be made the recipient of good wishes on setting forth on an adventure.

This again is quite a possible view, and is in fact the most generally accepted at the present time, though there are several others which also have their adherents. They do not, however, concern us. Our business is with the theorists and their attitude to the question.

Strangely enough most of them have evinced little interest in the Dedication, and seem quite ready to accept one or other of the general views. The Baconians and Oxfordians, as far as I can gather from their writings, prefer the Southampton theory, while the Derbyite, Titherley, declares uncompromisingly for the William Hall view.

It is Calvin Hoffman, the supporter of Marlowe's claims, who introduces some novelty into the situation and links it up with his main theory.[1] He has no doubt that 'Mr. W. H.' stands for Sir Thomas Walsingham. His formula for demonstrating this is as follows:

$$Walsingham = Walsing\text{-}ham = W\text{-}h = W. H.$$

The substitution of 'Mr.' for 'Sir' he explains as necessary for secrecy, adding rather naïvely, apparently in order to eliminate Southampton, that it would be impossible to reduce an Earl to plain Mr., but it might be done in the case of a mere knight. An ordinary person would have supposed, if it were a matter of disguise, the greater the reduction of rank the better the disguise. There is, however, a much stronger argument than this to demolish Hoffman's theory. Why was secrecy necessary in Walsingham's case? Even if Marlowe were still alive and had really written the sonnets, no one beyond the few people in the secret could have had the faintest idea of this; and there is not the slightest reason why William Shakespeare, the ostensible author, or Thomas Thorpe, the publisher, should not quite openly dedicate a batch of poems to that great patron of the arts, Sir Thomas Walsingham. Nor would the personal reason operate in this case as it does in Southampton's. No one could imagine that Walsingham was the addressee of the first 126 sonnets, for he was not a young man of almost feminine beauty, and, since he was already married, Sonnets 1 to 17 would have been wasted on him. This argument therefore, like so many of Hoffman's, falls to pieces the moment it is subjected to criticism.

We may now turn to some individual sonnets, and examine the interpretations the various theorists put upon them, undoubtedly the most entertaining and instructive part of our analysis. To start with we will take Sonnets 50 and 51. The former begins:

> How heavy do I journey on the way,

and the latter:

> Thus can my love excuse the slow offence
> Of my dull bearer when from thee I speed.

[1] *The Man Who Was Shakespeare*, p. 139.

Both Titherley[1] and Hoffman[2] annex these. Titherley claims that they were written by Derby when he was compelled on one occasion to be parted from his wife, to whom he was devoted, for some months; and Hoffman claims that they were written by Marlowe to describe his feelings as he rode (at least according to the Hoffman theory) to Dover on his way to exile, leaving his dear friend, Sir Thomas Walsingham, behind. Now it is true that the sonnets in question do refer to a parting, but in such general terms as to fit the circumstances of any two persons with a bond of affection between them, no matter who or where. They can be claimed for both Derby and Marlowe just because they could be claimed equally well for anyone setting out on a journey and leaving a loved one behind. They could even be claimed for Shakspere the actor, parting from wife or daughter when leaving Stratford for another theatrical season in London; indeed the wife and daughter are non-essentials; a nostalgic feeling for his home-town personified would be quite adequate. Of course I am not claiming that such was the actual occasion of the two sonnets; I merely suggest it to demonstrate their inadequacy as evidence for anything.

Sonnet 76 provides material for both Hoffman and the Oxfordians. The second quatrain of this sonnet runs as follows:

> Why write I still all one, ever the same,
> And keep invention in a noted weed
> That every word doth almost tell my name,
> Showing their birth, and where they did proceed.

Hoffman[3] interprets the second of these lines as, 'And keep on writing in a famous disguise', and claims that Marlowe is bewailing the fact that he is obliged to write under an assumed name, but boasts that the perfection of the style almost betrays the true author.

In reply to this it is only necessary to point out that the second line of the quoted quatrain simply cannot support the interpretation that Hoffman attempts to put on it. Its meaning in the context is plain enough. It is just that the poet clothes his ideas in well-known phrases; that is, in phrases which repeated use has made all too familiar.

[1] *Shakespeare's Identity*, Appendix III.
[2] *The Man Who Was Shakespeare*, pp. 131 f.   [3] Ibid., pp. 135 f.

The Oxfordians press their claim in a manner that almost rivals the Baconian cryptologists for sheer fantasy. They rewrite the four material lines in the following rather unusual form:[1]

Why write I still all one, E VER the same,
And keep invention in a notED-WEED
That E VER Y-WORD doth almost tell my name,
Showing their birth, and where they did proceed.

This, they explain, is Oxford's signature, thus appended to the whole sequence. His name was Edward (de) Vere; therefore the E VER in 'ever' and 'every' is obviously intended for the surname with the initial letter of the Christian name, while ED-WEED and Y-WORD from 'noted weed' and 'every word', standing, of course for 'Edward', expand the initial into the full name.

This somewhat startling interpretation, however, involves the Oxfordians in two difficulties. The first, which they do not seem to have noticed since none of them makes any comment upon it, is that it is an important part of their theory that Oxford desired to preserve the secret of his authorship permanently, and actually expressed a wish to this effect in the sonnets.[2] It therefore seems strange that he himself should supply a clue to his identity in those very sonnets. This is another example of the theorists' persistent habit of snatching at anything that seems to offer a chance of making a point, completely oblivious to its incompatibility with the rest of their argument.

The second difficulty is that in Sonnets 135 and 136 the author makes play throughout with the name 'Will', explicitly stated – not merely hinted at by assonance in other words – and further emphasized by being printed in italics. Now this quite obviously could only have any point for the addressee of the sonnets in question if it were in fact the author's name;[3] otherwise it is meaningless. Yet this the Oxfordians strenuously deny, as indeed they must. They argue that Oxford, realizing that he has given his identity away in previous sonnets, is here

---

[1] M. Douglas, *Lord Oxford and the Shakespeare Group*, p. 132.

[2] M. Douglas, ibid., p. 155.

[3] This of course excludes all claimants except William Shakspere, the actor, and William Stanley, the Earl of Derby.

merely acknowledging the fact.[1] How the wording of either of the 'Will' sonnets can be made to bear such a meaning is exceedingly difficult to see, and the Oxfordians discreetly refrain from attempting to explain.

These details, however, are only of secondary importance as a means of refuting the theorists' claims. Their main refutation lies in Sonnet 76 itself. One has only to read the whole of it through to realize that it is perfectly straightforward and contains no hidden meaning whatever. It is in fact typical Elizabethan complimentary verse. The poet begins by asking the rhetorical question why his ideas and the language in which they are clothed have developed a monotonous sameness, so that the moment any readers see a new poem of his they know exactly what it will be like. He then proceeds to answer his own question by saying it is because he can write only of one thing – the beautiful addressee, and praise his, or her, charms. That is all; there is not the faintest hint of the extravagant and, of course, mutually incompatible meanings that Hoffman on the one hand and the Oxfordians on the other attempt to extract from it.

Sonnet 37 has received attention from the Oxfordians and the Derbyites, both of whom profess to find in it support for their respective theories. It contains the line:

So I made lame by Fortune's dearest spite.

In its context the phrase certainly seems to be a figurative one, but it is not impossible to take it literally. The Oxfordians unhesitatingly adopt the second course, and claim it as evidence for Oxford's authorship on the grounds that he once received a severe wound in a duel with Sir Thomas Knyvet, a kinsman of his mistress, Ann Vavasour.[2] In 'confirmation' of this they quote another line, one from Sonnet 74:

The coward conquest of a wretch's knife.

That all this is simply gratuitous assumption is obvious. Even if we concede that the lameness mentioned in Sonnet 37 was an actual physical disability rather than a spiritual one, there is no suggestion that it was the result of a duel; while the

[1] M. Douglas, *Lord Oxford and the Shakespeare Group*, p. 137.
[2] M. Douglas, ibid., p. 138.

quotation from Sonnet 74 could not possibly indicate a duel, which was a very punctilious affair. Moreover there were so many duels fought in the Tudor period, when all gentlemen wore swords and quarrelled easily, that participation in one can hardly be accepted as evidence for the authorship of a sonnet sequence.

Titherley[1] uses the same two quotations from the same two sonnets in the interests of Derby's claim. In this instance his reasoning is inferior to that of his rivals. His argument, extracted from the persuasive language in which it is couched, amounts simply to this. He first deduces from the sonnets that Derby was severely wounded in some street brawl, an incident for which there is no confirmatory evidence, and then uses this brawl as evidence that Derby wrote the sonnets because it is mentioned in them. That is, he first makes A prove B, and then B prove A, which is a logical fallacy if ever there were one.

Sonnet 125 supplies ammunition for no less than three groups of theorists, the Oxfordians and Derbyites again, with the addition of Hoffman on behalf of Marlowe. The two former pitch upon the first line, which runs as follows:

Were it aught to me I bore the canopy.

Both groups take the statement in a literal sense, and say that it refers to the carrying of a canopy over the head of the Queen when she took part in a State procession. The Oxfordians claim[2] that it is thus evidence in favour of their candidate, as he actually performed this office at the Armada celebrations. The Derbyites make exactly the same claim for their Earl,[3] who, as a Knight of the Garter, was also entitled to carry the canopy, and did so on the occasion of the Royal visit to Elvetham in 1591.

It must be conceded that if the line in question is intended literally, then it does make a point in favour of an aristocratic author, even if only a very doubtful point; but one has only to read the rest of the sonnet to realize that the line cannot be intended literally. The third line, for instance, is:

Or laid great bases for eternity.

[1] *Shakespeare's Identity*, Appendix III.
[2] M. Douglas, *Lord Oxford and the Shakespeare Group*, pp. 135 f.
[3] Titherley, ibid., Appendix III.

Could such a statement as this possibly be literal? And if it could not, then neither can the first line, which is intimately connected with it both in sense and grammatically. No competent writer would mix up the literal and the figurative in this way.[1] Now as a matter of fact Shakespeare sometimes uses the word 'canopy' for 'sky' or 'firmament'. He does so in *Coriolanus* (IV, ii) and in *Hamlet* (II, ii), and it is clear that he is doing the same here. If 'canopy' is given this meaning in line 1 of the sonnet, then that line and line 3 fit together perfectly, as they are intended to do. The sense of the two together is, 'Does it mean anything to me if I have held up the heavens or built foundations for eternity?' The poet is asking what – in the given circumstances in which the sonnet was written – did it matter to him if he had performed the greatest of deeds. This is a sentiment that any poet, noble or commoner, might well express.[2]

Of course canopies are of no use to Hoffman, and he ignores this line. He concentrates all his attention on the two words 'suborn'd informer' in the penultimate line of the sonnet. This, he claims, quite oblivious to its context, is a reference to Richard Baines, the agent who sent the report on Marlowe to the Privy Council (see p. 126), and is therefore evidence for Marlowe's authorship. Comment on such a far-fetched interpretation would be superfluous.

Sonnet 81, the next to be considered, is eagerly appropriated

[1] An equivalent to what Titherley and the Oxfordians ask us to accept would be a line such as, 'I will tear down the stars from heaven to adorn your hair, and buy you a half-crown box of chocolate creams.' No poet, unless he were deliberately writing burlesque, would pen such an absurd mixture.

[2] It may be added that the name 'canopy' was also sometimes applied to the wooden roof that covered the rear portion of the stage in the Tudor theatre, stretching from the back wall to two pillars which supported its front. This, if I may make a suggestion, offers the orthodox Stratfordians an opportunity to defend the actor's authorship along precisely the same lines as those adopted by the theorists in defence of their candidates' claims. The Stratfordians may assume that one of the pillars broke and the 'canopy' would have collapsed if Shakspere had not sprung forward and supported it until it could be shored up. They may go further and assume that this incident took place at the Fortune Theatre and that Shakspere injured his leg in the effort, thus acquiring inspiration for the line 'So I made lame by Fortune's dearest spite' in Sonnet 37. It is at least as convincing as Oxford's duel and Derby's street brawl.

197

by all the theorists. As in this case it is the whole poem, not a single phrase or line, that is involved, the whole must be quoted. It reads as follows:

> Or shall I live your epitaph to make,
> Or you survive when I in earth am rotten,
> From hence your memory death cannot take,
> Although in me each part will be forgotten.
> Your name from hence immortal life shall have,
> Though I, once gone, to all the world must die;
> The earth can yield me but a common grave,
> When you entombed in men's eyes shall lie.
> Your monument shall be my gentle verse,
> Which eyes not yet created shall o'er-read;
> And tongues to be your being shall rehearse,
> When all the breathers of this world are dead;
> You still shall live – such virtue hath my pen –
> Where breath most breathes, even in the mouths of men.

Now it is apparent that this, with a little ingenuity, might be twisted into a lament by a poet that the immortal verse he has written will make another famous, while he himself must always remain unknown. It is this strained interpretation that the theorists, Baconians, Oxfordians, Derbyites, and Hoffman in the interests of Marlowe, alike seize upon, all claiming that it represents their particular candidate bemoaning the fact that he must write immortal poetry for Shakspere to reap the credit. Durning-Lawrence[1] paints quite a pathetic picture of Bacon in this unfortunate situation, which reads a little oddly since it follows his chapters on the cryptograms and all the other clues he alleges Bacon left so that posterity should be in no doubt about the identity of the true author.

When, however, we turn from this free-for-all scramble, and examine Sonnet 81 with a mind unclouded by any preconceived theory, we find that it is capable of another and a much more natural and plausible interpretation. In it the poet declares that, no matter when he or the addressee may chance to die, and though he, the author, may be completely forgotten, the memory of the addressee will live on in the poem, which will

---

[1] *Bacon is Shakespeare*, pp. 70 f.

endure for ever. That this is the true interpretation receives some confirmation from the following lines in Sonnet 18:

> But thy eternal summers shall not fade,
> Nor lose possession of the fair thou ow'st;
> Nor shall Death brag thou wand'rest in his shade,
> When in eternal lines to time thou grow'st;
>> So long as men can breathe, or eyes can see
>> So long lives this, and this gives life to thee.

where the same idea is expressed, and no alternative interpretation is possible.

This does not exhaust the parlour tricks played by the theorists with individual sonnets, but reasons of space preclude our examination of further specimens. Nor are any further specimens necessary. Those we have examined are sufficient to show the utter worthlessness of the whole proceeding. Apart from the blunders and misrepresentations of which it is full, it is obvious that when the same references can be made to prove the authorship of two or more candidates, in actual fact they can prove the authorship of none.

The Baconians and the Derbyites, however, have another line of approach. They say that the sonnets as Thorpe published them are not in their correct chronological order, and that properly arranged they are found to tell the life story of Bacon or Derby as the case may be.

Now, while it is not by any means a necessary conclusion that the sonnets, as they have come down to us, are wrongly arranged, this is of course a possibility. We know nothing about the circumstances of their publication, nor whether the author, whoever he might be, personally saw them through the press. There may be a case for a re-examination of them to discover if there is a more natural arrangement than the present one. Some even among the orthodox Stratfordians hold that such a case does exist. But if the attempt is made, it must be strictly in accordance with the literary evidence of the sonnets themselves, and certainly not carried out by persons whose minds are full of preconceived ideas and who are bent on making changes solely with the object of proving their own point of view. That this is what the theorists do is evidenced by the fact that their rearrangements differ completely from one another.

The story the Baconians extract can be read in B. G. Theobald's *Shakespeare's Sonnets Unmasked* and Alfred Dodd's *The Personal Poems of Francis Bacon*. It is the usual type of 'secret history', with much the same details as those contained in the cryptograms – that Bacon was the natural son of Queen Elizabeth, the leader of the English Freemasons, and the rest; in fact Messrs Theobald and Dodd merely treat the sonnets as a series of cryptograms, and the only rearrangement of them that they make is one designed to bring the events they claim to discover in them into the order they claim these events happened, which can scarcely rank as a scientific method. As for the cryptogrammatic meanings themselves, they are open to all the criticism I have levelled at this sort of thing in Chapter III (see pp. 70 f.) and, of course, to the full force of the Friedmans' attack. No more therefore need be said about them here.

Titherley,[1] arguing the case on behalf of the Earl of Derby, is far less extravagant in his claims, and at least keeps within the bounds of the possible in the story he narrates, which is as follows:

Derby writes to the young Earl of Southampton urging him to marry and settle down. Derby himself lives rather a wild life as a young man, becomes embroiled in a street affray, and sustains a wound that might have proved fatal, and which leaves him with lameness, temporary or permanent. He takes a mistress, unidentifiable except as the 'dark lady', who is unfaithful to him, presumably with Southampton, and casts her off, an episode borrowed in its entirety from the orthodox account with the substitution of Derby for Shakspere. He falls genuinely in love with Elizabeth de Vere, but before anything can come of it, he is compelled to become secretly betrothed to Queen Elizabeth. Their marriage, however, distasteful to both, proves unnecessary, and he is free to return to Elizabeth de Vere.

This, unlike the Baconian fantasy, at least merits serious criticism. When, however, we subject it to this, obvious weaknesses soon make their appearance. If all the items mentioned in Titherley's list were facts established by independent evidence the sonnets might conceivably be considered to have

1 *Shakespeare's Identity*, pp. 299–327.

reference to them, though even so it would be an uncertain conclusion. Actually, however, the only item in the list known to be a fact is that Derby married Elizabeth de Vere; all the rest are mere suppositions based largely on the sonnets themselves, which are so vague that Titherley is obliged to plead that the meaning was deliberately disguised in order not to give away the secret. This, of course, is tantamount to a claim by Titherley that he has penetrated a disguise and discovered a secret which Derby's contemporaries, living close to the events, if these really happened, could not do.

An example of Titherley's method is that of the alleged street brawl, which we have already reviewed in detail (see pp. 196 f.). The entire incident is built up on two lines from two different sonnets – 'So I made lame by Fortune's dearest spite' from No. 37 and 'The coward conquest of a wretch's knife' from No. 74, both of which may well be figurative, and in any case are unable unaided to support Titherley's interpretation of them.

Much the same is true of the alleged betrothal of Derby to the Queen, which I criticized earlier in another connection (see pp. 92 ff.). Titherley deduces this very improbable circumstance from a few sonnets like the following (No. 57), which he claims are addressed to the Queen:

> Being your slave, what should I do but tend
> Upon the hours and time of your desire?
> I have no precious time at all to spend,
> No services to do till you require.
> Nor dare I chide the world-without-end hour
> Whilst I, my sovereign, watch the clock for you,
> Nor think the bitterness of absence sour
> When you have bid your servant once adieu;
> Nor dare I question with my jealous thought
> Where you may be, or your affairs suppose,
> But like a sad slave, stay and think of nought
> Save, where you are how happy you make those.
> So true a fool is love, that in your Will,
> Though you do anything, he thinks no ill.

One is tempted to wonder if Titherley has never been in love or called the girl of the moment his queen. As a matter of fact this is typical romantic love poetry, and can be paralleled not only in the love poems of the Elizabethan age, but of almost every other literary period as well. There are striking echoes of it in the love duologues between Valentine and Silvia in T. G. of V. Any poet might have addressed it to any lady. There are no real grounds for assuming that it is addressed to Queen Elizabeth;[1] still less for building such a weighty political theory upon it.

This brings us to the final point in the discussion; that is, the group of sonnets Nos. 78 to 86. If these are the complaints of the author that his patron has transferred his favours to another poet, and it is almost impossible to twist their meaning into anything else, then clearly the authorship of the noble Earls and Bacon is completely ruled out. Either Shakspere or Marlowe might have written them, but not the titled amateurs, who, of course, would have no patron, and Marlowe, as we have already seen, is excluded on other grounds, chiefly that he was not alive at the time to write them.

This concludes our survey of the case in the light of the sonnets. It will readily be recognized that there is nothing in these to lend the least support to the claims of the theorists. The deductions the latter attempt to make from them are far-fetched and unconvincing in the highest degree; some are childishly absurd. Moreover there are too many uncertainties and unsolved problems concerned with the sonnets themselves for them to be accepted as reliable evidence for anything.

[1] It must be remembered that, according to Titherley himself, the betrothal between the Queen and Derby was distasteful to both parties, and only entered into for political reasons. It was therefore most unlikely to evoke passionate poetry. The claim is just one more example of the many contradictions into which the theorists are led in their frenzied efforts to find evidence for their various cases where no evidence exists.

CHAPTER X

Richard II and the Missing Link

We have already had occasion (see p. 20) to refer to the attitude
of Queen Elizabeth towards the play *Richard II*, and Baconians,
Oxfordians, and Derbyites all mention it as an example of the
danger incurred by a dramatist in Tudor times and as a motive
for their particular candidate to keep his authorship secret.
There is, however, much more in the story than this, and
properly the further details concern Bacon alone. I should
therefore have treated it in the chapter on the Baconian case if
Titherley had not made one of his buccaneering raids upon it.
Of course, as we have repeatedly seen, all the theorists on
occasion make use of the same factors as evidence in support of
their different candidates, but most of them confine these
operations to factors that could apply equally well to anyone.
Titherley has no such limitations; he appropriates almost every
point that is raised, no matter how impossible it may be to connect it with Derby, as he did in the case of the 'Promus' (see
pp. 165–167), and, as we shall see later, he does in the case of the
Northumberland Manuscript (see pp. 228–234). He calls this the
Inductive Method. I suspect the Baconians have another word
for it.

Be that as it may, Titherley's intervention brings the subject
under the heading of 'evidence common to two or more
theories', and since the matter is a very interesting one and the
ultimate situation possibly unique in the annals of controversy,
a chapter to itself is by no means unjustified.

The play *Richard II* must have been written by 1595, for
there is documentary evidence of its performance that year.
It seems to have been very popular, for Quarto editions of it
were published in 1597, 1598 (two), 1608, 1615, and 1634. The
earlier Quartos did not contain the 'Deposition Scene', which
first appeared in the 1608 Quarto, when James I was on the
throne. Events, however, as will be apparent, make it certain

that this scene formed part of the play as originally written, and it was probably omitted from the earlier Quartos by order of the Censor, the reason being that the Elizabethans, including the Queen herself, recognized parallels between her and Richard, though they may not be very obvious to us today.

When the Earl of Essex, after his return from his unsuccessful expedition to Ireland, fell into disfavour with the Queen and resolved on rebellion, one of his supporters, Sir Gilby Merrick, believing that the play might stir up mutinous feelings in the citizens of London and induce them to side with Essex, approached the Lord Chamberlain's Company with the proposal that they should revive *Richard II*. The players objected that it was a very old play and no longer likely to attract an audience, but consented to stage it when Merrick offered them a sum of money to do so. It is clear that this performance must have included the 'Deposition Scene', for after the rebellion had been crushed Elizabeth was furious about it, and ordered an inquiry into the circumstances in which it had been produced. From this the actors escaped without loss of royal favour since they were obviously innocent tools, but Merrick was executed.

Queen Elizabeth was also at the same time incensed about another literary production. This was a small book or pamphlet which had been published more than a year before the rebellion, in 1599 to be exact, with a dedication to the Earl of Essex signed by John Hayward, and with his initials, J. H., on the cover as author. It was entitled *The First Part of the Life and Raigne of Henry IV*, and openly spoke of a claim to the throne superior to that of the Queen. After Essex's rebellion Hayward was arrested and imprisoned.

Bacon, who had been a friend and protégé of Essex, but had refused to follow him into rebellion and took part in his prosecution, felt that some explanation of his position was necessary, and wrote an *Apology*. In the course of this he states that the Queen expressed some doubts about the authorship of Hayward's book, and threatened to have Hayward racked to force him to reveal the true author, a course of action from which Bacon was able to dissuade her.

It is on this statement, strange as it may seem to those unfamiliar with the workings of their minds, that the Baconians pounce as evidence of Bacon's authorship of *Richard II*. His own statement is not good enough for them. They insist that it was not Hayward's book the Queen meant when she said she doubted the authorship, but the play *Richard II*; and this in spite of the fact that Bacon never mentions the latter, and does mention both the book and the proposed torturing of Hayward. B. G. Theobald[1] indignantly demands how the Queen could possibly have any doubts about the authorship of the book 'seeing that the title-page informs the reader that it was written by J. H.; and that it was naturally supposed to have been written by the writer of the Latin dedication to the Earl of Essex, plainly signed J. Hayward'. We can only rub our eyes in wonder on seeing this statement, and ask when, according to the Baconians, a name attached to a book was evidence of its owner's authorship. On the contrary, surely it is the very essence of their theory that someone else's name on its title-page is proof positive that a book was written by Bacon. There are a number of books with W. S. on the title-page which, among others, the Baconians declare to have been written by Bacon. Queen Elizabeth was only showing herself a good Baconian by suspecting Bacon's authorship of the book ascribed to Hayward, if that is what she did do.

Theobald continues the argument on exactly the same lines. He writes:[2] 'When the case of Essex came before the Lords Commissioners, Bacon wrote to the Queen and begged to be excused from taking part in it, in view of his friendship with Essex. But the Queen curtly refused, and he was compelled to obey. Accordingly the Lords allotted to him the very part of the case which concerned this matter. Naturally this caused him great pain, and all the evidence shows that he took the utmost care to say as little as possible against Essex consistent with his public duty to point out the treason of which Essex was so clearly guilty. He says that the Lords Commissioners decided "that I should set forth some undutiful carriage of my lord, in giving countenance to a seditious pamphlet, as it was termed, which was dedicated unto him, which was the book before-mentioned of King Henry IV. Whereupon I replied to that allotment, and said to their Lordships, that it was an old matter

[1] *Enter Francis Bacon*, p. 62.   [2] Ibid., pp. 63–64.

and had no manner of coherence with the rest of the charge, being matters of Ireland, and thereupon that I having been wronged by bruits before, this would expose me to them more; and it would be said I gave in evidence mine own tales". Really! What tales could these be? Evidently they were connected with the history of the deposing of Richard II and the accession of Henry IV; but Hayward's book could not be the tale in question, for as we have already seen, his name as author was put to the dedication, and his initials were on the title page.'

'Really!' – to borrow his own favourite expletive. One wonders what kind of spectacles Theobald was wearing when he read Bacon's *Apology*. At the risk of some repetition we must examine this precious argument a little more closely, for it will amply repay our study. The account upon which it is based, we must remember, comes from Bacon himself, and, summarized, gives us the following items of information:

(1) The Queen, much incensed, discussed Hayward's *King Henry IV* with Bacon. There is no doubt that it was the book ascribed to Hayward that was under discussion, for its title, the dedication to Essex, and Hayward's name are all mentioned. The Queen, however, suspected that Hayward was not the real author, and declared her intention of having him racked to force the truth from him.

(2) Bacon, a reluctant member of the Commission appointed to deal with the case of Essex, was allotted the task of bringing forward this very book as evidence against the accused nobleman. There is again no doubt that it is Hayward's book that is meant; its title is given and the dedication to Essex is mentioned. The play, of course, had no such dedication.

(3) Bacon protested against this, partly on the grounds that the book was irrelevant to the charge (the book had been written nearly two years before the rebellion, and, unlike *Richard II*, had played no part in that event; it was therefore, as Bacon said, 'an old matter'), and partly because it would be embarrassing to him personally. When the subject of the book was raised previously there had been rumours that he was its real author; and if he were obliged to put it forward at the trial, these rumours would recur with the addition that he had

used what he himself had written as evidence against his former friend.

This is the plain sense of what Bacon wrote, as anyone can test by reading the material section in the *Apology* for himself. *There is not a word about the play 'Richard II' in the whole passage.* Theobald must have read this, since he quotes it at some length, yet so distorted is his vision by his *idée fixe* that he actually claims it as evidence that Bacon wrote *Richard II* and heads his Chapter 'Bacon's virtual admission that he wrote *Richard II*'. This is simply nonsense. If Bacon virtually admitted anything it could only be the authorship of the book ascribed to Hayward, for this is the only work discussed. But of course Bacon was not admitting anything; on the contrary he was protesting against having Hayward's book fathered on him. As usual on analysis, the whole Baconian case falls to pieces.

Titherley also attempts the feat of trying to make bricks not only without straw, but without clay as well. His case for Derby's authorship of *Richard II* is of the same kind as that offered by Theobald for Bacon's, and rests on evidence quite as invisible to any eyes but his own.

He takes for his material some notes made by William Lambarde, Keeper of the Rolls, of a conversation he had with the Queen, shortly after the Essex rebellion on the subject of Merrick's production of *Richard II*. The notes are very rough, and contain no mention of any name. Titherley[1] thus describes the incident: 'The Queen opened with the angry remark, "I am Richard II, know ye not that?" To which Lambarde replied, "Such a wicked imagination was determined and attempted by a most unkind Gent; the most adorned creature that ever your Majestie made." He might have meant the Earl of Essex, but the Queen in her reply seems to have meant "Shakespeare" (Derby), by saying darkly, "He that will forget God, will also forget his benefactors: this tragedy was played 40^{tie} times in open streets and houses." Essex, of course, had nothing to do with those forty productions.'

Now, since Titherley admits that Lambarde 'might have meant Essex' – there is no 'might' about it, he certainly did; there was no one else at the time to whom the words 'the most

[1] *Shakespeare's Identity*, p. 50.

adorned creature that ever your Majestie made' could apply –
since Titherley admits this, the whole argument turns on the
Queen's second speech.

In our criticism of this we will pass by without comment the
fact that on equally good, or rather equally bad, grounds both
the Baconians and the Oxfordians could have written the
identical paragraph, the former substituting ' "Shakespeare"
(Bacon)' and the latter ' "Shakespeare" (Oxford)' for Titherley's ' "Shakespeare" (Derby)', if it had occurred to them to do
so, and turn our attention at once to the speech itself. We may
begin by pointing out that this consists of two separate and distinct parts[1] – (i) a comment on an unnamed person, and (ii)
another on the play, *Richard II.*

As to the first, however 'darkly' she spoke, the Queen certainly did *not* mean ' "Shakespeare" (Derby)'. Her words are
an obvious reply to Lambarde's remark, and she could not
possibly fail to understand that he was referring to Essex, for,
as we have already stated, its wording could apply to no one
else. Nor can the Queen's own remark; certainly it cannot refer
to Derby. Essex might well be said to have forgotten God, since
he had dared to take up arms against the Lord's anointed, in
doing which he had also forgotten all the benefactions he had
received from the human Queen. But neither of these charges
could be made against Derby; he had received no outstanding
favours from the Queen, and for what he had received to the
best of our knowledge he had always been loyal and grateful.

The sentence then is an interjection in reply to Lambarde's
remark, but the Queen's mind is still running on the subject of
the play, with which she had opened the conversation. She at
once returns to this, and the second sentence has no connection
with the first. Her thought would seem to be as follows – if
Merrick could think its production so useful to Essex's cause,
what disloyalty might have been bred by all the productions it
had had in the past, no matter how unwitting those responsible
for them might have been. We know from history that Queen
Elizabeth was exceedingly nervous about depositions and
executions of monarchs; it was this that made her so reluctant

[1] In Tudor times a colon was frequently used where today we use a full-
stop.

to agree to the execution of Mary Queen of Scots when pressed by her Ministers; and no doubt this was the main reason why the 'Deposition Scene' was not printed in the Quartos of *Richard II* published in her reign.

This is the plain meaning of the matter as it stands, and *nowhere is there any reference to Derby or any suggestion of one.* Moreover, in putting forward his interpretation of the Lambarde Note, Titherley seems to have overlooked the fact that, according to his theory, it was fear of the Queen and the need to keep his authorship secret from her that caused Derby to father his plays on the actor Shakspere. Yet if what he claims here is true, the Queen knew all about it. Nevertheless, in spite of her great rage over one of the plays, she took no action against Derby; he was not even summoned to the Inquiry, as were the actors. We have in fact just another example of that confusion of thought which we so often encounter in the theorists' arguments. Cannot they see that if the secret was as generally known as their frenzied attempts to produce evidence for it compel them on occasion to suggest, it could have been no secret at all, contemporary references to the truth could never have been suppressed, and we should never have had a Shakespeare Problem?

I said near the beginning that attempts to prove Bacon's and Derby's authorship of *Richard II* merited a chapter to themselves, and the result amply justifies this. Had their respective cases been treated along with other matters, the poverty of the evidence by which they are supported might have been somewhat obscured. In isolation it stands out in all its nakedness. Theobald, seeking evidence of authorship for Bacon, can produce Bacon but no *Richard II*, while Titherley, seeking evidence of authorship for Derby, can produce *Richard II* but no Derby, which is quite a Gilbertian situation.

CHAPTER XI

The Hidden Hand in *As You Like It*

In Act V, Scene i, of *As You Like It* there appear a few lines of dialogue spoken by Touchstone and William, with Audrey also on the stage. The passage is as follows:

TOUCHSTONE. Art thou learned?

WILLIAM. No, sir.

TOUCHSTONE. Then learn this of me – to have is to have; for it is a figure of rhetoric that drink, by being poured out of a cup into a glass, by filling the one doth empty the other; for all your writers do consent that *ipse* is he; now you are not *ipse* for I am he.

WILLIAM. Which he, sir?

TOUCHSTONE. He, sir, that must marry this woman.

No doubt many generations of readers and playgoers have believed, as I did myself when I first began to study Shakespeare, that this piece of dialogue was part of the play, and that Touchstone was informing William, with a certain lack of tact, that Audrey had changed her mind about her matrimonial intentions, and was going to marry him (Touchstone) instead. But these generations of readers and playgoers would be quite wrong, at least according to the theorists. This apparently simple and straightforward bit of dialogue is in reality charged with secret meaning, which they have discovered and, in due succession, given to the world.

Durning-Lawrence[1] claims that Touchstone represents Bacon; the rustic William, Shakspere of Stratford; and Audrey, the Shakespearean plays; while the pouring of the drink from the cup (Bacon) into the glass (Shakspere) represents the credit of the authorship's being diverted to the wrong man. In support of this he invites us to note that Audrey has previously declared that William 'has no interest in me in the world'. The

---

[1] *Bacon is Shakespeare*, pp. 43–46.

rest of the scene, he says, is designed to show that William, though he has some wealth, is not learned, which means that he is totally illiterate; and finally not he, but Touchstone (Bacon) shall marry Audrey, that is be recognized as the true author of the Shakespearean plays.

Percy Allen[1] claims that Touchstone represents Oxford, while sharing with Durning-Lawrence the view that William represents Shakspere of Stratford, and adopting the same interpretation of the transference of the drink from the cup to the glass. He points out that Shakspere was twenty-five, the age to which William confesses, in 1589, the year in which, according to the Oxfordian theory, A.Y.L.I. was written. He then paraphrases the dialogue quoted at the beginning of this chapter as a monologue by Touchstone (Oxford) as follows:

Are you learned enough to have written these plays? No! Well, water being poured from a cup into a transparent glass, by filling the one doth empty the other. All the writers, Harvey, Chapman, Jonson, and others are whispering that '*ipse*' *is he*, or that the works were written by a courtier or a learned person, and it is clear that you are neither of these nor, in fact, '*ipse*' *for I am he.*

Hoffman[2] claims that Touchstone represents Marlowe, and, of course, that William represents Shakspere of Stratford; then following exactly the same lines as the other theorists, including the use of the cup (Touchstone) and glass (William) metaphor, he interprets Touchstone's speech as Marlowe informing Shakspere that he (Shakspere) did not write the plays, but that he (Marlowe), *ipse*, did.

If all these theories are true, then the little piece of dialogue quoted must indeed be the most remarkable ever written. It is certain that never before has so much meaning been contained in so few words. But perhaps, before allowing ourselves to be reduced to speechlessness with wonder and admiration, it may be as well to examine the theories and ascertain if they do actually represent the truth about the passage. We will begin

[1] Quoted by M. Douglas in *Lord Oxford and the Shakespeare Group*, pp. 98 f.
[2] *The Man Who Was Shakespeare*, p. 168.

with three general criticisms applying equally to all, and then analyse each theory separately in some detail.

In the first place, as we had occasion to remark in dealing with the sonnets, a factor that with equal facility can be twisted into evidence for several incompatible views, can in reality be evidence for none of them. Any passage in any literary work containing a phrase meaning 'you are not the man' could be worked up in exactly the same way, and as soon as we place the interpretations of the A.Y.L.I. passage by the three different schools of thought side by side their absurdity is apparent. Titherley, with a caution perhaps engendered by his scientific training, refuses to fall into this trap, though, of course, by merely claiming that Touchstone represented Derby and then proceeding according to the usual formula, a case as convincing, or rather as unconvincing, as any of the others could have been made out for Derby.

Again, it is obvious that in offering such stuff as this as evidence the theorists have completely forgotten the very foundation of all their various theories. According to these the true author of the plays or, in the case of Marlowe, his agent sought Shakspere out and paid him to pose as the author so that the true author might avoid serious trouble, perhaps the loss of his life; Shakspere certainly did not, because he could not, *steal* the plays. Yet, according to their modern sponsors, all the true authors, represented by Touchstone, stand up before public and private audiences and berate poor Shakspere as if he had done them a personal injury, and at the same time proclaim their own authorship at the top of their voices. Could anything be more incredibly silly? It is of no use for the theorists to argue that all this was very cleverly disguised. If they, after the lapse of centuries, can discover it so easily, it would surely be even more apparent to contemporaries who knew the persons concerned. At least there would always be the risk of the wrong people penetrating the secret, and if there were not, what was the good of putting in stuff that no one could understand? The whole argument is just a colossal example of the confusion of mind from which the theorists suffer, and of their childish clutching at every straw of supposed evidence no matter how incompatible it may be with the rest of their case.

The third criticism is of the interpretation the theorists give to the 'cup and glass' metaphor. Why, except to bolster up their own cases, do they identify the former with Touchstone and the latter with William? Surely it is obvious that the reverse is intended, and that the brilliant Touchstone is the glittering crystal glass into which the drink, representing Audrey, has just been transferred, while the boorish William is the plain opaque cup, now, alas, left empty. It is in fact Touchstone who has done the stealing of what was originally William's, *not* the converse. Yet apparently the vision of the theorists is so clouded by their preconceived ideas that they cannot even read the plain sense of the passage they quote, nor see that it simply cannot bear the interpretation they put upon it.

We may now turn to the detailed examination of the individual theories. Little need be said about that of Durning-Lawrence. It consists, as is usual with him, of *ex cathedra* pronouncements. He says Touchstone represents Bacon, William represents Shakspere, and Audrey represents the Shakespearean plays, without deigning to offer one shred of evidence in support of his statements. The identification of Audrey with the plays is particularly amusing when we remember that just previously, in Act III, Scene iii, she is described as 'foul', 'sluttish', and 'not poetical'. If that really represents Bacon's considered opinion of the plays, the Baconians would seem to be acting a little unkindly in trying to drag his authorship of them to light.

Turning now to the Oxfordians, we must begin by denying M. Douglas' claim that Percy Allen *discovered* this interpretation of the A.Y.L.I. passage. It is obvious that Durning-Lawrence had preceded him, and he has done little more than adapt it to the Oxfordian view by the simple expedient of substituting Oxford's name for Bacon's as the person represented by Touchstone. He has, however, dropped the ludicrous identification of Audrey with the Shakespearean plays, and he does make an attempt, even if a very poor one, to find a little supporting evidence, for which we must spare a glance.

In the first place he points out that William informs Touchstone that he is twenty-five years old, which is the age Shakspere was in 1589, the year in which he claims A.Y.L.I. was written. This is his whole evidence for identifying William with Shakspere. We may reply that even if it were true, he is making a very fragile foundation support a very heavy superstructure. Twenty-five admirably fits the dramatic situation as the age for a prosperous young farmer to contemplate matrimony, and if it happened to be Shakspere's age at the time the play was written, so it was of hundreds of other men also. A very mild coincidence would be a far more probable explanation of the circumstance than any other, though it would not be impossible for Shakspere, as author, deliberately to give William the same age as himself. But this is really beside the point, for we cannot accept Allen's claim as true. 1589 is only the date of the play by the Oxfordians' own particular method of calculation, and this, as we have seen (pp. 81–86), is almost certainly worthless. The accepted date is ten years later, when Shakspere would have been thirty-five.

The paraphrase of the Touchstone speech is just another example of embellishing a quotation in favour of a particular interpretation such as we have found in Titherley (see pp. 92–95) and Hoffman (see pp. 201–202), and have criticized in detail in the case of the former. The same criticism applies here. There is nothing more to say about the Oxfordian case.

Hoffman cannot be dismissed so briefly. The much-quoted Touchstone–William passage forms only a small part of his argument, and as there are at least two genuine Marlowe references in A.Y.L.I., his case demands more serious attention. We will accord it this, and deal with his points in the order in which he himself raises them. His method is the usual one adopted by the theorists in such cases; namely, to select a number of references in the play and interpret them in such a way as to make them apply to his candidate and thereby prove the latter's authorship of the play.

He begins his argument[1] by quoting from Act III, Scene iii, a speech by Touchstone addressed to Audrey:

> I am here with thee and thy goats as the most capricious poet, honest Ovid, was among the Goths.

Hoffman states (i) that these lines are not banter, (ii) that they have nothing to do with Audrey, and (iii) that they are full

[1] *The Man Who Was Shakespeare*, pp. 167 and 168.

214

of significance, because Ovid was Marlowe's favourite poet, and, by a coincidence, Ovid had suffered banishment just as Marlowe was suffering it. Hoffman claims that the real meaning of the speech is as follows:

> I, Marlowe, am banished to this goatish, wild, yet pastoral country just as strangely enough my idol, the whimsical and capricious poet, honest Ovid, was banished to the barbarous Goths.

We will deal with the third point first. Ovid may well have been Marlowe's favourite Latin poet, but he was equally the favourite Latin poet of nearly every other Elizabethan dramatist and of many people who were not dramatists. He was one of the first Latin poets to be translated into English when the Classical revival began, his works were a text-book in every Grammar School, and his *Metamorphoses* was the source of the plot or of some episode in it of a large number of Elizabethan plays, as well as of a multitude of similes and references. There was not a dramatist of the period who might not equally naturally have made the pun on 'goats', 'capricious', and 'Goths'. Moreover, Marlowe only suffered banishment according to Hoffman's theory; all the evidence, as we saw in Chapter VI, is against the idea that he did so in fact. In this instance Hoffman is perpetrating the logical fallacy of endeavouring to prove his theory by his theory.

Again, the statement that the speech has nothing to do with Audrey is patently false. It has everything to do with her. She was a goat-girl, and Touchstone, paying his ironic court to her, had just, in the manner of a devoted lover, volunteered to round up her flock for her. The speech he makes at the opening of the scene runs as follows:

> Come apace, good Audrey. I will fetch up your goats, Audrey.

And the remark Hoffman quotes arises naturally out of this.

Finally, in spite of Hoffman's denial, the scene is pure banter and nothing else, as anyone reading it or seeing it acted is immediately aware. There are three rustic characters in the play – Corin, William, and Audrey – and every time he encounters one of them Touchstone indulges in talk of a similar nature to the one under discussion. In a previous scene he had bantered Corin in exactly the same way, and in a later scene he was to try the same trick on William. If Hoffman can see any essential difference between the Audrey scene and the acknowledged bantering of the other two, he should surely have stated what it is. Needless to say he makes no attempt to do so.

Hoffman's first argument therefore collapses utterly. His second,[1] which has a similar fate, is taken from the same scene, and is based on the following few lines spoken by Touchstone:

> When a man's verses cannot be understood, nor a man's good wit seconded with the forward child Understanding, it strikes a man more dead than a great reckoning in a little room.

This is, of course, one of the two undoubted references to Marlowe in the play, a fact that not even the most bigoted Stratfordian would wish to deny. The quarrel between Marlowe and Frizer was stated in Danby's Report (see p. 134) to be over the 'reckoning', and its scene was a room, probably a small one, in a house in Deptford. According to Hoffman's theory Marlowe and Walsingham concocted the faked murder in collaboration, and therefore Marlowe would know all the details, including the two just mentioned.

If there were any truth in Hoffman's theory of the assassination, this would still be a very doubtful statement. In such a case Marlowe might have known the general idea of the plot, but in the haste of his flight and the agitated state of mind in which he would naturally be, he was unlikely to be capable of taking in such minor details as the size of the room in which the murder was to take place and what the alleged quarrel was to be about, even if these had been mentioned, which is in the highest degree improbable.

Hoffman, however, not only postulates Marlowe's knowledge, but also Shakspere's ignorance, which is more to the point. 'Would William Shakespeare,' he asks, 'had he written the play, have been privy to the circumstances of Marlowe's "assassination"? Would he have known "of the great reckoning in a little room"? How? Remember there is no evidence that Shakespeare and Marlowe ever knew or were interested one in the other. Since Danby's Report had been quietly laid away,

[1] *The Man Who Was Shakespeare*, pp. 168 f.

how could Shakespeare have gained access to it? It has been seen that none of Marlowe's contemporaries knew anything of the real facts behind Marlowe's murder; for several years after his death they believed that he had died of the then raging plague. It would have been impossible for William Shakespeare to gain knowledge of this beautifully kept secret.'

In reply to this I would point out that on pages 91 to 93 of his own book Hoffman has the answer to the rhetorical questions he himself poses. On those pages he quotes three contemporary accounts of Marlowe's murder. From the first two of these, Beard's *Theatre of God's Judgements* and Meres' *Palladis Tamia*, it is clear that the authors knew that Marlowe was stabbed and that the wound that caused his death was a head wound. In the third, Vaughan's *Golden Grove* – which incidentally was published in 1600, the identical year, according to the accepted view, when A.Y.L.I. was written – we find that the author knew much more. He knew that the murder took place in a house in Deptford and that the wound was in the region of the eye. He also gives the murderer's name as Ingram, which is quite correct, though this was his Christian, not his surname.

From these three references, of which I shall have more to say later (see p. 222), it is obvious that the details of the assassination and Danby's Report on it were by no means 'the beautifully kept secret' that Hoffman claims. It is indeed highly probable that all the facts were known to the public though few people, if any, had them all correctly, and many garbled accounts were floating about. Such things happen even today, and in the Tudor age, when there were no newspapers to provide any check on rumour, the situation would be aggravated. It is, however, quite clear that the author of A.Y.L.I., even if he were the Stratford actor, could easily pick up enough information to make the very meagre reference under discussion. Vaughan alone could provide him with most of it and other details as well.

Hoffman's next point[1] is the one I have already mentioned earlier in this chapter along with the Baconian and Oxfordian arguments on the same topic – the Touchstone speech containing the '*ipse*' remark. I have given a general criticism of the

[1] *The Man Who Was Shakespeare*, pp. 170 f.

common line of argument at that place (see pp. 212–214), and there is only one additional point of Hoffman's that requires to be treated here.

Hoffman, having paraphrased the Touchstone speech according to the usual formula of the theorists to make it suit his own purposes, continues, 'There is no reason buried in the motivation of the play that warrants this abstruse banter. . . . Unless it is interpreted in the light of the imposture, the words have not the barest justification; they should never have been written.'

The answer to this is simply that the statement is not correct. There *is* a reason in the motivation of the play for the banter. The speech in question, which is typical of Touchstone's style when conversing with the rustics, is directly leading up to his announcement that he, not William, is going to marry Audrey. Nothing could be plainer.[1]

The next point Hoffman makes[2] concerns the second genuine reference to Marlowe in the play. It is contained in the following speech by Phoebe in Act IV, Scene v:

> Dead shepherd, now I find thy saw of might,
> 'Whoever loved that loved not at first sight?'

As the second line, which is obviously the 'saw of might' referred to in the first line, is a quotation from Marlowe's *Hero and Leander*, and as it is said to be the 'saw' of the 'dead shepherd' (i.e. 'poet'), the orthodox interpretation has always been that

[1] Even if there had been no motivation in the play for the speech, it would still not have constituted evidence for the 'imposture' or for anything else. Perhaps Mr Hoffman will explain what 'reason is buried in the motivation' of *The Merchant of Venice* that warrants the following speech by Launcelot Gobbo (II, v):

> I will not say you shall see a mask; but if you do, then it was not for nothing that my nose fell a-bleeding on Black-Monday last at six o'clock i' th' morning, falling out that year on Ash-Wednesday was four year in the afternoon.

Or would he say the words 'should never have been written'?

As a matter of fact there are in all periods numerous plays which include speeches that have nothing to do with the motivation of the plot, but are merely put in for humorous effect.

[2] *The Man Who Was Shakespeare*, pp. 174 f.

the 'dead shepherd' was Marlowe. This puts Mr Hoffman in a dilemma. He cannot ignore the matter, yet he can hardly maintain that Marlowe would call himself a 'dead shepherd' in the very play in which, according to the Hoffman theory, he is engaged in giving strong hints that he is very much alive.

This is certainly an awkward dilemma for any theorist to encounter, and Hoffman's attempt to escape from it can hardly be called a happy one. It is both far-fetched and, on the face of it, highly improbable. According to him the 'dead shepherd' is Sir Philip Sidney, who had fallen in battle about twelve years before, and the 'saw of might' is these lines from one of Sidney's sonnets

> Not at first sight, nor with a dribbled shot
> Love gave the wound, which while I breathe will bleed;
> Best known worth did in time of mine proceed
> Till by degrees it had full conquest got;
> I saw and liked, I liked but loved not.
> I loved, but straight did not what love decreed,
> At length to love's decree I forced, agreed,
> Yet with repining at so partial lot.

Now it is obvious that the love described in these lines is of slow development, not an impetuous yielding at first sight; in fact the very antithesis of Marlowe's line, quoted by Phoebe when she lost her heart instantaneously at the very first sight of the disguised Rosalind. It is of course true that Sidney says, when at last he came to love, he regretted the lost time. It may even be that this sonnet suggested his own aphorism to Marlowe; about that we know, and can know, nothing. All this is completely beside the point. The fact remains that it is Marlowe's line that is quoted, that is called the 'saw of might', and consequently he must be the 'dead shepherd' who is referred to as its author, and no amount of sophistry or special pleading can get rid of this stubborn fact. The orthodox view fits the words exactly, and the words fit the accepted view of Marlowe's fate.

There are two more details concerned with A.Y.L.I. out of which Hoffman attempts to make capital for his theory. The first of these is the surname of the hedge-priest, Sir Oliver

Martext, or Mar-text. Hoffman asserts[1] that this means 'Marlowe's Text', and was intended to give a broad hint of the identity of the true author. One may be excused for feeling a little impatience when offered such an interpretation as this of a very simple word. 'Mar' in Tudor times, as it still does today, simply meant 'spoil' or 'ruin', and it is used in the Shakespearean plays a number of times in this sense. An example is Gratiano's remark in Act V of *The Merchant of Venice* – 'I 'll mar the young clerk's pen'. Only a few years before A.Y.L.I. was written there had been an attack on the Bishops by a Puritan writer who used the pseudonym of 'Martin Marprelate' with obvious significance. 'Martext' is an excellent name for a comic parson, implying that he ruins every text he preaches on. The author of the Shakespearean plays, following the tradition of the old Moralities, often made use of these descriptive names for comic characters – Slender, Simple, Froth, Le Beau, Dull, and Toby Belch are examples. Other writers, such as Ben Jonson, made even more use of this convention; in fact it was a common literary practice of the time and for long afterwards, and we need nothing further than this simple straightforward explanation to account for the name of 'Martext'.

The second of the minor points that Hoffman makes[2] is that *As You Like It* was registered for publication with the Stationers' Company in the year 1600, but was not published then or subsequently till it appeared in the First Folio in 1623. It was marked in the Stationers' Register as a book 'to be staied', though no reason for this was given.

Hoffman's explanation of this fact is that someone in the secret, probably Walsingham himself, heard of the intended publication, and either having already read the play or insisting on doing so before it was printed, realized the danger of the hints that Marlowe had given of his authorship, and stopped further proceedings.

It is a pretty theory, and might well seem convincing to anyone who had read nothing but Hoffman's account. The moment, however, that we begin to investigate the matter, we find the picture that has been presented to us lacks a number of

[1] *The Man Who Was Shakespeare*, pp. 175 and 176.
[2] Ibid., p. 177.

important details. When the full entry in the Stationer's Register is examined, it is at once obvious that it lends no support to his contention. The page is headed:

My lord chamberlens mens plaies Entered

The date 1600 is given together with the names of two non-Shakespearean plays entered earlier in the year; and then comes the entry referred to, but *not* quoted, by Hoffman. It runs as follows:

4 Augusti

As you like yt, a booke
Henry the ffift, a booke
Every man in his humour, a booke } to be staied.
The Commedie of muche A doo about
nothing a booke

Four plays were therefore registered at the same time – three of Shakespeare's and one of Ben Jonson's[1] – and all of them were 'to be staied'. Now neither *Henry V* nor *Much Ado About Nothing* contain any of what Hoffman calls 'dangerous hints', and not even he has ventured to claim *Every Man In His Humour* for Marlowe. Yet, since the four plays are bracketed together on the same date in the Register, it is idle to pretend that *As You Like It* could have been 'staied' for a different reason from the other three; they are all obviously on the same footing.

Nor is there any difficulty about the reason why they were to be stayed. Registering plays with the Stationers' Company with such a proviso was one of the devices adopted by the actors of that time to protect their plays from piracy. It meant that no publisher could enter a pirated edition of such a play with the Stationers' Company, and therefore could not legally print it. It does not seem to have been a completely watertight protection, but it was certainly some, and was often resorted to by the various companies of actors. The explanation then of this particular entry of *As You Like It* is perfectly simple, and is most

---

[1] *Every Man In His Humour* was first produced by the Lord Chamberlain's Company, and would therefore be the property of that Company in the same way as Shakespeare's plays were, which explains its presence with the others in this entry.

emphatically not evidence for Hoffman's theory of Marlowe's authorship.

There is another point about *As You Like It* that must be considered before bringing this chapter to a close. It is a point I should have expected Hoffman himself to raise. Had he limited himself to it, he might have made a more effective case than he has done with all the mare's nests he has displayed to our view; but since he has not raised it, I will do so for him, though naturally my conclusion is unlikely to be identical with the one he would have reached.

The point is this. However the fact may be explained, the play certainly has Marlovian associations. There are two indisputable references to Marlowe in the dialogue, and there may be others, such as Rosalind's remark about Hero and Leander in Act IV, Scene i, though this is more doubtful. Now why should Shakespeare, whoever he may have been, suddenly betake himself to making references to Marlowe in this particular play, a thing he had never done before and never repeated; and why should he expect these references to interest his audiences, for, in spite of the opinions of the theorists about the purpose of references in plays, I really cannot rid myself of the belief that an author puts them in primarily because he knows that they will entertain his public?

There can, of course, in the present state of our knowledge, be no complete answer to these questions, but we may gain a hint or two from certain proved facts. We have already seen (p. 217) that the third of the three books mentioning the death of Marlowe, Vaughan's *Golden Grove*, contains a good deal of information about that event, and, what is more, that this information is correct according to the Danby Report. We have also seen that Vaughan's book was published in the same year that *As You Like It* was written. It would therefore seem highly probable that about this time something had brought the Marlowe case again before the public. Perhaps the real facts about it, at first ignored and later garbled as a result of the severe outbreak of the plague, were officially announced. This would explain both Vaughan's knowledge and the general interest, and would also be sufficient to call forth a passing reference from the later playwright, who, whether the two were acquainted or not, could not be unaware of the great debt the drama owed to Marlowe.

Be all this as it may, our analysis in this chapter has plainly shown that there is no evidence whatever for a hidden hand in *As You Like It*, and that the efforts of the theorists to manufacture some fail completely.

CHAPTER XII

The Northumberland MS

The document known as the Northumberland MS is another piece of evidence, which, while properly belonging exclusively to the Baconians, has been appropriated by Dr Titherley in the interests of Derby, though in this case his piracy is more than redeemed by the valuable work he has done on the manuscript itself. Before, however, dealing with such matters, it is necessary for me to give in outline the story of this manuscript.

It came to light in the year 1867 at Northumberland House in the Strand, and consists of a number of sheets in Elizabethan script, which, since his name heads the outer sheet, were almost certainly once the property of Francis Bacon. The packet when found comprised twenty-two sheets of paper, folded double, and placed one upon another, with an outer sheet laid flat on the top. The pages were neither numbered nor joined together, so it is impossible to say how many may have been in the original bundle. The writing on these sheets, none of which is that of Francis Bacon, is in two or more hands, and generally suggests the work of scriveners or other professional penmen. On some the writing is quite clear, on others much faded, which suggests that two different kinds of ink were used, and several have been damaged by fire. None of them contains anything of interest for our purpose.

All such interest is concentrated entirely in the outer sheet that had served as a cover for the others. It evidently suffered to some extent in the fire already mentioned, for one corner is burnt, and there is a strip about an inch wide along the bottom and a narrower strip along the right edge that are severely scorched. The sheet is covered with a great mass of writing in at least two, possibly three, hands. It would appear to have been begun as the inventory of a collection of manuscripts belonging to Bacon, but ultimately became a mere piece of scribbling paper, containing a vast medley of disjointed words

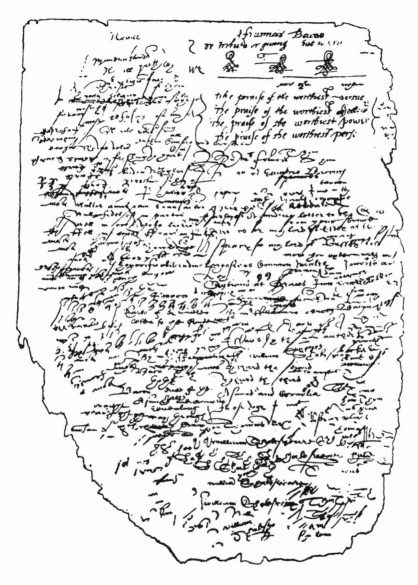

the praise of the worthiest vertue
the praise of the worthiest affection
the praise of the worthiest power
the praise of the worthiest person

Northumberland Manuscript, f1

and phrases. At least half of these are written upside down or at various angles in relation to the original script, and they often foul one another, making decipherment impossible. In addition there has been a great deal of fading and partial obliteration. There is also a little writing on the reverse side, which, unlike that on the front, is clear and legible.

In 1904 F. E. Burgoyne, Librarian of the Lambeth Public Libraries, published a facsimile of the manuscript and what is called a transcription of it, though this consisted of only a few of its most prominent features, and was therefore misleading in some respects. These features consisted of items from the inventory, which included some of his Essays and other works by Francis Bacon, to which Burgoyne added the *Ile of dogs* by Thomas Nashe and two items – *Rychard the second* and *Rychard the third* – with no author's name attached. Later investigations, however, make it almost certain that these three items belong, *not* to the inventory as Burgoyne supposed, but to the subsequent scribble. In this case the inventory consisted only of Bacon's own works, and it is thus unlikely that any MSS of the others were ever in his possession. This view is supported by the fact that no such MSS were found in the pile covered by the document. All the other items certainly come from the scribble, and consist, with a few odd phrases in addition, of the names 'William Shakespeare' and 'Francis Bacon' written several times both in full and in abbreviated forms, a misquotation from *The Rape of Lucrece*, and a mis-spelt version of the long word from *Love's Labour's Lost* (Act V, Sc. i), here reduced by the loss of seven letters to 'Honorificabilitudine'.

It is perhaps not surprising that the Baconians snatched at this document as evidence for their claims, though, of course, since we know nothing of its origin, and it can, as we shall see, be interpreted in several different ways, it cannot really be considered as evidence of anything. Still, it does bring together the two names of Shakespeare and Bacon, and contains references to several of the works ascribed to the former.

B. G. Theobald[1] naturally emphasizes these points, and, accepting Burgoyne's ascription of the two 'Rychards' to the inventory, infers from the fact that these plays, unlike the other

[1] *Enter Francis Bacon*, pp. 66–70.

works mentioned, have no author's name attached to them that Bacon wrote them, and that the secretary who made the inventory purposely left them in this anonymous state in order to preserve his master's secret. But even if they do belong to the inventory, which, as already stated, they almost certainly do not, this argument will not do at all. Why, we may ask, did not the secretary put in the name of William Shakespeare as the author? According to the Baconians it was Bacon's pseudonym, and it was certainly the name under which the plays were made public. To have used it in the case of the two 'Rychards' would have preserved Bacon's anonymity far more effectively than by treating these plays differently from the other works mentioned, which would in fact be more likely to attract special attention to them. Moreover, what was the use of his excessive care at this point, when immediately underneath this same secretary proceeds to write the names 'Bacon' and 'Shakespeare' side by side several times. This was surely giving the game away – *if there were any game to give away*. It is quite clear that we have here just another example of what we have so often before encountered in the theorists' arguments – the frenzied clutching at anything that might be twisted into something resembling evidence, regardless of its incompatibility with the rest of their case.

This is a particularly glaring example, for the incompatibility here is positively pushed under our noses. Theobald immediately takes up the question of the names, and contends that as they are the only two to be found in the scribble, in the peculiar circumstances in which they were written it is an obvious conclusion that they are both meant to apply to the same person, namely Bacon. I can only ask, if this were really the case, would Bacon's secretary, who must be credited with a little commonsense, so recklessly write on a scrap of paper what might well betray his master's vital secret, and then leave that paper about for anyone to read, as must have happened with this particular page for it to be used as a cover for other documents. Why, in any case, should he write those two names? There was obviously no purpose to be served by such an action, and, with all the dangers in which it could involve Bacon, to do so 'just for fun' would be a prank unworthy of a schoolboy.

The mere suggestion of such a thing is ludicrous. Whatever the reason for the mention of the two names, it is not the Baconian one.

There is, however, no need to labour this point except as an illustration of the strange working of the Baconian mind, for Theobald's statement that Bacon's and Shakespeare's names are the only two mentioned in the scribble is incorrect. There are several others, some of which are also repeated more than once and written in both full and abbreviated forms. No blame, however, attaches to Theobald for this misstatement, for the only transcription of the document available at the time he wrote was the incomplete one by Burgoyne, and this contains only these two names.

There is no problem involved in the quotation from *The Rape of Lucrece* – which in any case is inaccurate – for this had certainly been published long before the Northumberland MS was compiled, and the mis-spelling of the long word from *Love's Labour's Lost* suggests that it had been heard spoken on the stage rather than seen in print or writing. I shall have something more to say later in the chapter about these two items, and also about 'Bacon', 'Shakespeare', and the other names referred to in the preceding paragraph.

From this discussion it will be apparent that, even without any further complications, the interpretation of the Northumberland MS is not the plain sailing Theobald fondly imagined. But there *are* further complications, and to these we must now turn.

They are the result of Titherley's intervention. Obviously the transcription of the Northumberland MS, in the very imperfect state in which Burgoyne had left it, had nothing to offer in support of the Derbyite case. Titherley therefore resolved to complete it, and to include, as he himself tells us, every word, every fragment of a word, and even every smudge. And there is no doubt he has performed the task nobly, though his elucidation of some of the words, owing to fading and obliteration, was obliged to be left doubtful.

I give here a summary of his results and conclusions.[1] First he detects three hands in the writing. Two of these he labels A and

[1] *Shakespeare's Identity*, pp. 291–298.

B, and designates as those of Bacon's secretaries; the third is, of course, his own particular 'King Charles' head', that of Derby, though he admits that secretary B's hand resembles Derby's sufficiently closely to make it uncertain which was responsible for some of the groups of words.

Of the great jumble of words and phrases which make up the main part of the document, he states that a large number, in the absence of all clues, are completely meaningless. Such are 'Dyrmont',[1] 'Dyr',[1] 'revealed', 'Adam',[1] 'speech', and 'brought', all apparently unrelated to anything else. On the right-hand portion of the sheet, however, when in the inverted position, he finds a number of words and phrases, which, though chaotic in their arrangement, are at least associated by being legal terms. They are 'fraud', 'revercon', 'in fee', 'taile for me', and the phrases 'your defenc formost self' and 'Justice of Earle', together with the somewhat incongruous remark 'o liar, liar'. Among these the word 'Earle' occurs three times, once as 'D Earle', and there is also 'lo D'. All these are either in the writing of B or in that of the hypothetical third hand.

Among the similar medley of expressions written with the sheet in its normal right-way-up position, Titherley found a number of names, which included 'earle of Arundel' (twice), 'Thomas turner' (several times, sometimes in an abbreviated form), which also occurs on the reverse side of the paper, 'Anthonie ffitzherbert', and 'Nevill' (twice). There is also the pair, 'Asmund and Cormelia', which, if it is the title of some play or poem, as it may well be, is also, like the two 'Rychards', without an author's name. The names that are repeated more than once are, like those previously transcribed by Burgoyne, written sometimes by A and sometimes by B.

These are, of course, only the merest fraction of the vast host of incongruous words and expressions that make up this chaotic document. They are, however, quite enough to reveal its quality and to enable the reader to follow Titherley's interpretation of it, and we shall encounter a few others in the course of our examination of this interpretation.

[1] Chambers has suggested that 'Adam Dyrmonth' was the name of the secretary responsible for the scribble, which only goes to show how many are the ways in which this puzzling document can be interpreted.

Before proceeding to the interpretation, however, it is necessary to explain that Derby, a younger son, inherited his title unexpectedly from his brother, and that the will of the latter involved him in an expensive lawsuit with his sister-in-law, which dragged on for fifteen years. It is this lawsuit that forms the basis of Titherley's interpretation of the manuscript. The legal terms it contains, several of which could in fact refer to the inheritance of an estate, coupled with the phrases 'D Earle' and 'lo D', give him his first clue. He states that Derby's was the only Earldom at the time beginning with the letter 'D', and from this he builds up the whole genesis of the Northumberland MS.

Bacon is, of course, the lawyer acting for Derby in the case, and one morning Derby calls to see him on business. He finds the room occupied by the two secretaries, whom Titherley identifies as John Davies, the poet, and Thomas Turner, whose name, as we have seen, occurs several times in the document. The two are engaged in compiling an inventory of manuscripts for Bacon, but lay down their pens and rise respectfully as the noble Earl enters. I give the rest in Titherley's own words.

He writes: 'One of them, say B, left the room to tell Bacon of the Earl's call. While waiting for an interview Derby . . . seeing the paper (upside down) before him on the table, without taking the trouble to turn it round, first tried a borrowed pen on it (with "th" etc.) and then jotted down a few notes – "Can rt me", "defenc formost", "shall", "lest" – connected with the business of his visit, also one connected with poetry ("is no distch"). After a while B returned, announcing that Bacon was engaged at the moment but could see the Earl at 3 o'clock, and B, seating himself at the table beside Derby, confirmed the appointment by writing half-way down the left margin (inverted) "at 3 you readie". Then during a legal conversation between them, B made a number of further notes at odd spots on the still inverted sheet – "revercon", "in fee", "taile for me", and "o liar, liar", all connected with the suit, and completed Derby's "defenc formost" by adding "your" and "self"; also adding "D Earle", etc. Some of the remarks relate to general talk, such as "and liberties", "your Sovereign", "borow", and "ham" (possibly a present by Derby to Bacon). These notes, echoes as they are of the great legal embarrassment that was clouding the Earl's horizon, were probably intended to prepare the way for the afternoon interview with Bacon and assist him with his momentous brief. Secretary B may be judged from some of his earlier entries at the top of the sheet (upright) to have been religious and possibly puritanical, but he was undoubtedly a strong partisan of the Earl, a great admirer of "Shakespeare". It was he who not only wrote "D" and "lo D" several times, but "liar", "justice", and "fraud" in relation to the Earl's "defenc"; it was also he who afterwards wrote (upright, below) the words "revealing day through every cranny peepes and", thus slightly misquoting line 1086 of "Lucrece". Since A twice wrote the possessive word "your" over "Shakespeare" (upright, below) and "yo" just under "W. d" near the top, it is clear enough that B was what we should now call a Shakespeare "fan", devoted to the Earl of Derby. Yet A (i.e. John Davies), as is known from several of his later poems and epigrams, was devoted to the Earl's late brother and his litigious widow Countess Alice, and so his feelings towards her opponent Derby must have been at least mixed. Having listened to all the lively talk between Derby and B about the lawsuit, at its close it must have been A (Davies) who accompanied Derby to the door on leaving, because scraps of their parting conversation, overheard by B, still seated at the table, were clearly jotted down by him; at least this is a reasonable interpretation of the disconnected remarks about "Imprisonmt", "prince", "e d", "manoring", and "seafourth", found on the back of the sheet. From the tenour of these remarks it may be supposed that Davies playfully criticized the Earl on leaving, just as later about 1611 in his Epigram he gently chided "Will Shake-speare" for playing "kingly parts in sport" (see pp. 92–94); but after the Earl's departure, when he returned to the table there seems to have been some animated conversation about the Earl, only a small fraction of which would be committed to the paper. As Davies was a poet as well as a scribe his mind would revert from Derby the litigant and princly sportsman to Derby the poet. First, recalling the long word from "Love's Labour's Lost" (V, i, 45) he wrote "H", "your lovinge ffriend", and then "Honorificabilitudine" (shortening the word by seven letters) in a bit of free space in the middle of the sheet (upright). Then lower down on the right, in the free space below "Essais etc", he boldly wrote "William Shakespeare", "do princes backe". To which B added "ra[ces"] and, recalling Derby's earlier remark, "Rimd dis[tich"], then "Rychard the second" and "Rychard the third" (plays which like *Love's Labour's Lost* had not yet been published), then twice "Asmund and Cormelia" (possibly a lost Shakespearean poem). In the talk ensuing between the two secretaries there was apparently some damaging comparison between Shakespeare and Nashe, whose "Ile of dogs" Davies considered an "inferior plaie", but the main interest was still Shakespeare whose name Davies continued to write several times below, the whole space being eventually filled by fragmentary forms, some of which seem to have been contributed by B (i.e. Turner).'

What is one to say about this interpretation? We have to remember that it admittedly rests on no external evidence, but is built up entirely on disjointed words and phrases selected from the jumble represented in facsimile on page 225. It seems impossible that the same person who made the admirable transcription of the document could be guilty of penning such a farrago of nonsense when he came to interpret it. Perhaps this kind of lapse is an 'occupational risk' of all who set out 'to make a case' for something. It may be that most theorists fall into the trap at some time; enthusiasm is a poor guide. However, it is not our business to explain Dr Titherley, but to analyse his interpretation of the Northumberland MS, and to this we turn.

We will pass over the statement that Derby walked into the office of the greatest lawyer in the land, picked up the pen of one of the secretaries, and tried it out on a document they were preparing, without even glancing at the latter – since he wrote on it upside down – to see how important it might be. Perhaps a haughty Tudor aristocrat would behave in this way, particularly if he were carrying a ham as a present for Bacon, who accordingly would be less disposed to resent the liberty. I say we will pass over all this as well as over the host of other minor absurdities, which in any case bear witness to their own spuriousness, and turn at once to the main point. This is the two conversations – the one between Derby and Secretary B, the other between the two secretaries after Derby had left. I invite my readers to go carefully through the whole passage again, and then to ask themselves if it is conceivable that any conversation was ever conducted, anywhere at any time, on the lines suggested by Titherley – a conversation in which one party makes a remark at the same time jotting down odd detached words from that remark on a sheet of paper, presumably in order to assist his hearer in understanding it, and then politely passing the paper to the other party for him to reply in the same way? Yet this is precisely what Titherley describes as happening over and over again. For instance, Derby makes a remark and writes 'defenc formost', and then Secretary B takes the paper and, while replying verbally – for Davies is listening to 'all the lively talk' – adds 'your' before Derby's phrase and 'self' after it. Again in the second conversation, Secretary A writes 'do princes backe' to accompany some remark, and Secretary B, snatching the paper, triumphantly adds 'races'. And the same absurdity is evident in all the other combined verbal and scribal operations alleged to be contained in the manuscript, such as Turner's jottings on the parting conversation between Derby and Davies at the door, as well as his so-called confirmation of the afternoon appointment – 'at 3 you readie', as if he were dealing with a half-wit or a very young child who could not possibly take in the meaning of the spoken words without the reinforcement of a visual aid.

Once again, what are we to make of the 'legal notes' that Titherley states Secretary B took about the lawsuit 'to prepare the way for the afternoon interview with Bacon and assist him with his momentous brief'. They are just odd disjointed words and phrases jotted down here, there, and everywhere at random about the sheet. There is no connection whatever between them, no clue to what they referred, and no system or order in their arrangement. Moreover, no sooner had Derby left than the two secretaries grabbed the sheet and began scribbling around and over these precious notes until they had reduced them to a state of almost complete illegibility. What possible purpose could they have been meant to serve in these circumstances? If Bacon really were Derby's advocate and made use of these 'notes' in the conduct of the case, it is not surprising that it dragged on for fifteen years.

In point of fact, however, it is in the highest degree unlikely that Bacon was Derby's advocate. His only recorded connection with the case in question is that he signed, as one of the witnesses, the receipt of the Master of Rolls *for the documents put in by the other side.* He would hardly have been invited to perform this office if he were the opposing Counsel. Titherley's only evidence for the claim is what he himself has manufactured out of 'D Earle' and the so-called 'notes on the lawsuit' contained in the manuscript, together with his identification of the 'third hand' as that of Derby. But, as we have already seen (pp. 101–102), the evidence of handwriting is often very doubtful, and it is particularly so in this case, for, as Titherley himself admits, that of Secretary B resembles what he calls Derby's so closely that sometimes they are indistinguishable. For myself, I doubt the existence of a third hand, and incline to the belief that the so-called third script is merely that of Secretary B writing with another pen.

As for the 'legal notes', such as they are – there are a vast number of words on the sheet, and it would be surprising if a few were not to be found that, with a little ingenuity, could be adapted to fit almost any theory. Moreover, even if it could be proved – which of course it cannot – that Bacon acted for Derby and Derby's handwriting was on the sheet, this would not be evidence for Derby's authorship of the Shakespearean plays. There is not a word on the sheet to give the faintest hint of any such thing; everything advanced by Titherley on the subject is what he himself has read into it.

Before bringing this chapter to a close, I cannot resist the temptation of giving my own interpretation of the Northumberland MS. I admit that it is pure unsupported conjecture, but it is a natural and simple one; it covers all the facts, and it avoids all the difficulties the strained and far-fetched interpretations of the Baconians and Titherley encounter. If it does nothing else, it will at least prove how easy it is to produce theories.

I suggest that the two secretaries were having a quill-sharpening session. They collected all their pens, and sat down at a table on which lay a sheet of paper, begun as an inventory of Bacon's manuscripts but for some reason abandoned. This they both use to try out each pen as they sharpen it; if a pen is not quite satisfactory when tried, they subject it to further trimming and then test it again. In this way the paper would soon be covered with a mass of words. Being lawyers, they naturally write down many legal phrases, quite haphazard and having no association with one another, which would account for the chaotic positioning of these phrases. Their employer's name also figures naturally in this connection. Quill-sharpening, however, does not demand great mental concentration; they soon begin to talk on general subjects, and odd scraps from the conversation find their way on to the paper – not to assist the understanding of the hearer, as Titherley, against all reason, assumes to be the purpose – but because the words they are speaking communicate themselves almost automatically to the random movements of the pens which are being tested. Presently the talk turns on the drama, and it would be surprising if the most popular dramatist of the day and some of his plays were not mentioned. The repetitions are naturally explained as successive attempts to get a refractory pen right; the same words or part of the same words would be written several times to test the result by comparison. When the quill-sharpening is finished, the two secretaries leave the paper lying about, for it contains no momentous secret and is of no importance whatever. Eventually it is used as a cover for the pile of manuscripts with which it was found.

Such is my interpretation, and it is not merely author's pride that makes me think it may well be the correct one. But whether it is or not, one thing is certain – the Northumberland MS is nothing more than a page of idle scribble, and, while exceedingly interesting as a literary curiosity, has no bearing on the problem with which we are concerned. It only intrudes into this discussion because of the desperate anxiety of the theorists to erect an imposing façade of argument regardless of the material with which it is built.

CHAPTER XIII

The Feudal Aristocrat

The claim that the author of the Shakespearean plays must have been a feudal aristocrat is, of course, the particular preserve of the Oxfordians and Derbyites. The other claimants, though of diverse social status, belonged to the ranks of the 'new men'.

As A. J. Evans has a foot in both the Oxfordian and Derbyite camps, we may appropriately allow him to state the common position of the two. He writes,[1] 'There is no avoiding the conclusion that Shakespeare was an aristocrat – it is self evident. . . . Kings, queens, dukes and Court life are clearly the *milieu* in which Shakespeare is happiest. . . . The point of view is that of a nobleman . . . there is an air of feudalism in almost every play. . . . The plays are exactly what might have been expected from a courtier and a scholar. If a man from the lower classes wrote them, it is amazing that he avoided introducing scenes from his own humble environment and still more amazing that he could have acquired such intimate knowledge of a mode of life so far above his own.'

Earlier in his book[2] Evans had written, 'Only an aristocratic Shakespeare could have written *The Tempest*, which is aristocratic in tone throughout, reflecting as it does the point of view of a great lord accustomed to handle men and give orders to his inferiors.

From this it will be gathered that the case of the theorists is comprised under three heads, as follows:

(1) That the setting of the Shakespearean plays is almost invariably that of the upper ranks of society.

(2) That the attitude of the author in writing the plays is always that of a nobleman born to command.

(3) That the Stratford actor could not possess the necessary knowledge and experience to depict the scenes and personages

---

[1] *Shakespeare's Magic Circle*, pp. 141 f.   [2] Op. cit., pp. 115 f.

in the plays, and that if he had been the author they would have taken a very different form.

We will examine the validity of each of these in turn.

With regard to the first, Evans is, of course, perfectly correct in stating that the setting of many of the Shakespearean plays is in courts and palaces, and that the *dramatis personae* are kings, queens, dukes, and other lofty personages. But Shakespeare is by no means unique in this. The same is true of a large majority of Elizabethan dramatists, as a glance at their plays will prove. Would Evans deduce from this that all these other dramatists were also disguised noblemen, like the Pirates in the Gilbert and Sullivan opera? The truth is that the plots – almost all of them borrowed, not original, in Shakespeare's case – demanded such settings, and the audiences demanded such plots. It was among kings, queens, and other exalted persons that exciting incidents happened, or were believed to happen, and the citizens who attended the public theatres wanted to see exciting incidents, not a dull picture of their own workaday world.

In the case of tragedy there was an additional and more fundamental reason for this state of affairs, though it may not always have been consciously recognized even by the dramatists themselves. Wyndham Lewis,[1] quoting Bradley, states that it was part of the tradition of drama from the time of Aristotle onwards that the hero of tragedy must be an eminent person. Bradley says, 'The story of the prince, the triumvir, the general has a greatness and a dignity of its own. His fate affects the welfare of the whole nation or empire, and when he suddenly falls from greatness to the dust, his fall produces a sense of contrast, of the powerlessness of man, and of the omnipotence – perhaps the caprice – of Fortune or Fate, which no tale of private life can possibly rival.'

We see therefore that there were a number of very good reasons for the author of the Shakespearean plays, no matter how humble his birth, to choose to write the types of play he did, and that in so doing he was only following the same fashion as the greater part of his contemporaries. So far then as their contention in this matter is correct the theorists are fully answered. But their contention is not wholly correct.

[1] *The Lion and the Fox*, pp. 117 ff.

The author of the Shakespearean plays, contrary to the dog-matic assertion of Evans, did write of persons and scenes of lower stations in the social scale. The amateur dramatic society of the hard-handed workers of Athens in M.N.D. is one case, the sheep-shearing festivities in W.T. is another, and there are several others, including the London tavern scenes in Hen. IV. It is also to be remarked that Shakespeare often drew on 'low life' for his imagery. There are, for instance, seventeen references to the butcher's trade in his plays. This is very significant, for a lowly-born poet, while adding to his store of images as he rose in society, might well permit some references to his past to slip into his work, but we can scarcely picture noble lords deliber-ately visiting the local shambles in search of poetic symbols.

Again the leading *dramatis personae* of C. of E. are not nobles, but merchants and their families, and the Fords and Pages of M.W.W. are the same bourgeois type as swarmed in and around Stratford-on-Avon or any other small provincial town. More-over, whatever rank their owners may be given, the houses and households of the Capulets in R. and J., of Baptista in T. of Sh., of Leonato in M. Ado – are in no way different from the estab-lishments of the ordinary well-to-do citizens, as can easily be verified by comparing them with the pictures given of such citizens' households by Dekker in *The Shoemakers' Holiday*, by the collaborators in *Eastward Ho*, and by a number of other play-wrights. They differ in many important details from the organization of the aristocratic household.

In this connection M. St Clare Byrne[1] gives a lengthy list of Shakespeare's slips in representing an allegedly aristocratic household, sometimes even of the Court itself, and his substitu-tion of the arrangements of a bourgeois household for the correct details. She also traces a growing knowledge of aristo-cratic households in the later plays, which suggests that the author was learning by experience, which in turn suggests a non-aristocratic author, for a true aristocrat would naturally have known everything from the start. Thus a study of Shake-speare's stage households, contrary to the theorists' claims, actually provides evidence in favour of the actor's authorship.

[1] Essay on 'The Social Background' in *A Companion to Shakespeare Studies*, pp. 189–204.

When all these items are added together it will be seen that Shakespeare devoted a considerable proportion of his work to the lower grades of society, and seems to have been quite as happy in their company as he was in the aristocratic *milieu*.

The second point, that the author's outlook is essentially aristocratic, is more difficult to deal with because the statement is so vague and can have different meanings for different persons. Evans' interpretation of it is superficial and limited to external qualities, such as the one already quoted – the ability to handle men and give orders to inferiors. But surely he knows better than to imagine such qualities are exclusively aristocratic. Francis Drake was no aristocrat, but I imagine the crews of his ships 'jumped to it smartly' when he gave an order. Besides, the playwright is not required to display this or any other 'aristocratic' quality himself, only to depict *dramatis personae* who display it. And this brings us to the crux of the whole matter.

It is the business of the dramatist, the novelist, and the narrative poet to depict all the various types of humanity necessary to his plot. The ability to do this will depend on two factors: (i) the opportunity to observe the types, and (ii) the sympathetic insight that enables him to put himself in their place, which we call his genius, and which is far the more important. The first of these will be dealt with in the next section. With regard to the second, all successful authors must possess it to some extent or they would not be successful. The author of the Shakespearean plays is very far from being the only one who has drawn aristocratic types successfully, and if he has done it better than anyone else, it is only because his genius is greater, not because he was one himself. Exactly the same is true of all the other types he depicted.

And this is a point that Evans conveniently overlooks. If Shakespeare could give us a portrait of the essential aristocrat in Prospero, he could also give us a portrait of the essential slave in Caliban, with all his smouldering resentment and suppressed mutiny, and most critics would maintain that the latter is the more successful. If Evans insists that Shakespeare must have been an aristocrat to draw the one, then he is logically bound to insist that he must have been a slave to draw the other; and so on through the whole dazzling gallery of portraits that he has given us. He must have been king and commoner, man and woman, victor and vanquished, philosopher and fool, and many other things as well; and so, of course, he was, not by accident of birth, but by virtue of the supreme genius he possessed.

So much for Evans' interpretation. Many Oxfordians, however, take a more profound view of what is implied by the term 'aristocratic'. They interpret it as meaning a reverence for tradition, a tenderness for the past, a pride in the history of one's country and the men who made it great, a loyalty to certain ideals, and other kindred qualities. Most Stratfordians would agree that such an attitude is found in the Shakespearean plays, but they would vigorously deny that only a nobleman could display it. They would contend that it was the natural attitude of a certain type of mind which might occur in any class. And this is true, particularly of Tudor times. It must be remembered that such ideas as egalitarianism and internationalism with the tendency to 'cry down' one's own country were quite unknown in those days, and patriotic feeling ran high even among the poorest classes. The very fact that the Stratford actor was so anxious to exploit his mother's connection with the local landed gentry that he applied for permission, as there is documentary evidence he did in 1599, to impale the Arden arms on the coat he had recently acquired for his family, would certainly suggest that he had the type of mind we have just been discussing.

On the other hand there are critics who trace in the Shakespearean plays the ill-concealed contempt of a representative of the bourgeoisie for the effete old aristocracy and all the outworn childish ideas of feudal chivalry. The first hint of this viewpoint is to be found in *Shakespeares dramatische Kunst* by the German critic, Hermann Ulrici, published as early as 1839, but perhaps the best presentation of it is that by Wyndham Lewis,[1] which should be studied by all interested in the subject. I can only give a very brief summary here.

Lewis begins by categorically denying that Shakespeare was the aristocratically-minded feudal poet that so many critics claimed. It was true that he had a tenderness for much in the

---

[1] *The Lion and the Fox*, pp. 235–246.

past, but he had a contempt equally strong for much more. He shared the aristocrat's dislike of the mob, as the prosperous bourgeoisie often do, but he despised the limitations and childish attitude of the old aristocracy. As an artist he often fell in love with his great creations – Othello and Antony – but with others, the heroes of *Troilus and Cressida* and especially the character of Coriolanus, he allowed his contempt full sway.

Describing his treatment of the latter, Lewis writes: 'Coriolanus, as a figure, is of course the super-snob. Of all Shakespeare's heroes he is the coldest . . . that never became anything but a schoolboy, crazed with notions of privilege and social distinction, incapable of thinking . . . but also congealed into a kind of machine of unintelligent pride. He is like a nietzschean, artificial "aristocrat" with little nobility in the sense that Don Quixote caricaturely embodied the noble, but possessing only a maniacal intolerance and stiffness.'

After an analysis of the play in support of this contention, Lewis sums up: 'Coriolanus . . . is a play about a conventional military hero, existing as the characteristic ornament of a strong aristocratic system. Shakespeare was neither for him nor against him on propagandist, feudal or non-feudal grounds. He was quite ready to curse the crowd with him; he was equally ready to examine with as little pleasure the child of a harsh practical system, abusing his many advantages, and showing how the top, as likewise the under, dog is unsatisfactory and foolish, the one very nearly worthy of the other – the violent, dull, conceited leader, and the resentful but cowardly slave.'

Lewis adds that Shakespeare's other military heroes, though redeemed by finer qualities, show the same basic attitude.[1]

It is possible that these critics go too far. I myself should certainly hesitate to go all the way with them. But if they can make out such a strong case against aristocracy from the plays, and they certainly can, it renders the facile assumption of Evans

---

[1] It should be remembered that this and the similar findings of other critics were not written to score points against the theorists; they were written in opposition to the views of fellow-Stratfordians who held that Shakespeare was aristocratic in outlook though not by birth. They therefore had no orthodox axe to grind.

and the other theorists that Shakespeare was a member of the old aristocracy and wrote as such, to say the least of it, decidedly unconvincing.

The third point, that the Stratford actor could not have possessed the knowledge and experience necessary to write the 'aristocratic' scenes and references in the Shakespearean plays, may be conveniently subdivided for treatment under the two following heads:

(1) The knowledge the Stratford actor certainly possessed.

(2) Defects in the 'aristocratic' scenes incompatible with the idea of an aristocratic author.

With regard to the first of these, it must be realized that conditions in Tudor times were very different from those of today. The privacy to which we attach so much importance simply did not exist, and the humblest person had ample opportunity to observe much of the lives of the great. Salzman[1] says, 'No monarchs were more accessible than they (the Tudors). It was far easier for the humblest peasant to have speech with Queen Elizabeth than for an ordinary man to obtain access to a minister of a Labour Cabinet. The most magnificent festivities were open to the public; so much so that on one occasion the mob laid hands upon the sacred person of Henry VIII, and stripped off all the gilt ornaments with which his dress was spangled; the which he treated as a joke.' And the same was true of the nobility at their provincial seats and London houses – their banquets and other festivities were public shows which anyone who could push his way in might attend. If therefore William Shakspere had belonged to the humblest stratum of society, he could still have observed at first hand much of the detail that makes up the 'aristocratic' scenes in the plays.

But William Shakspere did not belong to the humblest stratum of society. He was the son of a prosperous citizen with many business interests in Stratford-on-Avon, a Justice of the Peace, and a man who held in turn all the highest municipal honours, including that of Bailiff (Mayor), and would therefore be responsible for the entertainment of any notable persons passing through the town. Moreover, on his mother's side

[1] *England in Tudor Times*, pp. 5 and 6.

William was related to some of the local landed gentry;[1] and with such antecedents as these would not have to begin from the bottom of the social scale if he set out to learn the ways of the nobility.

As an actor he was called upon to perform, not only in the public theatres, but at the royal palaces, the houses of the nobles, and the Inns of Court. At certain seasons, and particularly when the plague was raging in London, the players went on tour, frequently performing at the country seats of the nobility, and being lodged there perhaps for several days at a time, when they would have innumerable opportunities for observing the ways of a great house.

Moreover, in Elizabethan and Jacobean times the royal players, of whom Shakspere was one, were sworn in by the Lord Chamberlain as Grooms of the Chamber. They did not as a rule perform the ordinary duties of this office, acting taking the place of these, but it gave them the *entrée* to the Palace and the right to wear the prescribed uniform. Shakspere's name in fact appears on one extant list of actors who received an issue of material for such a uniform (see p. 37). Although, as stated, the actors did not normally perform the ordinary duties of the Grooms, there is a recorded case when they did so. This was in 1604, when they were attached to the person of the Spanish Ambassador, the Constable of Castile; and there may well have been other cases, the records of which have been lost. In the light of these facts the Stratford actor's knowledge of the 'aristocratic' life cannot be denied; he not only had ample opportunity to study it from several angles, but was called upon to play his own part in it, and it may well have been his happiest *milieu*, as Evans says.

But here a *caveat* must be entered. It was the social and domestic side of this life only with which such a person would be familiar. The doors of the Council Chamber on the other hand would be closed to him; he would never see Elizabeth or James in solemn conclave with their Ministers, as Oxford and

---

[1] In 1602, when some question about the coat-of-arms cropped up, the Garter and Clarencieux Kings-of-Arms set down in writing that 'the man was A magistrat in Stratford vpon Avon. A Justice of peace he maryed A daughter of Ardern, and was of good substance and habilite.'

Derby would, or be called upon to take part in debates vitally affecting the welfare of the nation. As a consequence of this we should expect to find both types of scene – the social and the political – equally well depicted if the author were a noble lord; but if he were a humble player then we should expect a marked difference between the two, for whatever scraps of information he might pick up about the second, he could hardly fail to break down on technical details.

And this is exactly what we do find. The ball-room scenes in R. & J. and M. Ado, the wedding festivities in M.N.D., the roystering of Sir Toby and Sir Andrew in T.N., and others like them, are vivid and authentic; we feel that this is just what they would have been. When, however, we turn to the scenes of leaders in council the case is very different; we cannot possibly accept them as authentic. Even when nothing of an *outré* nature is introduced they never convince us that they are the real thing; and very often something *outré* is introduced, as when Gloster (Ric. III, Act III, Sc. iv) interrupts the meeting of the Council, which is arranging the details of the Coronation, to send the Bishop of Ely out for strawberries, for all the world as if he were Burbage interrupting a meeting of theatrical managers to order another round of drinks. And there are many other examples of the same kind – Henry and York squabbling like two children over who is to sit on the throne in the Parliament House (3 Hen. VI, I, i), with threats by Clifford to pull York off by force; the snowstorm of gages covering the floor of Westminster Hall, hurled down as a long succession of challenges by the whole crowd of bickering and abusive nobles present (Ric. II, IV, i); and much else of a similar nature.[1] It is true that some of these episodes are derived from the *Chronicles* of Holinshed and others with no more real experience of such matters than Shakspere; but if the author had really been a great lord who knew what actually happened in such circumstances he would undoubtedly have

---

[1] Moreover, the author seems to think that Montjoy (Hen. V, III, vi) was the French Herald's personal name instead of his official designation, a mistake the Stratford actor in particular might well make, since he lodged for a time with a family of French refugees of that name, but which would be impossible in the case of Oxford or Derby.

devised something a little more realistic and plausible; Shakespeare, whoever he was, never was a slave to his sources, and had no hesitation about improving on them.

The Roman plays are superior to the English histories in this respect, but this fact confirms rather than modifies the conclusion we have reached. North's *Plutarch*, which is the main source of the Roman plays, is much more helpful in such matters than Holinshed's *Chronicles*, which were the main source of the English histories. The superiority of the former therefore only serves to demonstrate the author's lack of political experience and his dependence for information on his sources.

This concludes the discussion on the claim that the author of the Shakespearean plays must have been a feudal aristocrat. It has had to be somewhat diffuse owing to the varying shades of opinion on both sides. The two facts that most clearly emerge from it are that any such claim is in the highest degree improbable, and that the personal experiences of the Stratford actor were quite adequate to enable him to write any of the scenes the plays contain, provided, of course, he possessed the necessary genius to do so.[1]

[1] I have in this chapter said nothing about the possibility of Shakspere's having a noble patron, and in consequence of further increasing his knowledge of the aristocratic life by visits to this patron's house, as Marlowe visited Walsingham. To do so would have been to beg the question, for, of course, it is the essence of the theorists' case that Shakspere was not an author and would therefore have no patron. Nor was it necessary for my purpose to invoke such assistance, although there is some, if not conclusive, evidence for it. As the facts related in this chapter have clearly demonstrated, Shakspere's known opportunities for acquiring the necessary information and experience were ample to explain everything that occurs in the plays.

CHAPTER XIV

Portraits and Monuments

One cannot but admire the pertinacity and optimism of the theorists. They will patiently rake over any rubbish heap, no matter how unpromising its material, in the hope of dragging from among the discarded scraps something that might be manipulated into a support for their various claims. Probably the best example of this unrewarding labour is their attempt to turn the so-called Shakespearean portraits to account.

Of these there are more than a dozen in existence, but only two have even the remotest claim to being genuine, and neither of these is very satisfactory. With most we shall not be concerned in any way, two examples being ample for our purpose.

The first is the well-known Droeshout, which appeared on the title-page of the First Folio in 1623, and has adorned many a volume since. It appears to be the work of a Flemish engraver named Martin Droeshout, who was brought to London as a child, and who later was responsible for the portraits of several Jacobean men of letters. The portrait in question, several original copies of which have survived, is an engraving done on copper plates, and exists in two states – a first, or 'proof', state, and a second in which a number of details have been added. It shows the face and shoulders of a man with a vacuous mask-like countenance, an abnormally high forehead, arched eyebrows, an exaggerated moustache, a small beard, and a jaw greatly in need of a shave. He is attired in a flamboyant tunic, which, strangely enough, seems to have two left (or two right) sleeves.

As Droeshout was only fifteen when Shakspere died, and it is unlikely the two ever met, it is obvious that this is not a portrait from life; in fact the description that it consists of two left sleeves and a mask would seem to be very near the truth. The Baconians, or to be fair to the more scholarly of them, the Durning-Lawrence section, have seized on this picture as evidence for their theory. They say it was specially designed by Bacon in order to reveal that Shakspere was merely a mask for him, and might, as far as the authorship of the plays was concerned, be considered his left hand.[1] Of course there is not a scrap of evidence for this absurd theory, and it is open to all the criticisms that we have seen can be advanced against the other forms of cryptogram (see p. 70 f.).

What actually happened cannot now be known. We must remember that in those days there was no photography and no press with its library of illustrations of stage celebrities. The artist, as already stated, had in all probability never seen the man whose portrait he was required to make, and there seems to have been no picture he could use as a copy. Perhaps he was provided with a line drawing made by one of the players[2] from memory, or there may have been a roughly moulded mask of Shakspere in existence – the heads of beheaded *dramatis personae* carried on to the stage may well have been made to resemble the actor playing the part – which would explain the mask-like appearance of the face in the engraving.

In this case it is possible that Droeshout drew in the tunic without a copy. He was a young and inexperienced artist at the time, and is not likely to have been paid much for his work; the First Folio bears all the marks of having been produced 'on the cheap', and presents a very different appearance from the sumptuous Folio containing Jonson's works, published a few years earlier.

The next portrait that we must consider is the one designated the Ashbourne or Kingston. This is a pleasant three-quarter-length picture of a man in Elizabethan dress, and bears a two-lined inscription in the top left-hand corner – 'Aetatis suae 47, A° 1611'. As 47 was the actual age of Shakspere in 1611, there have, of course, been suggestions that the portrait is of him. Since, however, nothing at all is known about the picture before it came into the possession of the Rev. C. U. Kingston in 1847, and as there must have been many other men who reached the age of 47 in 1611, it would be impossible to claim it as a portrait of Shakspere even if its date were certainly

[1] Durning-Lawrence, *Bacon is Shakespeare*, p. 12.
[2] Richard Burbage is known to have been an amateur artist.

genuine. Such, however, is not the case; some experts who have examined it say that it bears many of the signs of a forged antique.

This fact has not deterred the Oxfordians from trying to make capital out of it for their candidate. They state[1] that Father de Vere Beauclerk, a descendant of Oxford, noticed a resemblance between the head in the picture and that of Oxford in the portrait of him known as the Welbeck, and demonstrated by a series of photographs that the two heads could be superimposed with complete accuracy.

Furthermore, in 1940 Mr Charles Russell, who was at the time Secretary of the U.S.A. Branch of the Shakespeare Fellowship, an anti-Stratfordian organization, obtained permission to make an X-ray and infra-red ray examination of the picture. Having done so, he reported that it was a portrait painted by the Dutch artist, Ketel, but that the original had been faked in various ways. A signet ring on the finger of the sitter, with a boar's head – the crest of the Oxfords – as a device, had been painted out, as had the artist's monogram, while the arms of the Trenthams, the family of the Countess of Oxford, which had occupied the top left-hand corner, had been effaced and the place it had occupied covered with the second line of the inscription – 'A° 1611'. Russell's interpretation of these features was that the picture was a portrait of Oxford painted by Ketel in 1595, when Oxford was 47 years of age, and that later it had been tampered with, and the alterations described carried out.

Even if all the details adumbrated are correct – and in the interests of scientific truth they certainly ought to be checked by a second and completely independent investigator, free from all preconceptions – what do they really amount to? The most they can prove is that a portrait of Oxford has, at some time unknown after it was painted, been doctored by another artist to make it appear as that of someone else. There is nothing to connect it with the Stratford actor except the trivial coincidence of the age which could apply to innumerable other persons equally well. In any case it does not, and could not, throw any light whatever on the authorship of the Shakespearean plays.

[1] M. Douglas, *Lord Oxford and the Shakespeare Group*, pp. 56 ff.

That strange coincidences can occur in painting no less than in literature, and that they are uncertain props to support any theory, may be illustrated by the following facts, which, of course, are never mentioned by any of the theorists. There is in the Rylands Library, Manchester, a portrait belonging undoubtedly to the Elizabethan era and representing an exceedingly handsome and artistic-looking young man. The inscription at the top gives the age of the subject as 24 and the date as 1588, so that he was exactly the same age as William Shakspere. Moreover a comparison with the Droeshout portrait shows that the relative distances from the point of the chin to the lower lip, from the lower lip to the tip of the nose, from the tip of the nose to the lower eyelid, from the lower eyelid to the eyebrow, and from the eyebrow to the top of the forehead, are identical in both portraits, while the great domed forehead is also a common feature.

It may well be that some of the Bardolators have attempted on this evidence to claim that here is a genuine portrait of Shakspere, for there are wild and woolly men in all camps; but as Dover Wilson,[1] who has described it, points out, apart from the coincidences of age and certain measurements, there is nothing to connect this portrait of an unknown young man with the Stratford actor. Dover Wilson's plain statement of the facts, with a warning on the limitations of these, and his refusal to erect any theory upon them, is an example of scholarly caution that the theorists would do well to follow. The picture, of course, throws no light on the problem of authorship, and I merely mention its existence for comparison with the similar stories of portraits, including the one just reviewed and the one that is to follow, utilized by the theorists, and to demonstrate that such details are by no means solely the perquisites of the anti-Stratfordians.

The next episode we have to consider comes from Calvin Hoffman's[2] book. It does not concern Shakspere at all, but an alleged portrait of Marlowe, though naturally Hoffman endeavours to extract some support for his theory from the incident.

[1] *The Essential Shakespeare*, p. 6.
[2] *The Man Who Was Shakespeare*, pp. 65 ff.

He relates that in 1953, when he paid a visit to Corpus Christi College, Cambridge, he was shown a picture which had been rescued from a rubbish heap raised in the quadrangle by the workmen during structural alterations to the Master's Lodge, the first, he asserts, since Elizabethan times. It is painted in oils on a wooden panel, 2 feet by 1½ feet in size, and is the portrait of a young man. In the upper left-hand corner is the inscription, extending over four lines – 'Aetatis suae 21, 1585, *Quod me nutrit me destruit.*'

About this discovery Hoffman writes as follows: 'Now we know that Marlowe was 21 in 1585. We also know that, already an established playwright, he was the most celebrated alumnus of Corpus Christi, and that in 1585, there were only twelve students in the college of his year. It is also known that Marlowe matriculated at Corpus at the remarkably late age of sixteen (matriculation generally occurred at thirteen or fourteen). Therefore, since he was the most illustrious student at Corpus Christi at that time, and since his age tallies with that given in the portrait the chances are overwhelming that the portrait is of him.

'The Latin motto, *Quod me nutruit me destruit,* reappears (slightly varied) in *Pericles,* Act II, Scene 2, Line 33:

THAISA. A burning torch that's turned upside down;
The word, *Quod me alit me extinguit.*
SIMONIDES. Which shows that beauty hath his powers and will,
Which can as well inflame as it can kill.

The motto also appears in English in Shakespeare's sonnet, Number 73:

Consumed with that which it was nourished by,

and in many variations throughout the plays.

'What struck me most about this portrait was its strong likeness to the First Folio engraving by Martin Droeshout of the genuine author of the First Folio plays. . . . Not trusting my judgement at the time, I showed both pictures to portrait specialists. To a man, they said the two were portraits of the same individual, the only difference being one of age. In America the two pictures, enlarged several hundred times,[1] have been examined by Washington experts, and the conclusion reached was that a marked general resemblance, and a specific resemblance in the features undeniably existed.'

I may begin my criticism of this claim by pointing out that a number of the statements advanced to support it cannot be accepted as established facts; they are suppositions which themselves require proof before they can be treated as evidence for anything else. In the first place it is by no means certain that at 21, Marlowe was the glittering star Hoffman describes. There is no evidence that he wrote any of his plays while at Cambridge. He may have done, but all we know for certain is that when he left the University he went to London, and his first play, *Tamburlaine*, was probably produced in 1587, two years later than the date on the picture. Anything beyond this bare detail is mere assumption. As for the statement that there were only twelve students of Marlowe's year in the College, it is evidence of nothing. It can throw no light on whether the portrait is that of Marlowe or not, nor tell what he wrote or did not write; it is in fact completely irrelevant to all matters under discussion.

Again Hoffman does not inform us of the identity of the 'portrait specialists' and 'Washington experts' to whom he submitted his copies of the Corpus Christi and Droeshout portraits for comparison, or of the grounds on which they reached their conclusions. We cannot judge the value of their opinions, no matter how many hundreds of times they enlarged the pictures, when we know nothing of their standing or competency or of their technique. Moreover, Hoffman does not even mention, much less attempt to deal with, the difficulties and problems inherent in the Droeshout portrait itself (see pp. 246 f.). No doubt many Stratfordians would be duly grateful to him if he could relieve them of the burden of this atrocity, but I, who have the greatest admiration for Marlowe, would be sorry to see it inflicted on him.

[1] I assume that Mr Hoffman means that he submitted photographs of the two portraits to his experts, *not* the originals. As he himself has informed us that the Corpus Christi portrait measures 2 feet by 1½ feet, an enlargement of this several hundred times would require extensive premises to house it and a rather long 'run back' for any expert who wished to judge its general effect. I doubt if even America could provide the necessary facilities.

With regard to the Corpus Christi picture itself – it may be a portrait of Marlowe or it may not. The chances are very far from being as favourable to the former view as Hoffman would have us believe. His insistence on the fact that Marlowe was rather old for a student of those days could only be of value if the portrait were known for certain to be that of a student, of which there is not the slightest evidence; indeed what evidence there is tells rather against such a supposition. If it had been the case, we should have expected the picture to be in the Hall or some other prominent place in the College, not in the Master's Lodge, and that a name would be attached to it. While it is true that names are lacking on most Elizabethan portraits, this is because they were to pass into the possession of the sitter's family where no label would be needed. But in the case of the star scholar of a college, whose stay there would necessarily be only temporary, and whose portrait was to commemorate him for future generations of undergraduates, some identification would be essential. This lack of a label and its presence in the Master's Lodge lead me to believe that the picture is of some member of a former Master's family.

As for the motto by which Hoffman seeks to link up the portrait with the authorship of the Shakespearean plays – it is just a commonplace Latin tag. If the reader will turn to the scene in *Pericles* in which it occurs (II, ii) he will see that this represents a procession of knights on their way to the lists. As each knight passes, Thaisa reads out the motto on his shield, and Simonides makes a comment on it. The complete list is as follows:

(1) *Lux tua vita mihi.*
(2) *Piu por dubzura que por fuerzo.*
(3) *Me pompae provexit apex.*
(4) *Quod me alit, me extinguit.*
(5) *Sic spectanda fides.*
(6) *In hae spe vivo.*

The motto in question therefore is merely the fourth of six such mottoes. Moreover, though it has been emended by editors of more recent editions to read '*Quod* etc', as it does in the portrait, in the original version of *Pericles*, the 1609 Quarto, it reads, less correctly, '*Qui* etc', thus suggesting that the author was an inferior Latinist. Four of these mottoes, including the one with which we are concerned, are culled from the Emblem books of the day, and so were available for anyone to borrow. And the one in question was frequently borrowed by both Shakespeare's predecessors and his contemporaries. For example, Surrey had used it in his poem, *Of a Lady who refused to dance with him* – 'I shall be glad to feed on that which would have fed on me', and Thomas Dekker used it in his prose work, *Seven Deadly Sins of London* – 'He destroys that which feeds him'. The forms it takes in *Pericles* and on the portrait, being variants, not identities, may well have come from different sources. Finally, the question of how much of *Pericles* was written by Shakespeare is still a very vexed one. It would seem that the Editors of the First Folio did not think it amounted to much since they excluded the play from that volume.

From this it will be seen that Hoffman's evidence for Marlowe's authorship of the Shakespearean plays consists in this instance of two variants of a motto in general use, one of which variants appears on a portrait very doubtfully of Marlowe and the other in a passage very doubtfully by Shakespeare. Comment is unnecessary.

This is all that need be said on the rather tedious subject of the portraits. We may now leave them and turn to the problem of the Shakespeare Monument in the Parish Church at Stratford-on-Avon.

This monument stands against the north wall of the chancel, and is made of marble inlaid with touchstone. It consists of an inscribed base from which arise two Corinthian pillars with black shafts and gilded capitals. These support a cornice and pediment. In the centre of the latter is Shakspere's coat-of-arms, surmounted by a skull and flanked by figures symbolizing Labour and Rest. The base, pillars, and cornice enclose a space that contains the bust of Shakspere in coloured Cotswold stone. Both hands rest lightly on a cushion, the right holding a pen and the left covering a piece of paper which is spread flat on the cushion. The inscription, the author of which is unknown, runs as follows:

Ivdicio Pylivm, genio Socratem, arte Maronem:
Terra tegit, popvlvs maeret, Olympvs habet.

Stay Passenger, why goest thov by so fast?
read if thov canst, whom enviovs Death hath plast,
with in this monvment Shakespeare; with whome,
quick natvre dide; whose name doth deck y^s Tombe,
Far more than cost: sieh all, y^t He hath writt,
Leaves living art, bvt page, to serve his witt.

obiit ano do^i 1616.
Aetatis 53 die ap^r.

The monument was obviously erected between 1616 and
1623, for Leonard Digges refers to it in his poem prefixed to the
First Folio, which was published at the latter date. It is good
Jacobean work, and is stated to have been executed by Gheerart
Janssen the younger, who, as he carried on his business close
to the Globe Theatre, may have known Shakspere at least by
sight.

In 1749 repairs were carried out, as the monument had become impaired by the ravages of time. Much of the money for
this work came from local subscriptions, but some of it was
raised by John Ward, the grandfather of Mrs Siddons, whose
theatrical company gave a special performance of *Othello* for
the purpose.

All this seems straightforward enough, and the theorists
would probably have ignored the monument as something too
intractable for their purpose but for one fact. In 1665 Sir
William Dugdale, Garter King-of-Arms and an antiquarian of
some note, produced a book entitled *Antiquities of Warwickshire*,
which included engravings of the monuments in the Parish
Church of Stratford-on-Avon. The one of the Shakespeare
Monument shows pronounced differences from the monument
as it is today. The symbolic figures, for instance, instead of
being close to the centre of the pediment, are at the extreme
edges with their legs dangling in space. It is, however, the bust
that shows the most marked differences. The figure of Shakespeare, much more hairy on head and face, has neither pen nor
paper, and the hands merely rest on the cushion. The inscription, on the other hand, would appear to be the same as at
present, for Dugdale has represented this by dotted lines which
correspond exactly with the existing arrangement, except that
the date has been omitted.

Nicholas Rowe, who published the first biography of Shakespeare in 1709, includes a similar sketch, but as he obviously copied Dugdale's engraving this is of no importance.

Dugdale's work, when ultimately the theorists became aware of its existence, was naturally hailed as 'treasure trove', and Durning-Lawrence[1] exploited it to the full. However the best interpretation of it from the anti-Stratfordian point of view is that given by Titherley, who makes all the possible points without the hysteria which characterizes the Baconian champion. I have in consequence taken my account from his book.

Titherley assumes[2] that when Shakspere returned to Stratford permanently he brought with him plenty of capital, obtained partly from his earnings as an actor and sharer in the King's Company, but mainly consisting of what he had extracted from Derby honestly and dishonestly. With this he engaged in a number of business activities, principally that of a maltster, and soon became one of the most prominent citizens of his native town. When he died his fellow-citizens decided to erect a monument to him, which naturally showed him as he was – a maltster, with his hands grasping a sack (i.e. the cushion) containing the commodity in which he dealt. Shakspere, however, had boasted privately to his family that he was also a great writer, knowing that this could not be contradicted without betraying Derby's secret. His family therefore insisted on having this supposed fact inscribed on the monument, and were allowed to have their way.

The inscription, however, was so glaringly incompatible with the other details of the monument that, when the repairs were carried out in 1749, those responsible for the work decided on a reconstruction that would bring the two into line, and the present form of the monument is the result. Titherley hastens to add that no deliberate dishonesty is to be imputed to them on this account. Shakspere by that date was universally believed to be the author of the plays, and it would appear to them absurd to let such a contradiction between the bust and the inscription continue. Still, the fact remains that in the original monument he was shown, not as a poet, but as a maltster, and that is undoubtedly what he was.

[1] *Bacon is Shakespeare*, pp. 6–23.   [2] *Shakespeare's Identity*, pp. 122 f.

We may begin our criticism by pointing out that most of this is, like so many of the theorists' arguments, pure conjecture. There is no evidence that the monument was erected by Shakspere's fellow-citizens – it may equally well have been erected by his family, and, though he did engage in various business enterprises, there is no evidence that he ever carried on the regular trade of a maltster; while the only evidence for the rest is the engraving in Dugdale's book. Titherley's ready acceptance of this is hardly what one would have expected of a scientist. One would have supposed that, before basing any theory on Dugdale's representation of the Shakespeare Monument, he would have taken the elementary precaution of ascertaining how that artist treated the other monuments he depicts. If he had done so he would have found that Dugdale is exceedingly inaccurate, and that his pictures are full of discrepancies. To take one prominent example – in the great canopied monument erected to Sir George Carew and his wife, also in Stratford Parish Church, the discrepancies between his picture and the original are far greater than in the case of the Shakespeare Monument, as a comparison of the two will readily reveal.

It is easy to perceive how such inaccuracies could have crept in. Since Dugdale's illustrations are engravings, they could not have been done on the spot. They would have to be made from rough sketches and a few notes. It must be remembered that Dugdale was not dealing with Stratford alone; he was covering the antiquities of a very large area, and he would not be able to spend much time on each sketch, while his memory of individual monuments would be confused by the immense number he had to view. The discrepancies in the Shakespeare Monument are just the sort that would occur in such circumstances – the position of the symbolic figures on the cornice, the details of the head and hair of the bust, and the omission of the pen and paper. The pose is correct, and the position of the hands resting lightly on the cushion – *not* 'grasping' it, as Titherley states. We may therefore take it that the monument today is substantially the same as it has always been.

This view of the situation is confirmed as completely as it is possible for any event of the kind to be, namely by contemporary documentary evidence. Joseph Greene, who was headmaster of Stratford Grammar School in 1749, when the repairs to the monument were carried out, wrote in September of the same year:

> In repairing the whole (which was done by contribution of ye Neighbourhood early in ye current year) Care was taken, as nearly as cou'd be, not to add or to diminish what ye work consisted of, & appear'd to be when first erected; and really, except for changing ye Substance of ye Architraves from white Alabaster to white Marble, Nothing has been done but Supplying with ye original materials whatsoever was by Accident broken off; reviving the old Colouring, and renewing the Gilding that was lost.

Greene would hardly have made such a categorical statement unless it had been correct, for there was no Shakespeare controversy at that time with a theory that needed bolstering up. Moreover, if it had not been true, there were all the inhabitants of Stratford-on-Avon and its environs, to whom the monument had been familiar all their lives, to give him the lie.

Our examination of this matter therefore shows that once again the theorists have offered us nothing but a mare's nest, in the discovery of which chimerical eyries they are past masters.

CHAPTER XV

Four Miscellaneous Items

In addition to their arguments in favour of their own candidates and their denigration of Shakspere, the theorists have also launched a series of general attacks on the Stratfordian position. In this chapter I shall survey four examples of these attacks. This arrangement will have one distinct advantage for our purpose beyond the intrinsic interest of the items themselves, for two of them – Nos. 3 and 4 – are involved in the problem of the First Folio, which is the subject of the next chapter, and by dealing with them here I can avoid interrupting the discussion of that very complicated problem by lengthy digressions. The four items I have selected are as follows:

1 · THE REJECTED PLAYS

Hoffman[1] calls attention to eight plays published between 1595 and 1611 – *Locrine*, 1595; *Sir John Oldcastle*, 1600; *The True Chronicle History of Thomas Lord Cromwell*, 1602; *The London Prodigal*, 1605; *The Puritan*, 1607; *A Yorkshire Tragedy*, 1608; *Pericles, Prince of Tyre*, 1609; and *The Troublesome Reign of King John*, 1611 – all with Shakespeare's name or initials on the title page. He states that these have been rejected from the orthodox canon, yet the evidence for their genuineness is precisely the same as that for the accepted plays; that is, Shakespeare's name or initials attached as author, and he adds, 'The authority of the title page is obviously untrustworthy. The objective reader will perceive that the yardstick by which Shakespeare's authorship is measured both accepts and rejects at the same time. Such a yardstick is valueless.'

The reply to this is that what Hoffman calls the 'yardstick' is only one, and far from the most important, of the factors upon which the Shakespearean canon is based. The main factor is

---

[1] *The Man Who Was Shakespeare*, pp. 39 f.

inclusion in the First Folio. The items for this were selected by Heminge and Condell, two of Shakspere's fellow-actors and members of the same company, who would certainly know what plays were ascribed to him either in his own right or as a cover for one of the claimants. Other factors are the occasional references in contemporary works, such as Meres' *Palladis Tamia*, Accounts of the Court Revels, entries in the Stationers' Register, and the evidence of style. None of the plays in the First Folio have been omitted from the canon, and the only addition to it has been *Pericles*, which was made on the ground that the evidence of style suggests that Shakespeare had a hand in it. Hoffman's 'yardstick' is therefore a figment of his imagination.

As for the W.S. plays, there are two factors which can adequately account for these, and the probability is that both of them were concerned in the matter.

In the first place the initials W.S. were among the most common of Elizabethan times; indeed there was a surfeit of them to the great confusion of modern scholars. Maxwell, in his *The Shakespeare Apocrypha*, gives the following list in addition to William Shakespeare and William Stanley (Derby): Wentworth Smith, dramatist; William Smith, poet; Sir William Segar, man of letters and Garter King-at-Arms; William Slye, a fellow-actor of Shakspere's; William Smyght, described as a player; William Sheppard, another player; and several widely separated references to certain W. Smiths, some of which, however, may indicate the same person. The first three of these were all recognized authors, and some of the others may have been also, while it is in the highest degree probable that Wentworth Smith was responsible for some of the plays in question.[1]

The second factor is the publishing situation in Elizabethan times. There was no copyright law in existence such as there is today, and we know that many plays by various authors were pirated and printed surreptitiously by unscrupulous publishers, while there were many other dishonest tricks known to the trade, including that of publishing plays by inferior writers under the name of some popular author in order to increase

[1] As a matter of fact *Locrine*, *Thomas Lord Cromwell*, and *The Puritan* have all been ascribed to him.

their sales. This fraud too no doubt played a part in producing the W.S. plays.

In any case there is nothing in this matter that is, or could be, evidence either for or against anyone's authorship of the Shakespearean plays. It is not in any way connected with the problem, and we can only conclude that Hoffman raised the point because he did not know the circumstances or hoped his readers would not.

2 · LACK OF SHAKSPERE RECORDS

At the very beginning of this survey we saw that it was the complete failure to find anything, apart from the published works, to connect Shakspere with authorship that started the whole Shakespearean controversy. It is only natural then that this lack of records should be used by the theorists as an argument against his claims, Titherley writes:[1] 'Nor are there any records . . . showing that he wrote any letter, or had anything to do with books and writing. . . . It is simply incredible that prolonged research should have drawn a literary blank if he had possessed the supreme distinction of Shakespeare.'

The reply to this is that Titherley is simply perpetrating an anachronism. He is writing about the sixteenth and early seventeenth centuries as if the same ideas and conditions existed then as now, which, of course, they did not. Today we recognize the complete supremacy of the author of the Shakespearean plays, but this was not the case with his contemporaries. Ben Jonson, for instance, had some very hard things to say about him and his plays, and even among those who admired him the praise could hardly be called fulsome. Webster, who paid Shakespeare the sincerest compliment of imitation, contents himself in his preface to the published version of *The White Devil* with the 'modified rapture' of the following:

> I have ever truly cherished my good opinion of other men's worthy labours; especially of that full and heightened style of Master Chapman; the laboured and understanding works of Master Jonson; the no less worthy composures of the both worthily

---

[1] *Shakespeare's Identity*, p. 109.

excellent Master Beaumont and Master Fletcher; and lastly (without wrong last to be named) the right happy and copious industry of Master Shakespeare, Master Dekker, and Master Heywood; wishing what I write to be read by their light.

There are also comments of a similar nature by Drayton, Heywood, Beaumont, and others, all of which go to show that in his own day Shakespeare was considered as little more than an ordinary competent dramatist, certainly not as one who towered head and shoulders above his contemporaries.

Now the point is this. Most of the professional dramatists of the time are in exactly the same position as that which Titherley ascribes to Shakspere. There are no records to connect them with authorship, not even a letter to show that they had anything to do with books and writing. Nor is this really surprising. The professional dramatist of those days was not the celebrity he is today. He was regarded as a poor and somewhat disreputable relation of the literary family. His work was ephemeral, to be cut, expanded, revised, and sometimes rewritten by another hand, to suit the ever-changing requirements of the stage, and, when its drawing power was exhausted, to be sold to some publisher for what it would fetch. If the dramatists left any records other than their published works, it is unlikely that anyone would think them worth preserving. Letter-writing, for obvious reasons, was not the common practice it is today; still, no doubt the dramatists did write a letter occasionally, but it would be of a private nature, and if not destroyed by the recipient after reading, would not be likely to survive long. In any case, whatever the reason, this is the common position of many of the Elizabethan dramatists, as the theorists can verify by a glance at any dictionary of literary biography. There they will find some such words as 'Almost nothing is known about Blank apart from the plays that bear his name', repeated with monotonous regularity as the opening sentence of the various accounts.

In these circumstances it was highly probable that Shakspere, as a professional dramatist, would have suffered this common fate no matter what he had done. He made it doubly sure by removing himself from London and settling in that stronghold of Puritanism, Stratford-on-Avon, where, as Ivor

Brown tells us in his *Amazing Monument*, the theatre was taboo, and where worldly wisdom, which he certainly did not lack, would have forced him to suppress all evidence of his former connection with it.[1] It is therefore by no means surprising that no record of this connection is to be found if Shakspere were in fact the author of the plays; on the contrary, it would be surprising if any were.

3 · ADDITIONAL LINES IN THE FIRST FOLIO

The text of some of the plays in the First Folio, published in 1623, differs in places from that in any of the Quartos, and in *Richard III* and *Othello* there are considerable additions, which critics consider to be the work of the original author. Since Shakspere died in 1616 these additions have naturally attracted the attention of the theorists. B. G. Theobald[2] states the case for the Baconians, and asks how Shakspere, if he were the author, could possibly have added the lines concerned seven years after his death, and Evans[3] poses the same question on behalf of Lord Derby.

There is, of course, a perfectly simple answer to this question. Not only are there additions in the First Folio, but omissions as well. Hamlet's famous soliloquy, 'How all occasions do inform against me, etc.', with the related dialogue, is among the important passages not included. Moreover there are similar differences between the various Quartos, one of which is certainly well known to the theorists, for they quote it in another connection. This is the 'Deposition Scene' in *Richard II*. The first three Quartos were all published without this scene, and it was not until the fourth Quarto was issued that it first appeared in print. Yet we know from the fuss Queen Elizabeth herself

---

[1] In 1602 the Corporation decreed that a fine of 10s. was to be imposed on any actor venturing to perform within the town boundaries, and a few years later the amount was increased to £10 – a very large sum in those days. Moreover, it is to be noted that the inscription on the Shakespeare Monument makes no specific mention of plays, merely claiming that he was an author.

[2] *Enter Francis Bacon*, pp. 83 f.

[3] *Shakespeare's Magic Circle*, p. 111.

made about it at the time of the Essex rebellion it had formed part of the original stage play (see pp. 204 ff.). If the publisher of the 1608 Quarto had, like his predecessors, also omitted it – as he might well have done – and it had made its first appearance in the First Folio, then it would have been in exactly the same position as the passages to which Theobald and Evans refer, and would no doubt have been hailed by them as new material written after the death of Shakspere.

The variations in different editions occurred because of the peculiar procedure concerned with the acceptance and staging of a play in Elizabethan times. The subject has been studied from documents such as Henslowe's Diary, and an excellent account of it is given by Greg.[1] The author submitted a rough draft of his play to the company of actors who, he hoped, would stage it. This draft was usually full of erasions, corrections, and interlinings, so that the term 'foul papers' by which it became known was by no means a misnomer. If it were approved a 'fair copy' was made, usually by a professional scrivener, the company retaining both the 'foul sheets' and the 'fair copy', so that if some accident happened to the latter a new one could be made.

The 'fair copy', which had wide margins, was then prepared as the acting version. To suit the stage requirements cuts and additions were made, the latter sometimes by the original author, sometimes by another hand. These were written in the margins along with the stage directions inserted by the prompter. Cut passages were not necessarily obliterated, as they might well be used in a revival; in fact a revival scarcely ever took place without alterations more or less drastic being made. When this process had gone on for a considerable time, as it would do in the case of a popular play, a new 'fair copy' would have to be made, for the old one would have become too much of a muddle to serve its purpose, and the same routine would begin again. In this way there would in course of time be a number of different versions of the same play, some containing passages which would be absent in others.

There is thus no difficulty in explaining the discrepancies in the First Folio if the dead Shakspere were the author. It is

---

[1] *The Editorial Problem in Shakespeare*, pp. 22–33.

simply that the editors would be obliged to collect the manuscripts and printed versions used in its preparation from where-
ever they could be found and in whatever state they were, and
do their best with them. If, however, the living Bacon or Derby
were the author the case is very different. The text of the First
Folio contains many gross errors and corruptions, a number of
them carried over from the previous Quartos. Is it conceivable
that either of these learned gentlemen would pen lengthy
additions to their plays for publication in the Folio, and yet
make not the least attempt to correct the mass of errors that had
gradually accumulated in the text, like some foolish builder
adding a fine new wing to a house and neglecting to repair the
gaping breaches in the original edifice?

This is sufficient to demolish the argument of Theobald and
Evans, but we shall have to refer to the matter again in the
next chapter.

4 · PUBLICATION OF THE PLAYS

Another point the theorists advance against Shakspere's
authorship is his apparent lack of interest in the publication of
the plays. They assert that if he had really been the author he
would never have allowed such imperfect editions to be put on
the booksellers' stalls, that he would have seen that all his plays
were published, and that he would certainly have taken some
action against the pirates.

With their usual mental confusion in such matters they fail to
see that this charge applies with equal force to their own candidates if any one of these happened to be the author; and in this
case the motive would be even stronger, for they would be
amateurs who surely could not have borne to see their artistic
creations violated, while Shakspere, the professional, could not
have afforded to take any step that might interfere with his
earning a living. Nor can the theorists evade this issue by claiming that their candidates could not act without betraying the
secret of their authorship. They might not be able to act in
person, but as whichever was the author must have had an
agent to transact all the necessary business connected with
placing the plays in the first instance, there was nothing to

prevent him from taking the necessary action through this agent. The point made by the theorists then actually counts against their candidates; but it is capable of a perfectly natural explanation if the author of the plays were the Stratford actor.

To understand this it is necessary to examine the way in which plays in general were published in Elizabethan times, together with one or two additional points concerning the Shakespearean plays in particular. The printed versions of the latter, prior to the appearance of the First Folio, were all Quartos, and these have been divided by scholars into two categories – the good Quartos and the bad Quartos. The former consist of those published legitimately, that is with the permission of the owners; the latter of those published surreptitiously by some literary pirate.

A full account of both is given by Greg,[1] and also by the Franco-American scholar, Feuillerat.[2] It seems that plays, with rare exceptions, were bought outright by the various companies of actors and became their exclusive property. As publication was deemed to injure the box-office, the players did not usually permit this until the drawing-power of a play was exhausted, though when times were bad, as when the theatres were closed owing to an outbreak of the plague, financial difficulties might compel them to sell their scripts before this point had been reached. The copies sold were either the original 'foul papers' or some other much altered playhouse version. This accounts for the corruptions and confusions of even the good Quartos. The Elizabethan printers could turn out satisfactory work where they received clean manuscripts from the authors, but the plays they printed are invariably full of the grossest errors.

The pirated versions were obtained by unscrupulous publishers in various illegitimate ways. They included copies stolen by some dishonest playhouse employee; versions botched up from memory by some equally dishonest actor or group of actors; and shorthand versions taken down during a performance. All these methods would produce exceedingly corrupt texts. Any stolen copy could only be one of the playhouse

[1] *The Editorial Problem in Shakespeare*, pp. 22–33.
[2] *Composition of Shakespeare's Plays*, Introduction.

scripts containing all the alterations made for various performances; the memorized versions might be accurate where
the actor concerned was dealing with his own part, but would
be full of the grossest inaccuracies for the rest; while the
Elizabethan shorthand systems were very inadequate for such a
purpose. Moreover copies obtained by this method must have
been very rare, since the plays were performed in daylight, and
it would be almost impossible for a stenographer to complete
his task without being observed and expelled from the theatre.
As for checking piracy, we have seen (p. 221) that the actors
did what they could, but that in the absence of copyright laws
enabling them to prosecute after the event, it was very
difficult to prevent the practice.

The study of the Elizabethan system of publication, legitimate and illegitimate, thus makes it quite clear that the professional dramatist had as a general rule little control over his
plays once he had sold them to some company; they were in
fact no longer his to deal with. In this respect Shakspere would
be more favourably placed than most, for as a 'sharer' in the
company he would at least have a voice in the disposal of his,
though he would of course be bound by the vote of the majority.

To the disabilities of the dramatist may be added the fact
already mentioned, that plays were regarded as a very ephemeral form of literature, as is evidenced by the ridicule Ben
Jonson brought upon himself when he ventured to publish a
sumptuous folio of his. Shakspere, if he were the author, had
the long narrative poems, *Venus and Adonis* and *Lucrece*, together
with the sonnets, to secure for him immortal fame, as he
boasted in the last named; why then should he bother about
the publication of the plays, some of which were not entirely
his own work, especially when he had not the right to do so
without the consent of his fellow-actors, who would be most
reluctant to give it while the plays retained any box-office
value?

An examination of this problem therefore not only proves
the utter worthlessness of the theorists' contention, but also
makes it perfectly plain that the state of all the printed versions
of the Shakespearean plays, as well as the fact that a number of
them were never printed at all before the issue of the First

Folio, is exactly what would be expected if they were written by a professional dramatist subject to all the conditions and restrictions of the day.

Our survey then of the general arguments advanced by the theorists produces precisely the same results as we have found produced by their more specific arguments. None of them succeeds in weakening the Stratford actor's claim to the authorship of the Shakespearean plays, and some of them are positively damaging to the theorists' own contentions.

CHAPTER XVI

A Tug-of-War with the First Folio

The First Folio, which, as it stands, indisputably links Shakspere the actor to Shakespeare the dramatist, is for this reason considered to be the citadel of the orthodox stronghold; consequently the theorists have devoted their main efforts to the task of undermining its evidential value. Their attacks upon it have been many and various. Moreover, though having a common object and often borrowing the munitions of war from one another, they are of course in no sense allies; they sometimes disagree in tactics, and occasionally indulge in skirmishes among themselves. The story of this part of the controversy is therefore a very complicated one and by no means easy to present in a coherent and logical form. However, that task must be attempted, and it may be facilitated if we begin with a brief description of the Folio, and especially of the details around which argument has raged most furiously.

The First Folio was published in 1623. It was clearly a commercial venture, produced 'on the cheap'. Compared with the sumptuous volume of Jonson's works, published a little earlier, it makes a poor showing. The people behind it, as the colophon informs us, were W. Jaggard, Ed. Blount, I. Smithweeke, and W. Aspley, and it was printed by Isaac Jaggard, son of the first named, and Ed. Blount. The alleged editors were two of Shakspere's fellow-actors in the Chamberlain's, later the King's, Company, John Heminge and Henry Condell. It contained the whole series of canonical plays, with the sole exception of *Pericles*, in 908 pages of double columns, all very badly reproduced, with much mispagination, errors in printing, and many corruptions of the text. Probably 1000 copies were printed, of which about 200 survive, though not all of these are in really good condition.

The introductory matter consists of the following items:

(1) A representation of the Droeshout atrocity, which has already been fully discussed (see pp. 246 f.).

(2) Some lines on this 'portrait' by Ben Jonson in which, with more charity than he sometimes showed, he begs the reader to look, not on the picture, but the book.

(3) A Dedication addressed to the 'incomparable paire of bretheren', the Earls of Pembroke and Montgomery, signed by Heminge and Condell.

(4) An Epistle addressed to the 'great variety of readers', also signed by Heminge and Condell.

(5) Commendatory verses by Ben Jonson, Hugh Holland, Leonard Digges, and I. M.

(6) A list of the principal actors in all the plays.

(7) A catalogue of the plays themselves.

It is upon certain items of this prefatory material that the theorists deliver their attack. Their idea seems to be that if some doubt can be cast upon the truthfulness or sincerity of the writers the case for the authorship of the Stratford actor will automatically collapse. Of the arguments they use only a few are original; many are borrowed from the writings of Sir George Greenwood, whose whole case, as we have already noted (see p. 49), was so roughly handled by J. M. Robertson in *The Baconian Heresy* that the name of this latter work is never mentioned by the theorists, and is carefully omitted from their bibliographies.

The first position to be attacked is the editorship of Heminge and Condell. These two men were merely ordinary players, possibly of little education and certainly with no literary experience. It is claimed that they were brought in for no other reason than that they had been friends of Shakspere and fellow-actors in the same company, and that their names, still well known on the London stage, would attract the public and act as a kind of guarantee for the enterprise. The real editor according to most of the critics was Ben Jonson, though a few favour Ed. Blount, who had already done similar work.

As these points are conceded by the Stratfordians, who in fact were among the first to raise them, they are obviously not in themselves hostile to the orthodox position. This most of the theorists admit, but quote them as an example of the general

269

atmosphere of dishonesty that pervades the publication of the First Folio.[1]

The reply to this charge need not detain us long. Certainly the use of names in a capacity their owners do not fill does not conform to an ideal ethical standard; but it is a trick that has long been common in the publishing trade. The theorists cannot be unaware that most of the books which appear today under the names of famous sportsmen are not written by the sportsmen concerned. The latter merely lend their names and provide most of the material used, but the actual writing is done by professional journalists. The position of Heminge and Condell was very similar. Their names would undoubtedly be an attraction, and in addition they would be useful in laying hands on playhouse copies of the works required for the Folio, and in helping as far as possible to disentangle the muddles in the script – after all they had acted in the plays and must have had some knowledge of the text. To this extent then they probably did take part in the editing, and the deception, if in the circumstances it can be described as such, was of a very venial kind.

The same cannot be said for the Epistle 'to the great variety of readers'. Here there are undoubtedly flagrant untruths, equal to any of those on a modern blurb. Heminge and Condell say, or are made to say, to their readers that 'as where before you were abused with divers stolen and surreptitious copies, maim'd and deform'd by the frauds and stealths of injurious imposters, that exposed them, even those are now offer'd to your view cured and perfect of their limbs, and all the rest absolute in their numbers as he (Shakspere) conceived them; who, as he was a happy imitator of Nature, was a most gentle expressor of it; his mind and hand went together; and what he thought he uttered with that easiness, that we have scarce received from him a blot in his papers.'

In this three claims are indisputably made, as follows:

(1) That the Folio, unlike the previous Quartos, is a perfect text.

(2) That it is based on Shakspere's original autographs.

(3) That such was Shakspere's genius that these autographs contain scarcely a single obliteration.

[1] Evans, *Shakespeare's Magic Circle*, pp. 129-131.

The third of these claims is entirely incredible, and the first two are demonstrably false. The text of the First Folio, though it does show signs in places of some attempt at editing, is very far from perfect – it is exceedingly corrupt. If one thing is obvious, it is that most of it was printed from playhouse copies with their confused mass of interlinings, marginal alterations, additions, and cuts, made for the various performances the play had received (see pp. 263 f.), producing in the printed version many muddles of various kinds. Moreover, ten of the plays in the Folio were simply copied direct from the previous Quartos – though from the 'good', not the pirated editions – and reproduced even the printers' errors of the latter.

All this the theorists gleefully emphasize as evidence for the essential dishonesty of the Folio. Titherley writes,[1] 'The Folio editors uttered a most palpable untruth. . . . Not only did they utilize these reprobated Quartos, but much of their available manuscript was manifestly incomplete or in a very confused condition owing to alterations and theatre tampering; in some plays indeed the Folio text is in numerous places inferior to the Quarto texts, and the present writer has now proved . . . that the Folio was wholly printed from copies and *not from original autographs at all*' (Titherley's italics).

Yet such is the confusion of mind from which the theorists suffer when dealing with their pet subject that, in spite of all this evidence staring them in the face from every copy of the Folio, evidence which they themselves emphasize for their own purpose, they at once go into reverse and declare that their respective candidates, either directly or through some representative, handed over to the publisher carefully revised copies of the plays. We have already seen (p. 262) that according to B. G. Theobald Bacon wrote long additional passages for some of the plays,[2] and Evans makes a similar claim for Derby. J. T. Looney states that the full literary texts of Lord Oxford, who had died in 1604, had been preserved by his relations, the Countess of Pembroke and her two sons, 'the incomparable

---

[1] *Shakespeare's Identity*, p. 129.

[2] If Durning-Lawrence is to be believed, Bacon did much more. He was in the closest touch with Jonson, arranging for the insertion of all the cryptograms and other clues to establish his own authorship for future generations.

Paire' of the Dedication, who handed them over to Jaggard, and indeed financed the enterprise.[1] Titherley, in spite of his comments quoted in the preceding paragraph, states only six pages later[2] that Bacon may well have informed Jonson that Derby was the real author of the Shakespearean plays, and Jonson, finding that a number of the plays were no longer in the hands of the King's Company, may have requested Bacon, as an intermediary, to obtain for him the missing plays from Derby.[3] Finally Hoffman,[4] on behalf of Marlowe writes, 'Behind . . . there is a guiding hand; a hand that had supplied the plays to the publishers. In the light of what my argument has revealed this guiding hand could have been no other than that of Sir Thomas Walsingham; who not only gave the plays to the syndicate, but must have preserved them as Marlowe wrote them wherever the poet might be.'

The joint efforts of the theorists thus present us with the following pretty picture of the queue waiting outside the editorial sanctum of the First Folio. At its head is Francis Bacon, grasping in one hand his own manuscripts of the Shakespearean plays and in the other those of Derby; immediately behind is the Countess of Pembroke, supported by her two stalwart sons, bearing Lord Oxford's manuscripts of the same plays; while bringing up the rear is the burly figure of Sir Thomas Walsingham, his pockets bulging with Marlowe's manuscripts, again of the same plays.

Now it is obvious that all these suggestions that the original manuscripts, or fair copies of them, were handed over to the publishers of the First Folio are in flat contradiction to the chaotic state of the text of that Folio. Yet the theorists' claim is quite understandable, for it represents just what ought to have happened, and what certainly would have happened, *if any one of their theories had been true.* In that case the original manuscripts would have been available, and there could be no reason

---

[1] *Shakespeare Identified,* p. 379.   [2] *Shakespeare's Identity,* p. 135.

[3] This is really most unkind of Titherley. Having commandeered, as we have seen, some of the Baconians' pet arguments, he now adds insult to injury by reducing their candidate to a mere beast of burden to carry his rival's manuscripts to the publisher.

[4] *The Man Who Was Shakespeare,* pp. 196 f.

why at least fair copies of them should not have been entrusted to such a reputable literary figure as Jonson, who, as a matter of fact, was in the closest touch with Bacon at the time, assisting him in the preparation of a Latin version of his great philosophical works. That none were handed over is therefore strong evidence against the truth of the various theories, and the theorists' failure to recognize this shows how blind one may become under the influence of an *idée fixe*.

Evans alone seems to have some glimmering of the fact, and even makes an attempt to deal with it; but he only succeeds in entangling himself still further in the network of inconsistencies. He tells us[1] that Derby's autograph MSS could not be used because it would have jeopardized the secret of his authorship. This may be so; but what was to prevent a fair copy of Derby's MSS from being made by a secretary or scrivener? This must have been done in the first instance if Derby really were the author, or how did the plays ever see the light of day? Surely, when the great works were being given to the world in their final form, this method could have been repeated. Mr Evans is too naïve, and just as self-contradictory as any of the other theorists, for he seems to forget that he had already told us on page 111 of his book that Derby did in fact contribute a large number of additional lines to the First Folio. And to crown this series of self-contradictions and inconsistencies, on page 145 and those immediately following, he gives a warm welcome to Titherley's claim that hand D in the Additions to *Sir Thomas More*, a manuscript that would have to be seen by the Censor (see pp. 98 and 101 ff.), was an autograph by Derby.

The truth is that the First Folio makes a wreck of all the theories. It is not only obvious that none of the candidates contributed a single copy to it, but it is in the highest degree improbable that, if the plays had really been written by one of them, the author would have allowed them to be used by a man like Jaggard in such a shoddy enterprise. It would have been quite easy to prevent it without betraying anyone's secret. A word to Jonson would have been sufficient. Neither he nor any of those associated with him could have afforded to offend such powerful interests.

[1] *Shakespeare's Magic Circle*, p. 138.

Confirmation of this is to be found in the attitude of the 'incomparable Paire of bretheren', the Lords Pembroke and Montgomery. These two peers were closely related by marriage to both Oxford and Derby, and if either Oxford or Derby had written the plays no one was more likely to be in the secret than they. Yet they allowed the First Folio to be dedicated to them in a fulsome paragraph signed by Heminge and Condell, in which the latter termed the plays mere 'trifles' written by their 'friend and fellow Shakespeare'. The 'incomparable paire' would have looked supremely ridiculous, if nothing worse, had what the theorists maintain is the truth come out, as there would always be a danger that it might. Titherley says[1] that they probably accepted the Dedication 'with an indulgent smile', which is about as weak a defence as could be offered. An 'indulgent smile' is no doubt an amiable trait in its possessor, but it can hardly be regarded as an efficient instrument of criticism. I wonder what Titherley would say of any Stratfordian who tried to gloss over a difficulty with an 'indulgent smile'.

All the difficulties, however, which bristle in the path of the theorists, vanish completely if the author is a man of the theatre – that is, a William Shakspere of Stratford. In the first place, like most professional dramatists, he would probably have kept no manuscripts of his own. His 'foul sheets', as we have seen (pp. 263 f.), would become the property of the Company producing the play, and, as a busy man with his other interests as well as writing to a theatrical time-table, it is unlikely that he troubled to make a second copy, especially when, as a sharer in the Company, he would enjoy the unusual privilege of having access to the theatre copies at any time he wanted it. This would explain why the publishers had to work with such imperfect texts – there were no perfect ones. It would also explain why most of the alterations for the various revivals were done by the original author, and not, as in so many cases, by another hand – Shakspere as a member of the company was always on the spot. Finally it would explain the attitude of the Lords Pembroke and Montgomery. The former was Lord Chamberlain, and as such had a special responsibility for the

[1] *Shakespeare's Identity*, p. 128.

King's Company, which had formerly been the Lord Chamberlain's. It would therefore be a natural and gracious act that he should allow the Folio to be dedicated to him and his brother when requested by two faithful members of that Company; and if the plays were not written by a relative of his own, but merely by a former member of the same Company, no discredit could attach to himself and his brother however shoddy the production of the Folio might be.

It will therefore be seen that all the theorists' attempts to make capital out of the circumstances of the publication of the First Folio recoil on themselves, and not only make nonsense of their theories, but actually support the case for the Stratford actor's authorship. In blissful oblivion of this, however, they go gaily on their way, producing arguments based on other features of the First Folio, and these also we must submit to a critical examination.

The first is concerned with the commendatory poems. The problem confronting the theorists here is that all these most clearly identify Shakespeare the dramatist with Shakspere the actor, and, as this of course is fatal to their various cases, they must find some way to discount its effect. For most of them – Hoffman is an exception with which we shall have to deal later – it is only Jonson's poems that really matter. The other poets – Holland, I. M., and Digges – are unimportant; they were not in the secret, and accordingly wrote what they sincerely, though mistakenly, believed. Jonson had, however, at times satirized Shakspere unmercifully, so much so that the theorists believe he must have been in the secret – the Baconians and Oxfordians from the very first, Titherley from about 1620 when Bacon enlightened him. They regard him therefore as an ally, and ransack his complimentary verses for possible ambiguities, doublemeanings, and similar devices which could be used to prove that he did not mean what he said about Shakspere. Poor Jonson! Not one of them troubles to explain why he should have allowed himself to be put into a position that demanded such dishonesty. His literary standing was certainly sufficiently high at the time to enable him to refuse any offer that would outrage his artistic integrity. We are thus left to conclude that he must have done it, if he did do it, because he was that kind of man, and so belied in this instance all we can learn about his character from his conduct on other occasions.

We will begin our survey with the lines attached to the Droeshout picture that 'adorned' the title-page. They are as follows:

> This figure that thou seest put,
> It was for gentle Shakespeare cut;
> Wherein the Graver had a strife
> With nature to out-doo the life;
> O could he but have drawn his wit
> As well in brasse, as he has hit
> His face; the print would then surpasse
> All, that was ever writ in brasse.
> But, since he cannot, Reader, looke
> Not on his Picture, but his Booke.

On this Evans[1] has the following comment: 'It is not necessary to discuss here all the many possible meanings which can be read into these lines. I merely wish to point out that the engraving above them, together with the ambiguity of the lines, gives us good reason for believing that Jonson knew perfectly well that this was not a portrait of Shakespeare.'

Titherley[2] goes further, and mentions the possible ambiguities contained in the lines. His suggested alternatives to their face-value are as follows: 'for' (line 2) implying 'substitution', 'gentle' (line 2) applied to 'social position', 'out-doo' (line 4) meaning 'destroy', and 'hit' (line 6) in the sense of 'strike a blow'.

Now, as I have already made clear in Chapter XIV (see pp. 246 f.), I am in full agreement with Evans that the Droeshout is not a portrait of Shakspere – *or of anyone else*; and while I would not myself juggle with the face-value of words written more than three centuries ago unless I had unusually convincing reasons on my side – the theorists have none except the needs of their theories – I am in no way disposed to cavil at Titherley's suggestions. The Droeshout is certainly a *substitute* 'for' a portrait, and I have every sympathy with Jonson if he felt that the face, as represented there, ought to be 'hit' in the sense of *strike a blow*; while the artist has undoubtedly, though through no

---

[1] *Shakespeare's Magic Circle*, p. 133.   [2] *Shakespeare's Identity*, p. 125.

fault of his own, managed to 'out-doo', that is *destroy*, all signs of life in it. I will even concede that 'gentle' may be a mild satiric dig at Shakspere's *social* ambitions, perhaps an unconscious reminiscence of a similar satiric dig that long before Jonson had made at this trait of Shakspere's in *Every Man Out Of His Humour* (see pp. 43 ff.). What I do deny is that such remarks have any bearing on the question of authorship. If they really are double-meanings, which is of course very doubtful, far and away their most likely target is the ridiculous picture to which they are attached; this must surely have offended Jonson's taste, however satisfied Jaggard might be with it. The last couplet would certainly seem to support this interpretation.

It is, however, to Jonson's longer poem that the theorists have devoted most attention, as is natural, since it is in this that his greatest compliments to Shakespeare occur and where he most clearly identifies the dramatist with the actor. We may take a comment by B. G. Theobald[1] as an example of their methods. He begins by quoting the following four lines from the poem:

> Sweet Swan of Avon! What a sight it were
> To see thee on our waters yet appear,
> And make those flights upon the bankes of Thames,
> That did so take Eliza and our James.

These four lines, Theobald claims, are cleverly contrived so as to give two distinct meanings to two distinct classes of reader. The ordinary reader will take them at their face-value and believe that the dramatist and the actor are the same man; the enlightened few, who are in the secret, will recognize the secondary meaning which is subtly hidden in them and draw a different conclusion.

The clue to this hidden meaning lies in the word 'swan'. Poets were often likened to singing-birds, but a swan is emphatically not a singing-bird; therefore it could not really symbolize a poet-dramatist. This, Theobald says, is confirmed by the reference to 'flights', which are things seen as an actor is seen, not heard as the words of a dramatist are heard. Thus the person represented by a swan is definitely differentiated from the dramatist.

[1] *Enter Francis Bacon*, pp. 56–59.

277

This, however, is only the beginning of what may be deduced from the word 'swan'. Theobald tells us that there is a legend about these birds in Ariosto's *Orlando Furioso*, which Bacon actually quotes in his *De Augmentis*. According to this, medals bearing the names of famous men, when they come to die, are thrown into the waters of the River Lethe, where they would be lost and forgotten, but the swans of that river snatch them up and bear them to the Temple of Immortality.

Now, Theobald points out, some time before the publication of the First Folio, a poet named Weever, no doubt with this legend in mind, wrote the following epigram:

> Rome had her Roscius and her Theatre,
> Her Terrence, Plautus, Ennius, and Meander.
> The first to Allen Phoebus did transfer,
> The next Thames swans receiv'd fore he could land her,
> Of both more worthy we by Phoebus doome
> Then t'Allen Roscius yield, to London Rome.

On which Theobald comments as follows: 'The drift of this seems to be that before Phoebus Apollo could hand on the fame of the Roman playwrights here mentioned to a London dramatist, as he had handed on the fame of the Roman actor Roscius to Alleyn, a Thames swan seized it and carried it off.'

I can only conclude from this rigmarole that Theobald intends to imply that as soon as the 'enlightened' read the word 'swan' it sets up a train of thought which leads them inevitably through *De Augmentis* and *Orlando Furioso* to Weever's Epigram, and then they immediately realize that of course Jonson means that Shakspere had stolen Bacon's fame. Commonsense might wonder why Jonson took the trouble to inform the 'enlightened' of all this since they were already 'in the know', and to do so would add to the danger of betraying Bacon's secret. As, however, commonsense has little to do with this argument, we will leave the general idea and turn to the criticism of its details.

In the first place Theobald is quite wrong in his main statement. No matter what its vocal powers might be, 'swan' was in fact traditionally employed as an allegorical term for 'poet'. The N.E.D. actually gives 'bard, singer' as a secondary meaning of the word, and the Tudor Emblem books make frequent use of this bird as a symbol for a poet. Moreover, the commendatory poem in the First Folio was not the only occasion on which Jonson made use of the term. He did so in his *Ode Allegorike*, where its meaning is quite unmistakable. This is a complimentary poem addressed to the poet Hugh Holland, a former schoolfellow, which, while differing metrically from the commendatory poem, contains a number of similarities of idea and phrase, as the following quotation will show:

> Who saith our Times nor have, nor can
> > Produce us a blacke Swan?
> Behold, where one doth swim;
> > Whose Note, and Hue,
> Besides the other Swannes admiring him,
> > Betray it true;
> > A gentler bird, then this
> Did never dint the breast of Tamisis.
>
> Marke, marke, but when his wing he takes,
> > How faire a flight he makes!
> How upward and direct!
> > Whil'st pleas'd Apollo
> Smiles in his Spheare, to see the rest affect
> > In vaine to follow;
> > This Swanne is onely his,
> And Phoebus love cause of his blacknesse is.

Here the adjectives 'gentle' and 'sweet' reappear; there is the same association with rivers, especially the Thames; and since Holland was not an actor, the word 'flight' must stand for 'poem', that is for 'something heard or read, *not* seen on the stage'. Moreover a later verse, which begins 'Haste, haste, sweete singer', clearly proves that, in spite of its lack of musical education, Jonson *did* use 'swan' as a symbol for 'poet'. 'Swan of Avon' therefore means 'Poet from Stratford', and can mean nothing else.

This renders any reference to the legend in *Orlando Furioso* or Weever's epigram superfluous, for obviously 'swan', as used in Jonson's commendatory poem, has no connection with either of them. However, it may just be worth while to point out as an

279

example of what with the theorists passes for evidence that the swans in the legend, by rescuing the fame of great men from oblivion, do precisely the opposite of what Theobold accuses the 'swan', Shakspere, of doing – namely, stealing the fame of Bacon for himself.

Another quotation from Jonson's commendatory poem upon which the theorists have expended a great deal of ink is the famous line:

And though thou hadst small Latin and less Greek.

It is a most unpleasant line from their point of view, for clearly it can only apply to the dramatist; it would not matter in the least whether an actor knew these languages or not. Jonson therefore says, in so many words, that the author of the Shakespearean plays was a man whose Classical education was defective. If he knew, as the theorists maintain he did, that one of their candidates was the true author, there was no need for him to mention the matter at all, for of course the statement was quite untrue as far as Bacon, Oxford, Derby, and Marlowe were concerned. It was, however, perfectly correct as far as Shakspere, the Stratford actor, was concerned, and thus certainly makes it appear that Jonson regarded him as the author of the plays.

In the dilemma thus forced upon them the theorists resort to Sir George Greenwood, who, in *The Shakespeare Problem Restated*, had suggested that 'though' in the offending line might be taken to mean 'if', that is, as a supposition patently not true. The line would then read, 'And *if* thou hadst small Latin and less Greek (which of course is not so, you would still be a great writer,)' in which sense, Greenwood argued, it could be made to apply to a learned claimant.

In reply J. M. Robertson pointed out that such a construction was an impossibility in the English language; it was simply a violation of sense and usage. He wrote:[1] 'Need it really be pointed out that while "and if" *could* have meant "and though", "and though" could *not* mean "and if" in the sense suggested. "Though" can stand for "if" when put before a hyperbole – as in "though I speak with the tongue of men and angels"; not

[1] *The Baconian Heresy*, p. 563.

before a carefully quantified proposition such as "*small* Latin and *less* Greek" – a specification if there ever were one.'

Robertson goes on to show that if this somewhat strained usage had really been intended by Jonson, he would have written '*small* Latin and *small* Greek', or some other word of equivalent value to the second 'small'. When making a supposition, intentionally and obviously false, one does not *suppose* a false quantitive distinction between the two *false* details supposed.

Yet in spite of this scholarly annihilation of the whole argument, Evans calmly reproduces it *in toto*.[1] He does not attempt to refute Robertson's criticisms by producing unassailable examples of the disputed usage, which of course would be quite legitimate. He never even mentions Robertson, or that the interpretation concerned had ever been disputed. He merely repeats it without comment. This is clearly a case of deliberate suppression of evidence, or, as I am inclined to suspect, Evans has not read *The Baconian Heresy*.

Hoffman, as already stated, unlike the other theorists, does not believe that Jonson knew the 'true author's' secret. He therefore considers that Jonson's tribute is a genuine and unambiguous reference to the Stratford actor.[2] Not that he thinks Jonson wrote what he honestly felt about Shakspere; but he was hired to write a panegyric, and he gave his paymasters what they wanted. On the other hand, again unlike his fellow-theorists, Hoffman believes two – Holland and I. M. – out of the three minor poets concerned were, partly at least, in the secret. He believes this because both have lines in their commendatory poems regretting that the author of the plays died too soon, and Shakspere by Elizabethan standards had a fairly long life. He therefore thinks that Holland and I. M., although they did not know that the assassination of Marlowe was a fake, did know that the Shakespearean plays were written by him.

On such foundations are theories built. One cannot help wondering how Hoffman has managed to overlook so completely that most common of all commonplaces in panegyrics of this type, no matter how long the great man has contrived to

[1] *Shakespeare's Magic Circle*, p. 137.
[2] *The Man Who Was Shakespeare*, pp. 217 ff.

live, his passing is all too soon. A little reading of poems of this type would quickly open his eyes to the fact. Moreover Shakspere *was* a comparatively young man when he died even by Elizabethan standards. Hoffman seems to imagine – not only here, but in other parts of his book also – that, because the expectation of life was less then than it is now, people aged physically much more rapidly. This is nonsense. Many people did die young in those days, but it was only because medical science was less advanced; those who were healthy and escaped the prevailing epidemics lived just as long as people do today.[1] Finally, if Holland and I. M. believed, as Hoffman says they did, that Marlowe was killed at Deptford in 1593, but still thought that he wrote all the Shakespearean plays that had appeared at more or less regular intervals during the years that followed, when and in what circumstances did they think that Marlowe wrote them? On this not unimportant point Hoffman gives no information.

The points advanced by the theorists based on the commendatory poems which we have examined so far are exceedingly trivial, some positively puerile, and their refutation has accordingly given no trouble. It would, however, be unfair to pretend that this is all that can be said on the matter. It is perfectly true, as a number of theorists such as Titherley[2] claim, that never before had Jonson praised Shakspere and the plays in such glowing terms. On the contrary he had attacked and satirized both with great vigour. His complete change of attitude does constitute a real problem which demands serious investigation, and to this we must now turn.

We may begin by ruling out Titherley's speculation,[3] for which no evidence of any sort exists, that the change occurred because Bacon let Jonson into the secret that the plays were written by Derby. Such a suggestion is utterly alien to the

---

[1] The following is a short list, selected from men of letters only, of the ages reached by some of Shakspere's contemporaries: Thomas Hobbes, 91; Izaak Walton, 90; Gabriel Hervey, 85; Richard Herrick, 83; Thomas Campion, 83; and Anthony Munday, 79. This list could have been greatly lengthened by adding to it the names of some of the more obscure writers, and of course there must have been innumerable examples among unknown persons in all walks of life.

[2] *Shakespeare's Identity*, pp. 131–138.   Ibid., p. 135.

character of Jonson. Whatever his faults, the latter was artistically sincere, and the mere discovery that what he had thought bad was the work of a belted earl would not make him declare that it was good. Moreover the suggestion is absolutely negatived by the fact that Jonson's change of attitude was only a temporary one, limited to the First Folio. As we shall see, in his later writings he returned to his niggling criticism of Shakspere and the Shakespearean plays.

In any attempt to arrive at the truth of the matter we shall be obliged to take several factors into consideration. The first of these is the controversy that was maintained throughout the Elizabethan period, and longer, between rival schools of drama – the Classic and the Romantic. Jonson, as might be expected, was a neo-classicist, while the author of the Shakespearean plays, like most of the popular dramatists, belonged to the Romantic school. It is obvious therefore that the plays must have been distasteful to Jonson, who would not be able to evaluate them with an unprejudiced mind, and would naturally be ready to attack them when opportunity offered.

The second factor is of a somewhat similar kind. It is the literary squabble known as the War of the Theatres, which we have already had occasion to discuss (see pp. 44 f.). Here again Jonson and Shakspere were on opposite sides, and it was during the course of this that Jonson made his most bitter attacks on both Shakspere and the plays. Such attacks, of which there were other victims besides Shakspere and in which Jonson got as good as he gave, of course cannot be taken at their face value. They were written when tempers were high and the scoring of points all-important; they are not in any sense serious criticism.

The third factor is Jonson's character, about which we have a fair amount of information. He was notoriously both jealous and generous. He was given to cavilling and quarrelling, with a critical eye for other men's faults, and a high sense of his own value. He was quick to blame and condemn, but equally quick to forgive and praise. Shakspere was not the only person he attacked on one occasion and praised on another. He said he esteemed the poet Donne the best in the world for some things, but he told Drummond of Hawthornden that Donne deserved hanging for not keeping accent, and there are other episodes of a similar nature. Jonson even became reconciled with the detested Marston. It is therefore not at all remarkable that his attitude towards Shakspere should be inconsistent. In any case such an attitude is not unique in literary history; it can be paralleled by that of Carlyle towards Emerson, and, in a less degree, by that of Byron towards Scott.

The fourth factor is Jonson's personal friendship with Shakspere, for which the main evidence is his own plain statement of the fact in his *Discoveries* (see p. 285). In addition there are a number of anecdotes illustrating this friendship, such as the one that it was through Shakspere's good offices that the Lord Chamberlain's Company produced Jonson's Roman tragedy *Sejanus* when it had been rejected elsewhere. It is true that these anecdotes rest mainly on tradition, but the tradition is a strong one, and among the theorists Titherley at least is not disposed to reject it.[1]

From this review of the case three important facts emerge. They are:

(1) That Shakspere and Jonson had totally different ideas and ideals where the drama was concerned, and that what attacks the latter made upon the former were paralleled by those he made on other literary men with whom he disagreed.

(2) That Jonson's character was such as to lead him to praise at one time and condemn at another.

(3) That Jonson had certainly been on terms of friendship with Shakspere, and it is highly probable that he owed the latter a debt of gratitude.

In the light of these facts it is not difficult to suggest a reconstruction of Jonson's mental state during the preparation of the First Folio. He has been engaged by Jaggard to supervise the production and to lend the weight of his name to it, for the others concerned have no standing in literary circles. In this official capacity he naturally reads through the plays. As a result he is in a nostalgic frame of mind. Shakspere is dead, and all the irritation caused by his disorderly romanticism is for the time being forgotten. Memories of their friendship come crowding back. Moreover, Jonson also is an artist and a poet, and,

[1] *Shakespeare's Identity*, p. 131.

much as he may dislike the form and treatment of the plays, he cannot fail to see that they are good. And so, with the generous side of his nature uppermost, he pens his panegyric, a genuine tribute to the memory of his 'beloved, the author' – at least for the moment.

Of course this is only conjecture, but so are all the views put forward by the theorists, and mine at least fits the facts much better than theirs do; it is quite simple and natural, and free from all the inconsistencies, strained meanings, and far-fetched ideas to which they have resort.

This brings us to the final act in the drama of the First Folio, or perhaps it would be more correct to call it the epilogue. Somewhere round about 1630 Jonson wrote a series of essays under the title of *Discoveries*. One of these, No. 44, entitled 'De Shakespeare Nostrati', comprises the following:

> I *remember*, the Players have often mentioned it as an honour to *Shakespeare*, that in his writing, (whatsoever he penn'd) he never blotted out line. My answer hath been, would he had blotted a thousand. Which they thought a malevolent speech. I had not told posterity this, but for their ignorance, who choose that circumstance to commend their friend by, wherein he most faulted. And to justify mine own candour, (for I lov'd the man, and do honour his memory (on this side idolatory) as much as any.) He was (indeed) honest, and of an open and free nature; had an excellent *Phantsie*; brave notions, and gentle expressions; wherein he flow'd with that facility, that sometime it was necessary he should be stopp'd; *Sufflaminandus erat*; as Augustus said of Haterius. His wit was in his own power; would the rule of it had been so too. Many times he fell into those things, could not escape laughter; as when he said in the person of *Caesar*, one speaking to him; *Caesar thou dost me wrong.* He replied; *Caesar did never wrong, but with just cause* and such like; which were ridiculous. But he redeemed his vices with his virtues. There was ever more in him to be praised, than to be pardoned.

Now whatever may be said about this paragraph, it is fatal to the theorists' argument that by deliberate ambiguity in the First Folio panegyric Jonson carefully distinguished between the actor and the dramatist, thus implying that they were two different persons. It may be true, as Evans says, that '*Sufflaminandus erat*' applies to Shakspere's talking rather than to his writing. It may be true that Jonson's misquotation of the lines from *Julius Caesar* refers to Shakspere as an actor fluffing his lines – he would not be the only author-actor who has fluffed in his own plays. Both references are capable of other interpretations, but there is no necessity to trouble about them. Nothing can alter the plain sense of the opening sentences. *They constitute a rebuke to a dramatist for not sufficiently revising his work.* It does not matter whether Jonson was justified in this criticism or not; the fact that he made it proves that at this late date, and subsequent to his work on the First Folio, he believed Shakspere was the dramatist.

There is, of course, no doubt that when he wrote this paragraph Jonson's nostalgic mood had passed, which is only what we should expect in a man of his temperament, and that he had returned, as far as Shakspere was concerned, to the type of criticism he usually levelled at his contemporaries, with its sudden changes from praise to fault-finding. It is certainly far from fulsome flattery, but its acknowledgement of Shakspere as a dramatist is all the more impressive for our purpose because it finds fault with him as such.

The theorists have, of course, made frantic efforts to wriggle out of the dilemma in which Jonson has thus placed them. We will examine two of their attempts, for they are not without interest.

The first is that of Evans. He says[1] that Jonson, reading through the First Folio, was suddenly struck by the inconsistency of his own panegyric and other statements in the prefatory matter with his former jibes at Shakspere; and he feared that this might lead to a suspicion of the Stratford authorship, and so endanger Derby's secret. He therefore, possibly at Derby's request, made the paragraph in *Discoveries* deliberately puzzling to cover this.

I do not find Jonson's paragraph very puzzling, but I am exceedingly puzzled by Evans' explanation of it. I fail completely to see how it could cover any *gaffe* Jonson had made, if he did make one, in the First Folio. And if it could, it came far too late to do so. Some years elapsed between the publication of the First Folio and the writing of *Discoveries*, time surely for

[1] *Shakespeare's Magic Circle*, pp. 143 f.

any damage the former could do to Derby's secret, if Derby had a secret, to be done over and over again. If there were any two-and-two to be put together, it was the people who knew Derby personally, not a later generation, who were in the best position to add them up, and they had had about seven years to do it in. What possible protection could the paragraph in *Discoveries* be in such circumstances? As a matter of fact no one was likely to give Jonson's inconsistencies a second thought, for, as we have seen, he was equally inconsistent in his criticisms of other writers. The paragraph in question is typically Jonsonian, and such strained interpretations as that of Evans, based on no evidence of any sort, merely emphasize the hopelessness of this part of the theorists' case.

Our second example comes from Titherley.[1] His explanation of the paragraph is that Jonson's memory was failing, and that he had forgotten that Bacon had told him Derby was the real author of the Shakespearean plays. For twenty years or more, before Bacon enlightened him, he had believed that Shakspere had written the plays, and now, 'an aged aged man' of nearly sixty-four, he relapsed into the old illusion. In support of this Titherley points out that in the very volume of *Discoveries* itself Jonson complains that his memory is not what it was – 'is much decayed in me', are his own words.

Now as a young man Jonson had possessed a phenomenal memory. He could remember vast sections of books, word for word, after a single reading, and carry in his mind masses of information. It was probably this ability that enabled him to make himself a great Classical scholar while working twelve hours a day as a bricklayer. I am quite prepared to believe that he had lost these abnormal powers at the age of sixty-three, and that he might bemoan this loss as something of a calamity. But I simply cannot credit that he could forget such a simple yet startling fact as that Derby was the real Shakespeare communicated to him by no less a person than Bacon, and that in consequence he himself had carefully introduced into the First Folio a series of ambiguities and double-meanings hinting at this fact. To do so he must have become a mental defective, and the man who wrote *Discoveries* was certainly not a mental

[1] *Shakespeare's Identity*, pp. 137 f.

defective.[1] Moreover the First Folio would seem to have been very much in Jonson's mind when he wrote the paragraph in *Discoveries*, for his remark about Shakspere never blotting a line is almost a quotation from the Epistle of Heminge and Condell to 'the great variety of readers'. He does not appear to have forgotten that. The suggestion therefore that he could have forgotten that Derby wrote the Shakespearean plays, *if he had ever been told such a thing*, is manifestly absurd.

This concludes our review of the theorists' attack on the First Folio. I think it may be justly claimed that it has been repulsed at every point. Not only have they proved quite unable to shake that work's favourable testimony to the orthodox view, but they come out of the fray with their own theories looking even more threadbare than before.

[1] As a matter of fact Jonson wrote two more plays after he had written *Discoveries*, and although they are much inferior to his best work, they are such as only a man with normal mental powers and memory could have written.

CHAPTER XVII

Vice Versa

The contents of this chapter are not offered as *proof* of the Stratford actor's authorship of the Shakespearean plays. To provide such proof is not a matter with which I am concerned in this study. My purpose is to demonstrate the inadequacy of the theorists' cases, and one way of doing this is to show that evidence of exactly the same nature as they produce on behalf of their various candidates can also be produced for William Shakspere. It is such evidence that I have collected here. If it were actually put forward in defence of his authorship there is none of it I should regard as absolutely conclusive, and some that I should reject for the reasons I have rejected the same kind of thing when put forward by the theorists. I must ask my readers to bear this in mind throughout the chapter since, for purposes of comparison, I must argue each point as strongly as the theorists do.

We will begin with the type of evidence which is the mainstay of all the theories, and is particularly popular with the Oxfordians. This is the identification of some incident or reference in a play with some event in the career of the candidate, and then claiming that this proves him to be the author. The objection to such evidence, as I have repeatedly stated, is that if a sufficiently large body of literature is examined, and the Shakespearean works amply fulfil this condition, incidents and references can be found that will fit anyone. There are plenty to fit William Shakspere of Stratford.

My first example is taken from Act I, Scene iii, of *2 Henry IV*, where in a lengthy speech Lord Bardolph uses the building of a house as a simile for the reconstruction of the Kingdom. The speech runs as follows:

> When we mean to build
> We first survey the plot, then draw the model;
> And when we see the figure of the house,

Then must we rate the cost of the erection;
Which if we find out-weighs ability,
What do we then but draw anew the model
In fewer offices, or at last desist
To build at all? Much more in this great work –
Which is almost to pluck a kingdom down,
And set up another – should we survey
The plot of situation and the model,
Consent upon a sure foundation,
Question surveyors, know our own estate,
How able such a work to undergo,
To weigh against his opposite; or else
We fortify in paper and in figures,
Using the names of men instead of men;
Like one that draws a model of a house
Beyond his powers to build it; who, half through,
Gives o'er, and leaves his part created cost
A naked subject to the weeping clouds,
And waste for winter's churlish tyranny.

The accepted date for the writing of 2 *Henry IV* is 1597/1598, and in May of 1597 Shakspere purchased New Place, the second largest house in Stratford. There is evidence that when he bought it the house had fallen into a very bad state of disrepair, and he had to carry out considerable rebuilding and reconstruction.[1] The juxtaposition of the dates of the purchase of the house and the writing of the play is certainly suggestive. The simile is so detailed and factual that we feel it must have been based on a personal experience, and here we find that Shakspere had just such an experience shortly before the lines were written. In the light of this, how can his authorship of the passage, and so of the whole play, be doubted? But if confirmation is required, there is the bourgeois thrift that breathes through every sentence. To count the cost would be second nature to the shrewd business-man of London and Stratford, and the imagery is just the kind that he would instinctively think of; it would never occur to the extravagant Elizabethan nobles, who wore a small fortune on their backs at a Court masque and squandered a large one in a three-days' entertainment of the Queen.

[1] Murry, *Shakespeare*, pp. 33–35.

The second example comes from *Hamlet*, Act IV, Scene iii. It is the Queen's speech to Laertes, in which she gives him a false account of Ophelia's death, making it appear an accident and not suicide. She says:

> A willow grows aslant the brook.
>
>   *   *   *
>
> There on the pendant boughs her coronet weeds
> Climbing to hang, an envious sliver broke;
> When down her weedy trophies and herself
> Fell in the weeping brook. Her clothes spread wide;
> And mermaid-like, awhile they bore her up;
>
>   *   *   *
>
> Till that her garments, heavy with their drink,
> Pull'd the poor wretch from her melodious lay
> To muddy death.

When Shakspere was about sixteen years old a girl was found drowned after an unfortunate love affair. The inquest was held at Stratford, and her parents, in an attempt to prevent a verdict of suicide, pleaded that it was an accident. They said their daughter had fallen while climbing out along a branch of a willow tree which overhung the river in order to dip in the water some flowers she had gathered. The girl's name was Katherine Hamlett.

E. A. Armstrong[1] in his study of the psychology of Shakespeare's authorship makes use of this incident as an example of the effectiveness of a personal name in reviving memory-association. According to his view the name 'Hamlet' of his play revives in the mind of the author the memory of Katherine Hamlett from his youth, and this in turn recalls all that happened at the inquest, details which later are poetically woven into the story of Ophelia.

This seems reasonable enough. In any case there could hardly be a more certain and obvious origin of the Queen's speech, or in fact of the whole episode, than the account of that particular inquest. And Shakspere is the only one of the claimants who can be brought into any association with it.

[1] *Shakespeare's Imagination*, p. 112.

My next example is not without its humorous aspect, for, surprisingly, it is provided by the Derbyite, Titherley.[1] Dr Titherley, like all the theorists, when he mentions an incident in his candidate's career, adds a reference to the play in which he believes there is a reminiscence of this incident. Apparently the habit has grown upon him to such an extent that he does it unconsciously, for writing of the marriage, *not* of Derby, but of the Stratford actor, and mentioning that Anne Hathaway was eight years older than her husband, he instinctively adds in brackets 'cf. 12th. Night, II, 4, 29'. The reference here is to the conversation between the Duke and the disguised Viola, which contains the following lines spoken by the Duke:

> Let the woman take
> An elder than herself; so wears she to him,
> So sways she level in her husband's heart.

And a little later:

> Then let thy love be younger than thyself,
> Or thy affection cannot hold the bent;
> For women are as roses, whose fair flower
> Being once display'd doth fall that very hour.

Of course this reference admirably fits the circumstances of Shakspere's marriage, which might well have suggested it, and in consequence points to him as the author. Since, however, this is the very opposite of what Titherley is trying to prove, I can only assume that he drew attention to it in the way that he did in a fit of absence of mind. The incident should certainly impress upon him how much value is to be set upon this type of evidence.

Such instances could be multiplied many times, but the three examples I have given are sufficient to illustrate the point. Readers who are interested can find others in Middleton Murry's *Shakespeare*. We will now turn to another type of evidence, also popular with the theorists. This consists in taking a section of their candidate's life, and tracing its alleged influence on the plays written about the same time. I will take

[1] *Shakespeare's Identity*, p. 105.

such a section of the Stratford actor's life and apply it in the same way; and to add to the interest I will select a period that some of the theorists[1] actually quote as of such a dull humdrum nature that no one living it could possibly have written the glowing colourful plays the writing of which corresponds to it.

The period is that between 1598 and 1604, when Shakspere lodged in Cripplegate at the house of Christopher Mountjoy, a French Huguenot, who, with his wife and his daughter, Mary, had taken refuge in England from one of the persecutions of his Faith that so frequently broke out in France. The theorists describe Mountjoy as a wigmaker, though they are not alone in this – some Stratfordians do the same. It is, however, quite incorrect. That indefatigable literary detective, Dr Leslie Hotson, whose hunting grounds are the Record Office and other places where ancient documents lie hidden, and who never speaks without contemporary documentary evidence to support him, has investigated the status and circumstances of the Mountjoys, and I propose to give here a summary of his findings and the evidence upon which they are based.

Before doing so, however, it is necessary to mention a previous discovery made by Professor Wallace, which Hotson reports. This proves that Shakspere was not only a lodger, but also an intimate friend of the family. Mountjoy had an apprentice named Stephen Belott, described as 'a very honest and good fellow'. Belott wished to marry his master's daughter, and the match was favoured by the girl's mother. Her father, however, was opposed to this arrangement, and Mrs Mountjoy appealed to Shakspere to use his influence to straighten things out. He did so, and the marriage took place, though there was further trouble over it eight years afterwards.

Now we may turn to the documentary evidence that Hotson has brought to light.[2] This consists first of a number of legal documents in which Mountjoy is invariably described as a *tiremaker*. A tiremaker was certainly *not* a wigmaker. The 'tires' or headdresses of the Elizabethan ladies were beautiful confections of gold, pearl, and precious stones. The foundation was a coif, caul, hair-net, or hair-lace, cunningly woven of gold

[1] Titherley, *Shakespeare's Identity*, p. 106.
[2] Essay 'Not of an Age' in *Shakespeare's Sonnets Dated*, pp. 174 ff.

thread on which jewels were mounted. Hotson quotes a description of one of Queen Elizabeth's tires – 'A Jewel, being a ship of Mother-of-Pearl, garnished with rubies', together with some other contemporary descriptions.

It was from Venice that the tiremaker's art came, and it *was* an art; Mountjoy was an artist and a craftsman. In a lawsuit, the documents of which Hotson brought to light, he was described as one who practised the art or mystery of making and working gold and silver thread, 'commonly called Venice gold and silver thread'.

The headdresses made by the tiremakers inspired contemporary lyric poets to sing their praises, and it is an argument in favour of the Stratford actor's authorship of the plays that these reveal a certain familiarity with the tiremaker's art. In the *Merry Wives of Windsor* Falstaff is made to flatter Mistress Ford by telling her: 'Thou hast the right arched beauty of the brow that becomes the ship-tire, the tire valiant, or any tire of Venetian admittance.'

A subordinate part of the craft was called 'spinning upon silk'. It consisted of intertwining the gold or silver threads with silken strands. Hotson suggests that Shakspere had watched Mary Mountjoy doing this beautiful work, for he includes the technical terms in a couplet in *Pericles*:

> Be 't when she weav'd the sleided silk
> With fingers long, small, white as milk.

Critics, Hotson adds, have often considered the metaphor of the appearance of the murdered Duncan in *Macbeth* far-fetched and tasteless:

> Here lay Duncan,
> His silver skin laced with his golden blood.

No doubt it has both these faults, but if Shakspere had noticed the wefts in the gold and silver nets in Mountjoy's workroom, it would explain why such an unlikely image should occur to him.

There are two other technical terms from the tiremaker's art introduced into *Antony and Cleopatra* – 'Cloth of Gold', which was silk stitched or brocaded with gold thread, and 'Tissue', which was a fabric of woven gold on a light foundation of silk. Enobarbus' description of Cleopatra's barge contains these lines:

> She did lie
> In her pavillion, cloth of gold, of tissue.

And in *The Winter's Tale* Autolycus mentions the humbler and cheaper varieties of headdress:

> *Golden quoifs* and *stomachers*
> For my lads to give their dears.

And:

> Any silk, any *thread*,
> Any *toys for your head*.

It may be remarked here that it is a point in favour of the Stratford actor's authorship of the plays that he alone of the claimants is known to have had first-hand experience of the processes of the art which gave rise to these allusions.

Hotson's researches have revealed that the customers of the Mountjoys came from the *élite* and included the Royal Family. Among the documents he has discovered is one for the payment of a bill for fifty-nine pounds – a considerable sum in those days – to 'Marie Mountjoy tyrewoman' for tires for King James' wife, Queen Anne.

At this point it is well worth quoting Hotson in full. He indulges in a little speculative reconstruction after the manner of Titherley describing Derby and Bacon producing the *Promus* together at Gray's Inn (see p. 166 f.) and the making of the Northumberland MS (see pp. 230–232), but with very much more probability and factual evidence to support it. He says:

'We are now equipped to make a visit in imagination to Silver Street, say early in October 1604. What shall we find in the busy household of Christopher Mountjoy? In the shop and workroom, glittering with silk, Venice gold and silver threads, jewels, and tissue, the best hands and brains, including those of the young lovers (Stephen Belott and Mary Mountjoy), are active, preparing a rare ornament for the head of the Queen.

Upstairs their friend Shakespeare is hard at work on a tragic tale of lovers, furnishing *his* Venetian offering for the Queen – *Othello, The Moor of Venice.*

'By November 1, he and his company are ready, the fresh lines all learnt, and present the new play before James and Anne and their brilliant court in the Banqueting House at Whitehall. Perhaps at the performance the Queen is wearing the new Mountjoy head-dress. Four days later Shakespeare and his fellows are again before royalty, this time with the revived *Merry Wives of Windsor*, in which, as we have seen, Falstaff assures Mistress Ford that she is beautiful enough for a royal court. "Thou hast the right arched beauty of the brow that becomes the ship-tire, the tire valliant or any other tire of Venetian admittance." Within two weeks the Queen has paid Mrs. Mountjoy a large part of her bill, and thereupon the marriage of the two young fellow-craftsmen, prepared by Shakespeare, takes place.'

In addition to the material for his numerous references to tires in the plays and the imagery drawn from the processes of making them, Shakspere could have acquired in the home of the Mountjoys a knowledge of France and the French language; the idea for the two scenes in *Henry V* where the French Princess struggles with English, from hearing Mary Mountjoy speak her 'broken music'; and possibly some local colour of Venice, for Mountjoy, to supply the Royal Family, must have been a master of his art, and may well have studied it in its place of origin, Venice. Moreover, the name of his friend and landlord could easily have led Shakspere into mistaking Mountjoy for the personal name of the French Herald in *Henry V*, which, as I have already pointed out (see p. 244 fn.), he does do, instead of his official designation, a mistake no nobleman or lawyer could have made.

Be all that as it may, one thing is certain – there was nothing dull or humdrum about the romantic and colourful house where Shakspere lodged during the period when so many of the great plays were written; on the contrary it seems to have been the direct inspiration of much that is found in them.

The error over the Herald's designation in *Henry V*, to which reference has just been made, is not the only lapse in the Shakespearean plays. The theorists are fond of such comments as 'Only a nobleman or a great lawyer could have written this', and 'A country-bred tradesman's son could never have written that'. Ivor Brown[1] turns the tables on them and produces a number of instances where the comments 'Only a country-bred tradesman's son could have written this', and 'A nobleman or a great lawyer could never have been guilty of that', are quite appropriate.

We will examine one example. It comes from *Hamlet*, from the same speech of the Queen describing the drowning of Ophelia that we have already considered in another connection (see pp. 291 f.). In the course of the speech the Queen relates what flowers Ophelia had gathered:

> There with fantastic garlands did she come
> Of crow-flowers, nettles, daisies, and long purples
> That liberal shepherds give a grosser name,
> But our cold maids do dead men's fingers call them.

The offending line is the third one. Let us consider the situation. No less a person than the Queen of Denmark is speaking. She is breaking to a brother the tragic news of his sister's death, *and she pauses in the middle to make a smutty joke.* It is not the bawdy itself that matters – the Elizabethans were not squeamish – but the occasion of it. It is not only appallingly tasteless and inappropriate, but technically bad, for it interrupts the drama of the Queen's recital, besides being likely to evoke laughter among the audience at the wrong time. It is incredible that a great noble, brought up in a Court of most punctilious etiquette and trained from childhood in what was befitting for every occasion, would be guilty of such a lapse. But Shakspere, whatever veneer of culture he might have acquired and whatever innate refinement he might possess, could never escape completely from the environment of his youth. There would be occasions when he would be bound to nod, and this is clearly one of them. He had no doubt often laughed with the 'liberal shepherds' around Stratford at their suggestive name for

[1] *Amazing Monument*, pp. 195 f.

297

the flower in question, and, perhaps carried back by the memory of Katherine Hamlett to his boyhood's days, he slips in the coarse jest almost unconsciously.

Another type of so-called evidence of which the theorists make use is alleging that a certain reference in some contemporary writer's work applies to their particular candidate. They then claim that this writer had some personal association with their candidate and so would be likely to know if he wrote the plays, and finally they deduce that the reference proves that he did write them. Titherley's handling of the Davies epigram, which we examined in Chapter V (see pp. 92–94), is an example of this kind of thing, and there are many others. The weakness in every case is that, in spite of much straining on the part of the theorists, it is never certain that the reference is to their candidate and always most improbable that it means what they say it means.

I can produce one such reference in favour of the Stratford actor that is entirely free from these defects. There is no doubt that it refers to him, and there is no doubt that it treats him as the author of the Shakespearean plays. This is the commendatory poem by Leonard Digges prefaced to the First Folio. Even the theorists themselves concede both my claims, but say they are of no evidential value as Digges was merely a minor poet of no importance, and of course believed what all the rest of the ignorant general public believed.[1]

Now let us see what is actually known about Digges, largely brought to light by Hotson's researches,[2] and supported by his customary array of contemporary documentary evidence. Digges was the son of an eminent astronomer and mathematician. He went to Oxford University, where he was described as 'a great master of the English language, a perfect understander of the French and Spanish, a good poet, and no mean orator'. The most interesting thing about him for our purpose, however, is that while he was still a child his mother, left a widow, married Thomas Russell, second son of Sir Thomas Russell of Strensham. Thomas Russell lived at the

---

[1] Titherley, *Shakespeare's Identity*, pp. 124 and 127.
[2] *Shakespeare's Sonnets Dated*, pp. 111 f., and also *I, William Shakespeare*.

Manor House, Aldminster, four miles from Stratford, and was a friend of Shakspere, who appointed him one of the overseers of his will, and left him five pounds.

Leonard Digges must have known Shakspere personally, since the latter was a friend of his step-father. I do not claim that because of this he must have known whether Shakspere wrote the plays – though in similar circumstances most of the theorists would do so – but I do claim that he must have considered Shakspere capable of doing so, or he would not have risked his own reputation by writing the commendatory poem published in the First Folio, nor a second, which he wrote later and which was prefaced to the Second Folio.

Here we have documentary proof of Shakspere's friendly relations with a family of the local landed gentry, and a distinguished man of letters, who knew him personally, apparently entertaining no doubt that he was the author of the Shakespearean plays, the very thing of which the theorists have repeatedly denied the existence. It is true that most of these details are of comparatively recent discovery; they have, however been known long enough for writers on the subject since 1940 to take notice of them, yet not a word about them have the theorists said, another example of their besetting sin of *suppressio veri* – or is it possible that they never read the other side?

I do not intend to waste time and space in producing so-called cryptograms from the plays bearing testimony to William Shakspere's authorship, although it is as easy to do so for him as for Bacon or any of the other claimants. I have already quoted one example of this in the course of describing Nicholson's exposure of Donnelly's cipher (see p. 68), and interested readers will find a number of others given by the Friedmans to illustrate how easy it is to extract almost any desired name from a passage by the cryptologists' methods. Other types of evidence in support of Shakspere occur incidentally in various parts of the present work, such as the way in which certain difficulties associated with the publication of the First Folio vanish directly his authorship is assumed (see pp. 274 f.), and those who desire more need only turn to some recognized biography, like that of E. K. Chambers, to find plenty. I will only repeat here what I said at the beginning of the chapter – that I am not attempting to provide an absolute proof of Shakspere's authorship, merely to show that evidence at least as strong and of the same kind as that advanced by the theorists exists for it. And this I claim to have demonstrated beyond all possible dispute.

CHAPTER XVIII

Confusions and Conclusions

At various places, and particularly in the preceding chapter, I have made it clear that it is no part of the purpose of this study to provide positive proof that Shakspere, the Stratford actor, wrote the Shakespearean plays. As a matter of fact, though there are good grounds for such a belief, there is no *positive* proof that he did so. All we know *positively* is that the plays have come down to us bearing his name, that he was generally accepted as their author in his own day, and that he has been generally accepted as such ever since. In this respect, however, he differs in no way from many of his contemporaries and predecessors. The authorship of the works that bear their names rests on precisely the same foundation as his, and if theirs had been as pre-eminent as his no doubt the same sort of controversy would have raged around them; indeed it does to some extent, for we have seen that the more extreme Baconians claim the works of many other Elizabethan writers for their candidate exactly as they do those of Shakspere.

This state of affairs is in no way surprising in days before the art of biography had developed, and when there were no newspapers or periodicals with critiques of every new play produced and columns of gossip to keep the activities of authors constantly before the public. Apart from a few official lists of plays performed at the Court and a passing mention of titles and authors in such works as Meres' *Palladis Tamia*, all rather limited as sources of information, there are usually no records of plays except the published versions. It is therefore only in comparatively rare instances that we can find any evidence of authorship more positive than that on which Shakspere's rests before the last quarter of the seventeenth century.

In such circumstances I suppose that it is just within the bounds of possibility that a mistake in the ascription of authorship might occur – though hardly in the way the theorists suggest. That is why I stated in my Introduction that I should always keep an open mind on the subject and be ready to consider any new evidence, if such were forthcoming, on its merits. Unless, however, such hypothetical evidence were very different from anything the theorists have offered up to the present time, there would seem to be little likelihood of my having to change my opinion. Just how weak all their cases really are it has been the object of this study to demonstrate, and in this final chapter I propose to summarize the main points we have examined, and discuss what general conclusions may legitimately be drawn from them.

In the first place the whole story of Shakspere's association with the plays, if he were not the author, is manifestly absurd. Since he was a member of the Company which produced the plays he would be a most unsuitable person to act as a 'cover' for the true author. He would constantly find himself in embarrassing situations, such as being called upon to elucidate some obscure point or to rewrite part of a scene on the spot, and the recipient of other similar requests with which he would be totally unable to comply. If the 'true author' had employed a cover at all, he would have selected for the purpose some minor man of letters who had no connection whatever with the practical side of the theatre.

There could, however, be no need for such a cover, whoever the author might be, for the Shakespearean plays contain nothing that was likely to offend the Government; if they had, then it would have been vetoed at once by the Censor, to whom all plays had to be submitted, and who, as we have seen in the case of *Sir Thomas More*, was prompt to take action in such matters. In the one instance, that of *Richard II*, where a play, quite innocent in itself, was used for a treasonable purpose, the actors did not suffer any penalty and the author was not even interrogated. If one of the claimants were really the true author and desired to preserve his anonymity, a simple *nom-de-plume* would have served his purpose much better than any 'cover'.[1]

---

[1] The *nom-de-plume* 'Martin Marprelate' served its owner with complete adequacy. The author of the pamphlets published under that name (*c.* 1590) was never discovered despite the most strenuous efforts made at the time, and remains a mystery to this day.

The picture the theorists paint of Shakspere in their denigration campaign only adds to the absurdity of the 'cover' claim. The ignorant, drunken, rascally clown they present could obviously deceive no one, and would be infinitely more of a danger than a protection. No one but a lunatic would engage – and pay exorbitantly – such a person for such a purpose, and the theorists who use this argument prove nothing but the woolly state of mind in which they approach the problem.

Not all the theorists, of course, involve themselves in this latter absurdity, but all the theories contain a mass of inconsistencies and contradictions only slightly less obvious, demonstrating the mental blindness with which the determination to make out a case for something can afflict even intelligent men.

The most important example of these is the confusion between 'secret' and 'no secret', which we have had occasion to note again and again. Not one of the theorists is ever sure whether his candidate's authorship was so dangerous that his life depended on its never being suspected, or whether almost everyone from the Queen downwards knew all about it. No doubt the theorists adopt this course of necessity, since without the 'secret' there could be no reason for Shakspere's reputed connection with the plays, which is a stubborn fact, while unless the 'secret' were known to a number of people so that they could hint at it in their writings and in other ways, there could be no evidence for its existence. We may sympathize with the theorists in this dilemma, but their giddy gyrations cannot add conviction to their cases.

Another type of evidence we have found used by the theorists is that which becomes patently absurd the moment their various theories are brought into juxtaposition. This is the evidence that fits two or more of the claimants equally well – or equally badly, as the case may be. Examples of this type are the incidents alleged to have occurred in the production of the First Folio, the parallelisms found in the recognized works of the claimants and the Shakespearean plays, the interpretation of the Touchstone–William scene in *As You Like It*, and certain references in the sonnets. It is obvious that what may be used equally well to support two or more incompatibles can in reality support none. Even in the unlikely event of its being true for one case, this could not be known.

Then there is the type of evidence which is the mainstay of all the theories – the identification by the theorists of certain of the *dramatis personae* in the plays, mainly on some slight similarity in the name, with real persons associated in some way with their respective candidates, or some incident in a play vaguely reminiscent of an incident in the candidate's life, from which it is argued that only he could have written the play. The most elaborate example of this is Professor Lambin's alleged discovery of the origin of *Measure for Measure* and its association with Derby, but every one of the theories abounds in similar examples, and we have reviewed a great many in these pages. Such so-called evidence has been shown to be quite worthless, for it is clear that if a sufficiently large amount of literary material is taken, and the Shakespearean plays amply fulfil this condition, such references and incidents can be found to fit anyone; we found a number to fit Shakspere.

Moreover, as we have seen, many items the theorists offer in support of their respective causes are purely conjectural and based on no tangible evidence. They are just assumptions that their authors are compelled to make in order to reconcile awkward facts with their theories. Such are the whole of Hoffman's reconstruction of the story of Marlowe's assassination; Titherley's accounts of the emergence of the 'Promus' jointly at the hands of Derby and Bacon at Gray's Inn, the making of the Northumberland MS, and the story of Derby's secret engagement to the Queen; as well as all Durning-Lawrence's *ex cathedra* pronouncements. Obviously none of these imaginative efforts has any evidential value at all. And the same criticism may be applied to the fantasies of the cryptologists, and to the host of irrelevancies, logical fallacies, and misinterpretations through ignorance of the Tudor background, which, together with cases of *suppressio veri, suggestio falsi*, and even misrepresentation of the evidence, we have found disfiguring the pages of some of the theorists' works.

Of course there sometimes emerge from this mass of confusion, contradiction, and pure invention, other arguments – though surprisingly few of them – which do not completely outrage commonsense, and which demand serious examination. One example is that of the Hall and Marston satires, quoted by B. G. Theobald, but the most that this can be made to prove is that two contemporary writers hazarded a guess that *Venus and Adonis* was written by Bacon in collaboration with a new and unknown poet; it cannot prove that Bacon actually did write it, still less that he had anything to do with the Shakespearean plays. Again there is Titherley's discussion of the Addition to *Sir Thomas More* and the Oxfordian argument from a comparison of *Venus and Adonis* with a *Vision of a Fair Maid*, and a few others of a similar nature. The facts on which all these depend, however, are capable of more than one interpretation, and usually the theorists have selected the least natural and plausible of the alternatives. In no case do they amount to proof or even to evidence of anything; they are merely theories within a theory.

The other leg of the theorists' argument, upon which they are all in agreement, consists in the assertion that the plays show an academic knowledge and a familiarity with life in high places that a man with Shakspere's background could not possess; in other words that only an aristocrat or someone in a high official position like Bacon could have written them. This was not an unnatural attitude to take in the earlier periods of the controversy, when little was known about the Tudor background and still less about the particular background of Shakspere. In the light of all the recent discoveries made by Hotson and other investigators the situation is completely changed and the old view no longer tenable. We have seen that the plays contain nothing necessarily beyond the knowledge of Shakspere the Stratford actor, and that they do contain a number of defects and solecisms which would be impossible in the case of an aristocratic author.

The theorists' cases therefore all fall completely to the ground. Most of their arguments can only be described as puerile or absurd, and those that rise above this level never attain to the status of evidence, only of an opinion about the interpretation of certain facts. It was when my study drove these points home that I abandoned the neutral attitude (see p. 10) with which I started, and decided that I had become a convinced Stratfordian – at least while the situation remains as it is. For this complete failure of the theorists to establish even the faintest possibility for the validity of their claims is of the greatest significance. I have said that there is no *positive* proof that Shakspere was the author of the Shakespearean plays, and this of course is true; but the theorists have put forward what must surely be every available rival candidate for this office – the complete list, including those of all the minor theories, numbers fifty-seven – and they have devoted a very intensive research over a long period to the task of discovering evidence to establish one or other of these rivals' claims. If after all this effort, they can produce nothing better than the sorry stuff they have done, it can only be because there is nothing better to be discovered, and consequently no real evidence in favour of any of their claimants. The theorists have, in short, given us an additional and very strong reason for the belief that William Shakspere of Stratford is the true author of the Shakespearean plays, namely that there is no one else who could be put in his place.

Before bringing this book to a close there is one other point with which I wish to deal. Though they may not be great Elizabethan scholars, some of the theorists are eminent men in other walks of life, and certainly they are not fools. How is it then that they can seriously put forward such hopelessly inadequate and often ludicrous arguments as we have examined in these pages? In an attempt to solve this problem I have evolved a 'theory of theorists'. It is, of course, merely a personal opinion, formed as a result of studying their works, and rests on nothing more solid than the impression this experience made upon me. It may quite well be wrong, and if any theorist is offended by it, I apologize in advance. Still it does seem to explain not only the puzzling circumstance I have just mentioned, but the whole amazing development of the controversy, and for this reason I am emboldened to set it forth here.

My view is that the original Baconian theory was a sincere and genuine attempt to deal with what was a very real problem at the time. When it was first put forward very little was known of Shakspere and his background, and that little did not seem to fit the author of the immortal plays. Then came the Bardolators – cranks, if cranks ever existed – piling up absurd claims for, and absurd myths about, their idol. It was no wonder that some people turned away in disgust, and began to look around for another candidate. Bacon, as the most versatile genius of his day, was an obvious, if a somewhat superficial, choice; and, like any novelty, the theory was bound to make converts. Of course it soon developed its own cranks, and some of its arguments are the silliest the controversy has produced. On the other hand, I think this theory has also produced the best, though this perhaps is not very high praise considering the general standard.

With regard to the other schools of thought, I do not think that *subconsciously* they believe in their theories, though no doubt *consciously* they have persuaded themselves that they do. Sooner or later the Baconian theory was bound to produce imitators – such things always do – and once the game had started it would certainly spread as far as the available supply of candidates would allow it. There is undoubtedly a fascination in 'making a case' for something, no matter what, for there is a bit of an advocate in most of us. This view would largely account for the absurdity of so many of the arguments put forward by the members of these schools and for the numerous examples of *suppressio veri* that disfigure them. If at the back of their minds the protagonists were dimly aware that it was only a game, they might well feel that it did not require quite the same strict integrity that they would exercise over something more serious. This, however, would not prevent them from being emotionally involved in it – our emotions may be very strongly stirred by a game, and this is particularly the case when the game is a controversy such as the one with which we are concerned. The bitterness that this sometimes provokes is no bar to its being a sham fight.

I have not dealt with any of the minor theorists in this book, but, for the sake of completeness, I must include them in my 'theory of theorists'. I think what I have said in the preceding paragraph would apply to most of them, but there are a few about whom I have darker suspicions. I do not think they really believe their own theories. These are so extravagant and the arguments by which they support them equally so, that I incline to the belief that they are playing a gigantic practical joke upon their readers to see how much these will swallow; or, alternatively, they may be satirizing their more serious fellow-theorists. After all, Oscar Wilde perpetrated a rather similar trick, and he may well have some unavowed imitators.

Whether my ideas are right or wrong, I am no opponent of the various theories in the sense that I wish to stop them from being propagated. On the contrary, I believe they serve a very useful purpose. They are good entertainment, and they afford the thoughtful reader an opportunity for mental exercise and a little private research in the reference books. Most important of all, they will send many, who would probably never have made the venture without some such stimulus, to that fountain-head of pure English – the immortal works of Mr William Shakespeare.

Bibliography

ALLEN, Percy. *The Life Story of Edward de Vere as William Shakespeare*. 1930.

AMPHLETT, Miss H. *Who Was Shakespeare?* 1955.

ARMSTRONG, E. A. *Shakespeare's Imagination*. 1946.

BOOTH, W. S. *Some Acrostic Signatures of Francis Bacon*. 1909.

BROOK, C. F. T. *Shakespeare's Sonnets*. 1936.

BROWN, Ivor, and FEARON, George. *Amazing Monument*. 1939.

BYRNE, Miss M. St C. *The Social Background* in 'A Companion to Shakespeare Studies'. 1934.

CAMPBELL, J. *Shakespeare's Legal Acquirements*. 1859.

CASTLE, E. J. *Shakespeare, Jonson, Bacon, and Greene*. 1897.

CHAMBERS, E. K. *William Shakespeare, A Study of Facts and Problems*. 2 vols. 1930.

CHUTE, Marchette. *Shakespeare of London*. 1951. *Jonson of Westminster*. 1954.

CLARK, Mrs S. T. *Shakespeare's Plays in the Order of Writing*. 1931.

CORNWELL, A. B. *Francis the First, Uncrowned King of England*. 1936.

CRAWFORD, C. *The Bacon–Shakespeare Problem*, in 'Collectanea' (Stratford), 2nd series. 1907.

DEVECMON, W. C. *Re Shakespeare's Legal Acquirements*. 1899.

DILLON, Viscount. *Armour and Weapons* in 'Shakespeare's England', IV, Vol. I, 1916.

DODD, Alfred. *The Personal Poems of Francis Bacon*. 1931.

DONNELLY, Ignatius. *The Great Cryptogram*. 1888.

DOUGLAS, M. W. *Lord Oxford and the Shakespeare Group*. 1952.

DURNING-LAWRENCE, E. *Bacon is Shakespeare*. 1910.

EAGLE, R. L. *New Views for Old*. 1950.

EVANS, A. J. *Shakespeare's Magic Circle*. 1956.

FEUILLERAT, A. *Composition of Shakespeare's Plays*. 1953.

FRIEDMAN, W. F., and E. S. *The Shakespearean Ciphers Examined.* 1957.

GALLUP, Mrs E. W. *The Bi-literal Cypher of Sir Francis Bacon.* 1901.

GOLDWORTHY, W. S. *Shakespeare's Heraldic Emblems.* 1928.

GREENWOOD, George. *The Shakespeare Problem Restated.* 1908. *Is There a Shakespeare Problem?* 1916.

GREG, W. W. *The Book of 'Sir Thomas More'.* 1911. *The Editorial Problem in Shakespeare.* 1942.

HALLIDAY, F. E. *Shakespeare in His Age.* 1956.

HENDERSON, Philip. *Christopher Marlowe.* 1952.

HOFFMAN, Calvin. *The Man Who Was Shakespeare.* 1955.

HOLLAND, H. H. *Shakespeare Through Oxford Glasses.* 1923.

HOTSON, Leslie. *The Death of Christopher Marlowe.* 1925. *I, William Shakespeare.* 1937. *Shakespeare's Sonnets Dated.* 1949.

ISAACS, J. *Shakespeare as a Man of the Theatre* in 'Shakespeare Criticism'. 1936.

LEFRANC, Abel. *Sous le Masque de William Shakespeare.* 2 vols. 1919. *A la Decouverte de Shakespeare.* 2 vols. 1945 & 1950.

LEWIS, Wyndham. *The Lion and the Fox.* 1927.

LOONEY, J. T. *Shakespeare Identified.* 1920.

MAXWELL, B. *Studies in the Shakespeare Apocrypha.* 1956.

MUIR, Kenneth. *Shakespeare's Sources.* Vol. 1. 1957.

MURRY, J. Middleton. *Shakespeare.* 1936.

NICHOLSON, R. B. *No Cipher in Shakespeare.* 1889.

PENZANCE, Lord. *Biography of Shakespeare.* 1909.

POLLARD, A. W. *Shakespeare's Folios and Quartos.* 1909. *Shakespeare's Text* in 'A Companion to Shakespeare Studies'. 1934.

POTT, Mrs H. *The Promus of Formularies and Elegancies, by Francis Bacon.* 1883.

PROTHERO, R. E. *Agriculture and Gardening* in 'Shakespeare's England', XII, Vol 1. 1916.

ROBERTSON, J. M. *The Baconian Heresy.* 1913.

SALZMAN, L. F. *England in Tudor Times.* 1926.

SLATER, Gilbert. *Seven Shakespeares.* 1931.

SMITH, W. H. *Bacon and Shakespeare.* 1857.

SWINBURNE, A. C. *A Study of Shakespeare.* 1879.

SYMONDS, J. A. 'Introduction' to *Marlowe's Works.*

TANNENBAUM, S. A. *The Booke of 'Sir Thomas Moore' a bibliotic study.* 1927.

THEOBALD, B. G. *Shakespeare's Sonnets Unmasked.* 1929. *Enter Francis Bacon.* 1932.

THEOBALD, R. M. *Shakespeare Studies in Baconian Light.* 1904.

TILLYARD, E. M. W. *The Elizabethan World Picture.* 1943.

TITHERLEY, A. W. *Shakespeare's Identity.* 1952.

ULRICI, Hermann. *Shakespeares dramatisch Kunst.* 1839. Tr. by L. D. Schmitz as *Shakespeare's Dramatic Art.* 2 vols. 1876.

WALLACE, C. W. *Shakespeare and his London Associates as Revealed in Recently Discovered Documents.* 1910.

WILSON, F. P. *Marlowe and the Early Shakespeare.* 1953.

WILSON, J. Dover. *The Essential Shakespeare.* 1951.

Appendix

A complete answer to Mr Hoffman's claim that the similar lines he quotes from *The Passionate Shepherd* and *Merry Wives of Windsor* form the kind of parallelism that proves a common authorship requires more space than could be accorded to it in the text. To attempt to treat it there would interrupt the continuity of the general argument, destroy the balance of the chapter, and give to this single example a preponderance over the others which it does not merit. The matter, however, is decidedly interesting and not without its humorous side, and is certainly too good to omit altogether. I am accordingly treating it fully here.

The incident in *M.W.W.* in which the lines occur comes at the beginning of the first scene in Act III. The lines are not spoken, but *sung*, which is a very important point, by Sir Hugh Evans, the Welsh parson. Evans, in spite of his cloth, is a very worldly person – another important point – and there are slight indications in the dialogue that he is not quite sober at the time. He is without coat or gown and carries a rapier, for he has come to the spot to fight a duel with Doctor Caius. He tells his companion to go and see if his opponent is approaching, and when left alone bursts into song as follows:

> To shallow rivers, to whose falls
> Melodious birds sing madrigals;
> There we will make our beds of roses,
> And a thousand fragrant posies.

Mercy on me! I have a great disposition to cry. (*Sings.*)

> Melodious birds sing madrigals, –
> When as I sat in Babylon, –
> And a thousand vagram posies.
> To shallow, etc.

SIMPLE. (*Coming forward.*) Yonder he is coming, this way, Sir
Hugh.

EVANS. He is welcome. (*Sings.*)

To shallow rivers, to whose falls –

Heaven prosper the right! What weapons has he?

When we have the whole scene thus before us, it is easy to see
how Shakespeare came to use Marlowe's lines. Evans, before
embarking on such a serious matter as a duel, feels that his
mind should be filled with pious thoughts in case the termina-
tion should be fatal to him. To this end he decides to sing one
of the metrical versions – much in vogue at the time – of the
psalm 'By the waters of Babylon we sat down and wept', but
his worldly mind, being more familiar with popular ballads
than with the sacred songs of his Church, he inadvertently
bursts into one of these, which has a similar metre and is also
about rivers. This is obvious from the way in which he later
mixes up the two, and by his remark that he feels disposed to
cry, suggested by the word 'wept' in the psalm. Moreover, it is
just the sort of thing that might happen with a man like Evans
when he was already disturbed by the prospect of the duel and
perhaps not quite sober.

Marlowe's poem was well known and exactly suitable for
Shakespeare's purpose. If the joke was to be made quite clear
to the audience he had to use a verse that would be instantly
recognized as one in general use; he could not write anything
new for the occasion or the point might have been obscured.

Technically he may have been guilty of a plagiarism, but
there is nothing dishonest about it any more than there would
be if a modern dramatist gave one of his *dramatis personae* a
verse of a popular song to sing in the course of his play, which
in fact has often been done. Everyone in the audience would
be aware that the lines were Marlowe's, and if it is to have the
unpleasant epithet attached to it, it is a very venial example.

At least the facts which we have just reviewed, and which
Hoffman does not mention, make it quite clear that this so-
called parallelism cannot possibly be claimed as evidence for a
common authorship of the poem and the play as he attempts
to do.

Index